C++ and C efficiency

How to improve program speed and memory usage

David Spuler

Learning Resources
Centre

PRENTICE HALL

New York   London   Toronto   Sydney   Tokyo   Singapore

005.133
C++
SPU

Disclaimer
Although the author and publisher have made every effort to achieve accuracy in the development of this book, neither party makes a warranty of any kind, expressed or implied, about the contents of this book or its programs. The author and publisher do not accept liability in any event for any damages caused, or alleged to be caused, by the use of programs, methods or ideas in this book.

Acquisitions Editor: Andrew Binnie.
Production Editor: Fiona Marcar.
Cover design: The Modern Art Production Group, Melbourne, Victoria.

Printed in Australia by Impact Printing, Brunswick, Victoria.

1 2 3 4 5 96 95 94 93 92

ISBN 0 13 096595 2.

**National Library of Australia
Cataloguing-in-Publication Data**

Spuler, David, 1969- .
    C and C++ efficiency.
    Bibliography.
    Includes index.
    ISBN 0 13 096595 2.
    1. C. (Computer program language). 2. C (Computer program language) - Problems, exercises, etc. 3. C++ (Computer program language). 4. C++ (Computer program language) Problems, exercises, etc. I. Title.

005.133

**Library of Congress
Cataloging-in-Publication Data**

Spuler, David, 1969-
    C and C++ efficiency : how to improve program speed and memory usage / David Spuler.
    p.   cm.
    Includes bibliographical references and index.
    ISBN 0-13-096595-2.
    1. C (Computer program language). 2. C++ (Computer program language). I. Title.
QA76.73.C15.S658   1992   92-30846
005. 13'3--dc20   CIP

Prentice Hall, Inc., *Englewood Cliffs, New Jersey*
Prentice Hall Canada, Inc., *Toronto*
Prentice Hall Hispanoamericana, SA, *Mexico*
Prentice Hall of India Private Ltd, *New Delhi*
Prentice Hall International, Inc., *London*
Prentice Hall of Japan, Inc., *Tokyo*
Prentice Hall of Southeast Asia Pty Ltd, *Singapore*
Editora Prentice Hall do Brasil Ltda, *Rio de Janeiro*

PRENTICE HALL

A division of Simon & Schuster

Contents

Preface

This book examines the art of improving the efficiency of programs written in C and C++. Efficiency is examined at a number of levels of program development. The highest level is the design phase which involves choosing the correct data structures and algorithms for the given problem. The next level is making effective use of program statements so as to avoid obvious inefficiencies, and the final level is using programming tricks to extract the last drop of speed from your code.

Assumed knowledge

The reader is assumed to be reasonably fluent in C or C++. No introductory discussion of either C or C++ is given in this book; for such an introduction the reader is referred to a good general textbook (such as my own!). There are a small number of cases where aspects of the languages are discussed because even the experienced programmer may not be aware of the details.

Aims of the book

This book is intended to aid the professional programmer in writing code that is efficient in terms of space and time. It isn't a theoretical book about algorithm complexity — although choosing a fast algorithm is important, it is far from a panacea. This book is about practical methods of improving the efficiency in real-world situations.

The coverage of C and C++ in one work is uncommon, but efficiency is a topic where most comments apply to both languages. C++ is a superset of C and almost all of the efficiency improvement methods mentioned in Chapters 3, 4 and 7 relating to C are relevant to C++. Special techniques that are available because of the C++ extensions are discussed in Chapter 5.

Exercises are provided in most of the chapters to give the programmer a chance to think about some interesting problems and to apply newly-gained knowledge. Most of the exercises are answered in the appendix.

Organization of the book

The book aims to cover the practical aspects of efficiency, avoiding the theoretical aspects of the asymptotic complexity of algorithms for the most part. Algorithm complexity is covered briefly, in the discussion of searching in Chapter 8. Experience has shown that the process of writing fast programs is done poor justice by merely addressing asymptotic complexity. The constant factor is very important in practice, and most of the techniques in this book aim to reduce this constant.

Chapter 1 introduces the topic of efficiency by examining the correct way to approach improving the efficiency of a program.

Chapter 2 covers methods of measuring the amount of time and space being used by the program. This information is very useful in finding the areas of inefficiency. Methods of estimating time and space-efficiency are examined briefly, but, as is discussed in the chapter, there is precious little precise information that can be given about the art of estimation.

Chapter 3 covers some common methods of improving the data structures and algorithms used by a program, without making really fundamental changes to them. Most of the methods covered would apply equally well to other procedural languages, such as Pascal. The chapter is mainly about methods of reducing the constant factor in the complexity of algorithms.

Chapter 4 examines some of the specific methods that can be used in C (and also C++ because C++ is a superset of C). Experience with the C language has brought with it a heritage of tricks that can be used to improve efficiency.

Chapter 5 examines the methods of improvement of C++ programs that cannot be used in C programs. C++ offers more opportunities for efficiency via inline functions and pass-by-reference. However, the rigidity of method of defining C++ classes can lead to inefficiency if the programmer uses naive coding practices.

Chapter 6 covers efficient use of the ANSI C standard library. Though the standard library functions are efficient in most cases, there are some functions that are overly general and hence inefficient.

Chapter 7 covers methods of improving space-efficiency. The previous chapters have focused mainly on time reduction, and this chapter restores the balance. Techniques both general and specific to C are covered here.

Chapter 8 is the only chapter that examines efficiency from its highest design level — the choice of data structures and algorithms. Various abstract data types are coded using a variety of different data structures, and the benefits and disadvantages of each implementation are contrasted. In particular, the problem of searching for data is examined from the point of view of the relative costs of searching, insertion and deletion in different versions of the symbol table abstract data type. The common problem of sorting arrays, a favorite of algorithm texts, is also examined briefly.

Chapter 9 poses a small number of programming problems and then attempts to code them as efficiently as possible. The theory of computer game-playing is examined briefly and then an efficient implementation of a tic-tac-toe playing program is developed. The classic problem of determining if an integer is prime is examined and a number of solutions are given.

Chapter 10 assumes that the reader is the implementor of a C or C++ compiler and concerns itself with the methods that the compiler can use to improve efficiency. This chapter is a favorite of mine as I have a research interest in the area of compiler design, particularly static analysis.

Source code offer

A floppy disk containing C and C++ source code for most of the program examples in the book is available from the author for $20.00, including shipping and handling charges. Simply photocopy this page, fill in your address and the type of disk required, and send it to the following address. Please make checks and money orders payable to David Spuler.

Mail $20.00 to:			
Source Code Offer Spuler & Associates P.O. Box 1262 Aitkenvale 4814. AUSTRALIA			
Name: _____			
Address: _____			
_____			
_____			
Computer: Macintosh _____	IBM _____		
Diskette: 3.5" 800K _____	1.4M _____		
5.25" 360K _____	720K _____	1.2M _____	

Bug reports

A book is a very large document and it would be foolish to expect that it would be wholly correct, despite the massive amount of effort I have expended to assure its correctness. The author is interested to hear of all forms of errors, including typos, typesetting glitches, bugs in example programs, portability problems in programs, erroneous information, etc. As they are discovered, the problems can hopefully be corrected for later printings. The author can be contacted by postal mail at the address given above.

Acknowledgements

There are many people who deserve my thanks for their help in bringing this book to market. These people include personal friends, staff at Prentice Hall, and professional colleagues on the Internet.

A very special thank you to Anita Markovic for providing plenty of warm encouragement, not to mention proof reading many pages of a manuscript on a topic which reads as Greek to her. Dave Bonnell has my hearty thanks for reading many chapters of the book and proffering numerous useful suggestions. Cameron Gregory also tendered a number of useful ideas during the writing of this book. Thank you to Professor Gopal Gupta for tolerating my authoring tendencies when I should perhaps have been engaged in other activities.

Thanks to Andrew Binnie, Fiona Marcar, Chris Richardson and Liz Guthrie at Prentice Hall for co-ordinating the process of bringing out the completed book. In addition, the (anonymous) referees supplied by Prentice Hall were very encouraging and provided a number of useful suggestions for improvement. Peter Jones did an excellent job as the technical reviewer, particularly in cleaning up my C++ programming style.

A number of colleagues in the Internet groups `comp.lang.c`, `comp.std.c`, `comp.lang.c++` and `comp.std.c++` were very helpful. In particular, Steve Clamage and Luuk Trip provided useful material for the book. The FAQ list for `comp.lang.c` written by Steve Summit and also the FAQ list for `comp.lang.c++` written by Marshall Cline were both very valuable sources of ideas. The excellent group `comp.compilers` moderated by John Levine was especially useful in writing about compiler optimization in Chapter 10.

One individual who has contributed greatly to the writing of this book is Jon Bentley, author of the wonderful book *Writing Efficient Programs*. His book appears to be the first work to cover the area of efficiency as a whole, whereas previously most of the coverage of efficiency was to be found in research papers. His book has been an inspiration to my own.

David Spuler

Trademarks

Turbo C, Turbo C++ and Turbo profiler are all registered trademarks of Borland International. MS-DOS is a registered trademark of Microsoft Corporation. IBM is a registered trademark of International Business Machines Incorporated. UNIX is a trademark of Bell Laboratories.

Chapter 1

Introduction

No one likes a slow program. Although C and C++ programs are generally quite fast, good programming techniques can produce major improvements in execution speed. The main purpose of this book is to examine a large number of techniques for speeding up programs.

With falling memory prices, the amount of space a program uses is becoming secondary to its speed. This is particularly true of the UNIX system, where there is usually plenty of memory. However, in some situations (such as programming on a personal computer) there is the need to conserve memory. A number of techniques for conserving memory are also examined in this book, particularly in Chapter 7.

1.1 Why is C efficient?

Before beginning our discussion of efficiency techniques, it is interesting to discuss the origins of C and C++, and examine why these languages promote efficiency. Although it is certainly a mistake to state that C or C++ programs will *always* run faster than programs in other languages, the C and C++ languages provide several features that make it easy for the programmer to write efficient code.

The C language was originally developed at AT&T's Bell Laboratories by Dennis Ritchie and Ken Thomson. It was intended to remove the burden of programming in assembler from the programmer, while at the same time retaining most of assembler's efficiency. At times, C has been called a "typed assembly language", and there is some truth in this description. One of the main reasons for C's efficiency is that C programs manipulate objects that are the same as those manipulated by the machine: int variables correspond to machine words, char variables correspond to bytes, pointer variables contain machine addresses. Another example of a language feature that promotes efficiency is the register qualifier, which gives the programmer some control over register allocation (although as compilers improve, they will rely less and less on the advice of programmers).

1

The early versions of C had no official standard, and the de facto standard was the reference manual in the first edition of Kernighan and Ritchie's book titled *The C Programming Language*. For this reason, traditional C is often called K&R C. In 1983 an effort was initiated to formally standardize the C language, and in 1989 the final ANSI standard appeared. The ANSI standard is the definitive reference on the C language. Although many of the changes introduced by ANSI are related to the syntax and semantics of the language, some of the changes affect efficiency. As covered in Chapter 10, the compiler has more freedom to perform optimizations, such as using a faster function call mechanism because of changes to the rules of function prototyping.

The C language is not perfect, and there are still avenues for improvement. For example, traditional C performed all `float` operations using double precision arithmetic which is needlessly inefficient. Even in ANSI C where the new standard fixes the problem by permitting the compiler to use single-precision arithmetic, there is no mathematical library accepting `float` arguments. Users of the `<math.h>` library pay a performance penalty in conversions from `float` to `double`, and an "opportunity cost" in that faster algorithms could be used because less precision is required.

1.2 Why is C++ efficient?

C++ was designed by Bjarne Stroustrup in the early 1980s, and is almost a complete superset of C. One of the primary design objects of C++ was to retain the efficiency of C. Most of the extra features of C++ do not affect run-time efficiency, but merely give the compiler more work to do at compile-time. Since C++ builds on C, it benefits from C's use of data objects that are close to the machine: bytes, words and addresses.

C++ even contains some improved features that promote efficiency. The `inline` qualifier can be used by programmers to request that a call to a function be replaced automatically by inline code, thus removing the overhead of a function call, and introducing new opportunities for inter-function optimizations. The C++ concept of a *reference* type permits large objects to be passed to functions by reference to improve efficiency, and they are easier to use than pointers.

Only one aspect of the C++ class enhancements requires run-time support, which may reduce efficiency — `virtual` functions. However, `virtual` functions are quite efficient, and experienced C++ programmers find that their use is often more efficient than the equivalent C code needed to achieve the same effect. The efficiency aspects of `virtual` functions are discussed in more detail in Chapter 5.

At the time of writing there is no official ANSI C++ standard, although the process of standardization has begun. The draft version of the ANSI C++ standard is the reference manual from Bjarne Stroustrup's book titled *The C++ Language*.

1.3 A methodology for efficiency improvement

How should the huge number of methods of improving program efficiency be applied to a program? A programmer's time is usually far more important than the computer's, so the question is how to improve program efficiency with minimal extra time demands on the programmer. Unfortunately, the most effective method of improving a program — using better data structures and algorithms — often requires a good deal of extra programming effort. Of the code transformations in Chapter 4, those optimizations that improve the program by a significant amount should be tried first, and the smaller optimizations used only when it is important to squeeze out that last bit of extra speed. Hence, I suggest the following steps for improving the efficiency of a program:

1. Invoke the compiler's built-in optimizer.
2. Find a better data structure or algorithm.
3. Profile the code and optimize code at "hot spots".
4. Use the better code transformations.
5. Use less effective code transformations, if speed is crucial.

Most C and C++ compilers have an option to invoke an optimizer on the code. The optimizer, although it may not always yield a major increase in speed, has one very important advantage — the programmer need not change the code. Hence, if a small improvement is desired, the optimizer can often provide it without much effort. The optimizer is discussed in Section 1.6.

The choice of a better algorithm (usually with different data structures) for a program is not an easy method of program improvement. Simply identifying what would be a better algorithm is a difficult problem! And once identified, the new algorithm must be implemented by the programmer, costing precious man hours. However, this is the best method to achieve an order-of-magnitude increase in the program's performance.

The next step is to profile the code to determine which functions (or statements) are accounting for most of the program's time; these are the "hot spots" of the program. This identification of costly statements is best achieved by a profiler (see Section 2.1). However, if a profiler is not available, the programmer can usually guess where a program will be spending its time. Identifying frequently called functions and long loops is often adequate. Once the hot spots are identified, all efficiency measures, large and small, should be applied to this code. Any improvement to the efficiency of a statement, no matter how small, will improve the overall efficiency greatly if that statement is executed often.

Once the most costly functions and loops have been optimized, other statements can also be optimized, although the increase in speed will not be as noticeable. Some of the better code transformations to apply are loop optimizations, using pass-by-reference for passing structures or objects to functions, and replacing small functions with macros or `inline` functions.

1.4 Make it right first?

The speed improvement techniques in this chapter can be applied either as the programmer is writing the code, or after the development and debugging of the program. The second approach is often referred to as the "make it right first" rule. However, I believe that the first method is preferable simply because optimizing your program once it is working is a dangerous practice, and often introduces new bugs. Deferring efficiency improvement to the final development stage can also waste programmer time in improving the basic algorithms used in a program. Using efficiency techniques during the development of the program is a much sounder method of improving efficiency. Since many of the code transformation techniques sacrifice program clarity for a small increase in speed, it is only worthwhile applying these ideas to parts of the program that clearly need the extra speed.

1.5 Trade-offs in improving efficiency

The trade-off between program efficiency and programmer's time has already been mentioned. There are numerous other quantities that efficiency may affect:

- Space versus time-efficiency.
- Robustness of a program.
- Readability and maintainability of a program.
- Portability of a program.

There is almost always a trade-off between time and space when making programs run faster. Many of the algorithm improvements in Chapter 3 sacrifice space for extra speed.

Changing a program for efficiency can introduce extra bugs into a program (although you could argue that it might remove bugs too). If a piece of code has already been debugged, improving its efficiency may not be worth the risk to the robustness of a program.

Many of the program transformations used for efficiency can reduce the readability of a program. Naturally, this also makes it more difficult for a program to be maintained, and since the major cost in a program's development cycle is usually maintenance, improving efficiency may not be worth it in the long run.

Perhaps surprisingly, the efficiency of a program can usually be increased without affecting portability. There are some efficiency techniques in this book that use machine-specific information, but the portability problems are mentioned in these sections.

Almost all of the dangers of improving efficiency are dangers for the *programmer*. On the other hand, the *user* of a program will be well pleased by extra efficiency, and this alone makes efficiency improvement a worthwhile exercise.

1.6 The C optimizer

The first step to take when improving the performance of a program is to invoke the C optimizer that is available as an option in most compilers. This optimizer can be used for a good speed improvement that is simple to achieve and unlikely to introduce new bugs into the program (although some optimizers have been known to have bugs themselves). The improvement in speed is often quite noticeable, although this obviously depends on the implementation. In addition, some optimizers provide options to choose between optimization towards speed improvement or space reduction.

In the UNIX environment, the optimizer for the cc compiler is invoked using the −O option:

```
cc -O -c file.c
```

The use of −O causes all executable code generated to be optimized, in terms of space and time. The program should run faster, and require slightly less space to run. Note that some UNIX implementations support several levels of optimization — refer to the manual entry for the cc compiler.

In other environments the method of invoking the optimizer will depend on what compiler is used, although it is usually either a command-line option or a menu choice (for compilers integrated with a text editor). Consult your compiler documentation for information on how to use the optimizer.

1.7 Programmer efficiency

In our commercial world it is frequently the cost of our own time that is the greatest. Using our own time efficiently is far more important than writing fast programs. Although improving programming productivity is not the main topic of this book, a few methods are examined briefly here.

The basic method of reducing time spent programming is to build on the work of others. The use of libraries, including the wide variety of commercially available source code libraries, and the ANSI library, is a good way to build on the work of others. Asking other programmers, including those on the Internet, for code or ideas is also often fruitful. A literature search can be useful, although it is time-consuming. Books and research papers may well solve the problem at hand far more elegantly, efficiently and *correctly* than you could do yourself.

Building on your own work is the other main method of productivity improvement. How often have you coded up a binary tree? Have you ever written a sorting routine off the top of your head and then spent hours debugging it? You should perform tasks only once. This doesn't necessarily mean writing reusable code in its most general sense, but just having the source code available for the most common problems. Modifying code that has already been debugged is far more time-efficient than writing it from scratch.

1.8 Reducing compile-time

Reducing compile-time is a small method of improving the programmer's use of time. Although the speed of compilation largely depends on the ingenuity of the implementor of your compiler, there are a few techniques that can make your programs compile more quickly. One obvious method is to try different compilers, if any are available to you. For example, a UNIX environment may support both cc and gcc, or CC and g++.

A simple way to reduce compile-time is to avoid using the optimizer. To do so, consult your compiler documentation. Under UNIX, the optimizer is usually turned off by default, but when using a makefile, the default method of compilation is "cc -O" (i.e. optimizer on). This can be turned off by modifying your makefile to state explicitly how to compile your files.

Some compilers may also have options to control which libraries should be linked with your program. The default is often to link all libraries to the program, allowing the linker to pick out the functions that are actually used. If you are certain that you will not need functions from a certain library (e.g. the math library), change the option to prevent it being linked.

Some compilers support an option called *precompiled headers* whereby the compiler stores the state of internal tables, such as the symbol table, in a data file. Instead of then processing the text in the header files the compiler simply loads the data file and ignores the header files. This saves the compile-time used in processing the declarations in header files.

The best method of reducing compile-time during the testing-debugging phase of program development is to break the program into a number of files and use object files (the use of multiple files is also good programming style). In this way, only the files that need to be recompiled into object files are processed by the compilation phase, although all object files are usually still linked in creating the final executable. The method of achieving this automatic rebuilding of object files depends on the environment. The `make` utility is recommended in environments where it is supported (especially UNIX). In other environments, the compiler may support automatic reconstruction. For example, the integrated development environment of Turbo C++ supports "projects" and recompiles only those source files that have changed.

There are a few points to note when breaking a program into multiple files. The first is that it is important to organize these files correctly, and header files should be developed with common declarations. However, such issues are not the subject of this book and the reader should consult more general C textbooks (e.g. there is an entire chapter on this topic in my own book: *Comprehensive C*). The second point is that the use of object files do not allow faster compilation when rebuilding from scratch, and may even be slightly slower in this situation than keeping the whole program as a single file. Hence, object files are most effective during the testing-debugging phase of program development when the program is often changed slightly and recompiled.

Another method of reducing compile-time is reducing the volumes of files that the compiler must read via `#include`. Remove any unnecessary `#include` lines from the program (e.g. don't include <`math.h`> unless you actually need to). If a header file is included for a single declaration only, place the declaration explicitly in the file and remove the `#include` line (however, be warned that this change will lead to non-portable code, and is very bad style). It can also help to prevent multiple inclusions of header files, not by placing the traditional `#ifdef`-`#endif` pair *inside* the header file, but by surrounding the `#include` line, as below:

```
#ifndef INCLUDED_MYDEFS
#include "mydefs.h"
#endif
```

where `INCLUDED_MYDEFS` is defined in "`mydefs.h`".

1.9 Further reading

An excellent book on efficiency is Jon Bentley's book: *Writing Efficient Programs*. This book is a treasure trove of practical techniques for speeding up programs and reducing the space usage of programs. The techniques are presented using a variant of Pascal and are easily applied to C. In addition to covering a huge number of optimization techniques, it also provides real-life anecdotes about how professional programmers improved the efficiency of their programs, which are interesting reading in themselves.

The book, *Efficient C*, by Plum and Brodie presents a number of techniques for improving the time and space-efficiency of C programs. Many of the general techniques used by Bentley are covered, in addition to techniques specific to C. This book is particularly strong in its coverage of how to measure and estimate the time and space requirements of a C program, and three of its chapters deal specifically with these topics.

Many of the code transformation techniques in Chapter 4 come from the theory of code optimization in compilers. For example, code motion and strength reduction on induction variables are well-known code optimization techniques. The classic reference for compiler design is by Aho, Sethi and Ullman, and this book contains a good chapter on code optimization.

One aspect of efficiency is the choice of data structure for a problem. Knuth's book on data structures for sorting and searching presents much of the theory in the area of organizing data for fast retrieval. The book is also interesting in that it applies a number of efficiency techniques to the program code presented (e.g. use of sentinels; unrolling loops). All programs are presented in a mythical form of assembly language called MIX.

Kernighan and Plauger's book, *The Elements of Programming Style*, discusses numerous stylistic issues of programming, including various methods of speeding up a program. The book uses Fortran and PL/I as its programming languages, and most techniques are easily related to C.

Of the growing number of C and C++ books, a few contain discussions of efficiency, usually as part of a general coverage of the language. My own book, *Comprehensive C*, contains a chapter on efficiency from which this book has grown. Numerous other C books also contain sections on efficiency: David Masters' book contains a chapter entitled "Program Efficiency and Testing"; Herbert Schildt's book has a chapter called "Efficiency, Porting and Debugging"; Ken Pugh's book contains numerous sections on various aspects of efficiency. Undoubtedly, there are many other C and C++ books that cover efficiency to some extent. Of the many C++ books, there are a number that contain discussions of various aspects of efficiency. Bjarne Stroustrup's classic text *The C++ Language* covers all of C++ and mentions efficiency aspects in many sections. Jonathan Shapiro's book *A C++ Toolkit* has a chapter on performance tuning and another on memory management. James Coplein's book on advanced C++ programming covers efficiency in many sections. Further discussion of C++ books is given in the "Further reading" section in Chapter 5.

AHO, Alfred V., SETHI, Ravi, and ULLMAN, Jeffrey D., *Compilers — Principles, Techniques and Tools*, Addison-Wesley, 1986.

BENTLEY, Jon Louis, *Writing Efficient Programs*, Prentice Hall, 1982.

COPLIEN, James O., *Advanced C++ Programming Styles and Idioms*, Addison-Wesley, 1992.

KERNIGHAN Brian W., and PLAUGER, P. J., *The Elements of Programming Style*, McGraw-Hill, 1974.

KNUTH, Donald E., *The Art of Computer Programming (Vol. 3): Sorting and Searching*, Addison-Wesley, 1973.

MASTERS, David, *Introduction to C with Advanced Applications*, Prentice Hall, 1991.

PLUM, Thomas, and BRODIE, Jim, *Efficient C*, Plum Hall Inc., 1985.

PUGH, Ken, *All on C*, Scott, Foresman/Little, Brown Higher Education, 1990.

SCHILDT, Herbert, *C: The Complete Reference*, Osborne-McGraw-Hill, 1987.

SHAPIRO, Jonathan S., *A C++ Toolkit*, Prentice Hall, 1991.

SPULER, David A., *Comprehensive C*, Prentice Hall, 1992.

STROUSTRUP, Bjarne, *The C++ Programming Language (2nd edn)*, Addison-Wesley, 1991.

Chapter 2

Measurement and estimation

When changing a program to increase efficiency, it is important to have a means of determining whether the changes have noticeably increased the program's efficiency (or even decreased it!). Techniques for measuring program efficiency range from the stop-watch method to the use of sophisticated profiler software tools. If no profiler is available, the programmer can gain timing information by adding statements to the program, although there are many pitfalls in attempting to determine the time taken by a sequence of statements.

The measurement of the space-efficiency of a program is a far more difficult problem because few tools exist to examine how much space a program uses. Measuring the memory usage of the stack and heap is also difficult because of their dynamic nature. However, clever use of C or C++ programming constructs can yield reasonable results.

2.1 Profilers for C

When improving a program's performance, it is useful to know where the speed bottlenecks are. There is a saying that 90% of the time is spent in 10% of the code. Hence, any speed improvement should aim to speed up the functions that are most frequently used. The programmer can often tell where the program is spending most of its time (e.g. where one function is called by all others), but it is useful to have a software tool to analyze exactly where the program is spending its time. Many implementations of C come with a software tool called a *profiler* which is used to examine the performance of the program. The most common UNIX profilers are prof, pixie and gprof.

2.1.1 The prof utility

Under UNIX the standard C profiling utility is called "prof". This utility calculates the percentage time taken by each function. This is valuable information when considering which functions to make more efficient.

To use `prof`, compile the program with the −p option to `cc` (strictly speaking, the −p option is needed only at the link stage of compilation) and then execute the program. Provided the program terminates normally or via `exit`, a data file called "`mon.out`" will be generated. This file contains the data to be used by `prof` in preparing an execution profile for the program. To examine this profile, type the command:

```
prof
```

If your executable is not called `a.out`, but say, `my_prog`, the command is:

```
prof my_prog
```

This command will generate a profile of your program's execution from which the functions that use the most time can be identified. A sample from the output generated by `prof` is:

```
%time       seconds    cum %     cum sec   procedure (file)

42.1        4.4700     42.1        4.47    strcmp (../strcmp.s)
40.6        4.3100     82.7        8.78    CheckWord (spell1.c)
 5.9        0.6300     88.6        9.41    fgets (../fgets.c)
 4.3        0.4600     92.9        9.87    initialize (spell1.c)
 3.0        0.3200     96.0       10.19    tolower (../conv.c)
 1.5        0.1600     97.5       10.35    read (../read.s)
 1.0        0.1100     98.5       10.46    malloc (../malloc.c)
 0.8        0.0800     99.2       10.54    strlen (../strlen.c)
 0.5        0.0500     99.7       10.59    morecore (../malloc.c)
 0.1        0.0100     99.8       10.60    open (../open.s)
 0.1        0.0100     99.9       10.61    sbrk (../sbrk.s)
 0.1        0.0100    100.0       10.62    fstat (../fstat.s)
```

Note that the percentages calculated are only approximate because the profiler uses sampling techniques during interrupts and these samples might not provide a fully accurate picture. For example, if the program has a very small and fast function, this function might be completely missed.

2.1.2 The pixie utility

The `prof` utility only produces estimates based on statistical sampling of the program counter at regular intervals throughout the execution of the program. The `pixie` utility can be used under UNIX to get more accurate counts on the number of times each statement in a function is executed. It measures the number of times each *basic block* is executed. A basic block is a sequence of code containing no branches.

The `pixie` utility is applied to the already generated executable file. There is no need to recompile the executable with the −p option. The command:

```
pixie a.out
```

will generate a new executable file, "`a.out.pixie`", which when executed will generate a data file called "`a.out.Counts`". A data file of function addresses called "`a.out.Addrs`" is also generated. The next step is to run the new executable:

```
a.out.pixie
```

and then the count file can be examined using either `prof` or `pixstats`. Two possible commands are:

```
pixstats a.out
```

or the use of `prof` with the `-pixie` option:

```
prof -pixie a.out
```

Both of these commands will generate a variety of information. `prof -pixie` will generate an ordering of functions based on instruction cycle counts, another based on invocations, and a list of instruction counts for each basic block. `pixstats` generates a whole wealth of useful information including summaries of opcode distributions and register usage. For more information examine the manual entries for `pixie`, `pixstats` and `prof`.

2.2 Timing code

For several reasons it can be useful to time the execution of a program. In environments that don't support a profiler tool, the only way to gather information about a program is to add timing statements to it. Even if a profiler is available, it might only indicate which functions are consuming time, whereas timing instructions can be useful in determining exactly which statements should be optimized.

If the full execution time for a program is all that is needed, the UNIX `time` command can be used to calculate the time required by a program. There are two versions — a stand-alone utility in `/bin`, and a command built into `csh`. The command to run is usually:

```
time a.out
```

A different executable name can also be used and command line arguments can be specified. On non-UNIX machines the total execution time can easily be measured with a stop-watch.

Timing code can determine the relative efficiency of various operations and give you valuable information about writing code for your machine (e.g. whether shifting is faster than integer multiplication).

If a more detailed speed analysis is needed, it is possible to add C code to your program to monitor its own performance. The basic idea is to use the standard library functions declared in `<time.h>` to monitor the time before and after an action. The most useful function is the `clock` function which counts the number of clock ticks since the program began executing. The `time` function which keeps track of the real calendar time could also be used, but it is not a true indication of processor time on a large multi-user system such as UNIX. The `clock` function is correct for single user and multi-user systems.

The `clock` function returns a value of type `clock_t` which is declared in `<time.h>` (typically as `long` or `int`), and this integral value counts the number of clock ticks. The value can be converted to seconds by dividing by the constant `CLOCKS_PER_SEC`, also declared in `<time.h>`. The basic idea of timing C code is to call the `clock` function before and after an operation and examine the difference between the number of clock ticks. For example, the code below times the execution of a program (excluding the time used by the program's startup and termination sequences).

```
#include <stdio.h>
#include <time.h>    /* declare clock() and clock_t */

main()
{
    clock_t before;            /* Save old value of clock() */

    before = clock();
    ... /* rest of program */
    printf("Execution took %5.2f seconds\n",
                (double)(clock() - before) / CLOCKS_PER_SEC);
}
```

Note that some implementations don't conform to the ANSI standard and return the number of clock ticks since the first call to the clock function. This means that a single call to clock at the end of the program would return zero. Hence, it is more portable to measure the number of clock ticks between two calls to clock, one at the start and one at the end.

The clock function also has a problem with *wraparound* on many implementations. Because of its high resolution, the number of clock ticks quickly overflows the maximum value that can be stored by the type clock_t. On one system the clock function will wrap around after only 36 minutes. If the program being timed runs for longer than this period, the use of clock can be dangerous. One solution is to use the time function declared in <time.h>, but this usually only has resolution to the nearest second.

2.3 Instrumenting programs

Usually, the total execution time of a program is not enough information on which to base optimization techniques. It is usually necessary to know which functions are consuming the most time, or even to know how much time is used by particular groups of statements. The process of adding timing instructions to a program to examine its efficiency is called *instrumenting* the program.

Presented below is a small library of functions to keep track of time in code blocks using "clocks". The clocks are referenced by a character string name, and are started and stopped by the functions start_clock and stop_clock. At the end of the program the clock_report function can be used to generate a summary of the times used by each clock and the percentage of total run-time consumed by that clock.

```
#include <stdio.h>
#include <time.h>       /* declare clock() and clock_t */
#include <string.h>

#include "instrument.h"   /* include the interface header file */

typedef int bool;
#define TRUE  1
#define FALSE 0

/*-----------------------------------------------------------------*/
/* Structure representing a clock                                  */
/*-----------------------------------------------------------------*/
```

```
typedef struct clock_node {
    clock_t ticks;              /* number of clock ticks recorded */
    clock_t last_time;          /* time when clock last switched on */
    char *name;                 /* name of clock */
    struct clock_node *next;    /* next pointer for linked list */
    bool clock_on;              /* flag if clock started or stopped */
} clock_type, *clock_ptr;

clock_type *clock_head = NULL;  /* head of linked list of clocks */

/*-----------------------------------------------------------------*/
/*    Set a clock off recording time                               */
/*-----------------------------------------------------------------*/

void start_clock(char *name)
{
    clock_ptr p;

    for (p = clock_head; p != NULL; p = p->next) {
        if (strcmp(p->name, name) == 0)
            break;
    }
    if (p == NULL) { /* not found; so create new clock */
        p = malloc(sizeof(struct clock_node));
        p->name = malloc(strlen(name) + 1);   /* store the name */
        strcpy(p->name, name);
        p->ticks = 0;           /* No time on clock yet */
        p->next = clock_head;   /* add to front of linked list */
        p->clock_on = TRUE;
        clock_head = p;
    }
    else if (p->clock_on) {
        fprintf(stderr, "Error: clock '%s' already on\n", name);
        return;   /* no need to set last_time */
    }
    p->clock_on = TRUE;
    p->last_time = clock();     /* store the current time */
}

/*-----------------------------------------------------------------*/
/* Stop a running clock; update its count of elapsed time          */
/*-----------------------------------------------------------------*/

void stop_clock(char *name)
{
    clock_t ticks = clock();    /* record time first */
    clock_ptr p;

    for (p = clock_head; p != NULL; p = p->next) {
        if (strcmp(p->name, name) == 0)
            break;
    }
    if (p == NULL) {    /* error; clock name not found */
        fprintf(stderr, "Error: clock '%s' not found\n", name);
        return;
    }
    else if (!p->clock_on)
        fprintf(stderr, "Error: clock '%s' not started\n", name);
    p->clock_on = FALSE;
    p->ticks += ticks - p->last_time;   /* record elapsed time */
}

/*-----------------------------------------------------------------*/
/* Print out the profiling report based on all clocks              */
/*-----------------------------------------------------------------*/

void clock_report(void)
{
    clock_ptr p;
    clock_t total = clock();   /* total time for entire program */
```

```
        fprintf(stderr, "------- CLOCK PROFILE -------\n");
        for (p = clock_head; p != NULL; p = p->next) {
            if (p->clock_on)
                fprintf(stderr,"Error: clock '%s' not stopped\n",p->name);
            fprintf(stderr, "Clock '%s':  %5.2f secs, %5.2f%%\n", p->name,
            p->ticks / (double) CLOCKS_PER_SEC,
            p->ticks / (double) total * 100.0);
        }
    }
```

The actual implementation is quite detailed. Clocks are referred to by using a character string name, and the program actually implements an "associative array" of names and clocks. Each clock is stored on a linked list and starting up an unknown clock automatically creates a new clock and adds it to the linked list. Considerable run-time error checking is added to ensure that the clocks are being used correctly. Use of the library is simple: include the following "instrument.h" header file in the program, and link the object file from the C source code above.

```
/*----------------------------------------------------------*/
/* INSTRUMENT.H:  Header file for instrumenting library */
/*----------------------------------------------------------*/

void start_clock(char *name);
void stop_clock(char *name);
void clock_report(void);
```

The program that makes use of the instrumenting library must be modified to include calls to start_clock and stop_clock. For example, the program below records how much time is spent in a single function.

```
#include <stdio.h>
#include "instrument.h"    /* include the interface header file */

long sum(long n)
{
    long i, total = 0L;

    start_clock("sum");      /* Start the clock */
    for (i = 1; i <= n; i++)
        total += i;
    stop_clock("sum");       /* Stop the clock */
    return total;
}

main()
{
    long i, total = 0L;

    start_clock("main");            /* Start clock for main */
    for (i = 1; i <= 1000; i++)
        total += sum(i);            /* sum of sums */
    printf("sum of sums of 1..1000 = %ld\n", total);
    stop_clock("main");             /* Stop clock for main */
    clock_report();                 /* Print out the profile */
}
```

This example produces the following output:

```
------- CLOCK PROFILE -------
Clock 'sum':    0.43 secs, 89.52%
Clock 'main':   0.48 secs, 100.00%
```

Here we see the main disadvantage of this implementation of the instrumenting library: both the clocks have recorded some of the same time. The clock for "main" has still been counting the time used by the "sum" function. To avoid this problem it becomes necessary to rewrite the code to turn off the clock before a function call and turn it back on afterwards:

```
start_clock("main");               /* Start clock for main */
for (i = 1; i <= 1000; i++)   {
    stop_clock("main");            /* Stop clock before */
    total += sum(i);
    start_clock("main");           /* Start clock after */
}
stop_clock("main");                /* Stop clock for main */
```

This produces the more useful profile output:

```
------- CLOCK PROFILE -------
Clock 'sum':     0.45 secs, 78.91%
Clock 'main':    0.05 secs,  8.84%
```

An alternative is to improve the instrumenting library so that it counts using only a single clock at any one time. A useful profile of the entire program would then simply require calls to start_clock and stop_clock at the start and end of each function (taking care to place a stop_clock call before every return statement). This and other extensions to the library are explored in the exercises at the end of the chapter. Of course, all possible instrumenting libraries suffer from the same disadvantage in that the programmer must do a lot of work to generate a profile. An automatic profiling tool should be used if one is available.

2.4 Benchmark timing programs

Benchmark programs attempt to examine how quickly your machine executes certain instructions. For example, how would you determine whether the integer multiplication operation x*2 could be more efficiently replaced by x<<1? The obvious method is to time a single operation, as in:

```
#include <stdio.h>
#include <time.h>   /* declare clock and clock_t */

main()
{
    int x;
    clock_t before;          /* Save old value of clock() */

    before = clock();
    x << 1;                  /* perform shift operation */
    printf("x<<1 took %f seconds\n",
                (double)(clock() - before) / CLOCKS_PER_SEC);

    before = clock();
    x * 2;                   /* perform multiplication */
    printf("x*2 took %f seconds\n",
                (double)(clock() - before) / CLOCKS_PER_SEC);
```

Unfortunately, this program outputs 0.000000 for both operations. There are a number of reasons for the failure of the simple approach above:

- Single operations take less time than a clock tick.
- %f prints only 6 decimal digits of its value.
- The operations are possibly being removed by the compiler.
- The cost of calling `clock` is relatively large.

The main problem is that the amount of time taken by these single operations is so short that it is less than a single clock tick. Hence, both calls to clock return the same number of clock ticks and the difference is zero.

Even if the operations did take more than a clock tick, printing out the number of seconds using %f is the wrong approach because it prints out only the first 6 decimal digits of the fraction, and will still print zero for values such as 0.0000001. This problem can be solved by using the `printf` format specification `%.20f` to print out 20 decimal digits, or simply by printing the actual number of clock ticks as an integer.

Another problem is that if the compiler is clever enough to notice that the x<<1 and x*2 statements have no effect in the program above, its built-in optimizer may remove them. The compiler can be forced to avoid this optimization by declaring x as `volatile`. The `volatile` qualifier tells the compiler that all accesses to x are important, and that it should not remove any. The intended purpose of `volatile` is to allow the declaration of addresses for memory-mapped I/O, or for variables modified by other programs (e.g. a semaphore modified by another program running concurrently). However, we can use it here to force all accesses to x to occur by declaring x as below:

```
volatile int x;
```

Unfortunately, the computations of the << and * operators in x<<1 and x*2 are not being assigned anywhere, so the computations themselves could be optimized out, even though the actual read operations on x must occur because x is `volatile`. To force the << and * operations to occur, it is necessary to use their result somehow, such as by assigning it to the (`volatile`) variable x:

```
x = x << 1;
```

Unfortunately, the `volatile` qualifier is not supported by some older non-ANSI compilers. Programmers using such compilers may have to resort to compiler-dependent tricks to prevent the optimizer from removing operations. Fortunately, non-ANSI compilers will tend not to perform these optimizations because of their recognized dangers.

Although all of the above improvements will enhance the previous version, a far better method of improvement is to time a loop that performs a huge number of the operations, as follows; the code given here examines the relative speed of 10,000 shift and multiplication operations on `int` operands:

```
#include <stdio.h>
#include <time.h>

#define ITERATIONS 10000

main()
{
    int i;
    volatile int x;      /* volatile to prevent optimizations */
    clock_t before;

    before = clock();
    for (i = 0; i < ITERATIONS; i++)
        x = x << 1;
    printf("%d Shifts took %5.2f seconds\n", ITERATIONS,
                    (double)(clock() - before) / CLOCKS_PER_SEC);

    before = clock();
    for (i = 0; i < ITERATIONS; i++)
        x = x * 2;
    printf("%d Multiplications took %5.2f seconds\n",ITERATIONS,
                    (double)(clock() - before) / CLOCKS_PER_SEC);
}
```

Unfortunately, the above method of measuring the speed of operations is not completely accurate, because it also includes the loop overhead (incrementing i from 1 to 10,000) and the cost of the assignment of the result to x. The loop overhead can be minimized by placing many operations within the loop, as below:

```
#include <stdio.h>
#include <time.h>   /* declare clock and clock_t */

#define ITERATIONS 10000

main()
{
    int i;
    volatile int x;      /* volatile to prevent optimizations */
    clock_t before;

    before = clock();
    for (i = 0; i < ITERATIONS; i++) {
        x = x << 1; x = x << 1; x = x << 1; x = x << 1;
        x = x << 1; x = x << 1; x = x << 1; x = x << 1;
        x = x << 1; x = x << 1; x = x << 1; x = x << 1;
        x = x << 1; x = x << 1; x = x << 1; x = x << 1;
        x = x << 1; x = x << 1; x = x << 1; x = x << 1;
    }
    printf("%d Shifts took %f seconds\n", ITERATIONS * 20,
                    (double)(clock() - before) / CLOCKS_PER_SEC);

    before = clock();
    for (i = 0; i < ITERATIONS; i++) {
        x = x * 2; x = x * 2; x = x * 2; x = x * 2;
        x = x * 2; x = x * 2; x = x * 2; x = x * 2;
        x = x * 2; x = x * 2; x = x * 2; x = x * 2;
        x = x * 2; x = x * 2; x = x * 2; x = x * 2;
        x = x * 2; x = x * 2; x = x * 2; x = x * 2;
    }
    printf("%d Multiplications took %f seconds\n",ITERATIONS*20,
                    (double)(clock() - before) / CLOCKS_PER_SEC);
}
```

Unfortunately, this assignment operation is needed to prevent the optimizer removing the computations, as discussed above. The assignment can be removed in any "stupid" compilers where the computation will occur regardless of whether its result is used. The only truly effective method of removing the cost of the assignment from the measurement is to time another separate loop, and subtract its time from that of the other loops, as below. This method also automatically accounts for the loop overhead cost, so the multiple operations inside each loop are not needed (and in fact would be incorrect). Our final version of the benchmark program is also made more sophisticated to output the relative magnitude of the two operations:

```c
#include <stdio.h>
#include <time.h>   /* declare clock and clock_t */
#include <math.h>   /* declare fabs() */

#define ITERATIONS 10000

main()
{
    int i;
    volatile int x;     /* volatile to prevent optimizations */
    clock_t before;
    clock_t loop_cost; /* time of loop overhead and assignments */
    double time1, time2;

    before = clock();                   /* time loop overhead */
    for (i = 0; i < ITERATIONS; i++)
        x = 1;
    loop_cost = clock() - before;

    before = clock();
    for (i = 0; i < ITERATIONS; i++) {
        x = x << 1;
    }
    time1 = (double)(clock() - before - loop_cost) / CLOCKS_PER_SEC;
    printf("%d Shifts took %f seconds\n", ITERATIONS, time1);


    before = clock();
    for (i = 0; i < ITERATIONS; i++) {
        x = x * 2;
    }
    time2 = (double)(clock() - before - loop_cost) / CLOCKS_PER_SEC;
    printf("%d Multiplications took %f seconds\n", ITERATIONS, time2);

        /* Compare both times, and print out percentage difference */

#define ACCURACY   0.00001    /* maximum difference for equal reals */

    if (fabs(time1 - time2) < ACCURACY)    /* (almost) equal? */
        printf("Shift and multiplications took the same time\n");
    else
    if (time1 < time2)
        printf("Shifts faster by %5.2f percent\n",
                (time2 - time1) / time2 * 100.0);
    else
        printf("Multiplications faster by %5.2f percent\n",
                (time1 - time2) / time1 * 100.0);
}
```

Finally, note that on some machines the code above may indicate that shifts and multiplications cost the same. This is most likely an indication that the compiler automatically optimizes any multiplications by powers of two into left shifts. To get the true cost of a multiplication, the expression should be:

```c
    x = x * x;
```

but on a compiler that does perform the optimization of multiplications to shifts automatically, the programmer will seldom be able to make any changes that the compiler does not, so the relative cost of shift and multiply is unimportant.

2.5 Examining assembly output

Another way of examining the relative costs of particular operations for a particular compiler is to examine the assembly language produced by the compiler. Many compilers have an option to produce assembly language output. For example, under UNIX the command:

```
cc -S main.c
```

will produce the assembly language listing for the C file and store it in a new file "main.s". Without the -S option, the assembly output would have been passed to the assembler to create the machine code executable.

Examining assembly language instructions produced for C operations can be very enlightening. For example, you can determine whether the compiler uses a special increment instruction for the ++ operator. Whether or not the compiler is performing various optimizations can also be examined.

Counting the number of assembly instructions is a simple measure and gives a reasonable indication of how efficiently an operation will be performed. A better method is to determine the number of *cycles* used by each instruction, but this requires a rather more intimate knowledge of the assembly language being used.

Many useful things can be discovered by examining assembly output. For example, does the expression x*2 generate a multiply instruction or a shift instruction (or an addition instruction)? Does the compiler notice that x=x+1 can be replaced by x++? Is the % operator implemented by a sequence of instructions? Using the relational operators (e.g. >, <) in expressions such as:

```
flag = x > y;
```

will often produce a sequence of instructions because of the need to assign flag the value either 0 or 1. The instructions may well look like the following pseudo-assembly language:

```
        LOAD    10($sp)         # Load x (from stack)
        CMP     12($sp)         # Compare with y (on stack)
        BGT     $1              # Branch if greater than
        LOAD    0               # Result of > operation is 0
        JUMP    $2
$1:
        LOAD    1               # Result of > operation is 1
$2:
        STORE   14($sp)         # Store in flag (on stack)
```

However, in situations such as:

```
if (x > y)
        ...
```

the instructions need not be as complex, because there is no need to store the value 0 or 1 anywhere. The assembly language could be similar to:

```
        LOAD   10($sp)           # Load x (from stack)
        CMP    12($sp)           # Compare with y (on stack)
        BLE    $1                # Branch if NOT greater than
        ...                      # Code for if statement body
  $1:
        ...                      # Statements after if statement
```

2.6 Measuring code size and static space

In general, it is more difficult to measure how much space a program is using than to measure how much time it is using. However, most environments provide some means of determining the size of instructions and static data in an executable program. If nothing else, the size of the executable file can be a reasonable guide.

Under UNIX, a useful command is the size command, which examines an executable program and reports the memory used by its instructions and its global or local static variables. However, it does not (and cannot) report the stack or heap usage because the amount of such memory used is dynamic, and hence cannot be found by analysing the executable. The command:

```
size a.out
```

produces output similar to the following:

```
text    data    bss    dec     hex
20480   8192    0      28672   7000
```

The "text" value refers to the machine code instructions for the program code. Both the "data" and "bss" areas refer to global and local static variables. The "data" area refers to variables which have been explicitly initialized; the "bss" area refers to variables with implicit initialization which default to zero.

If the code size is needed on a per function basis, most UNIX environments support the nm command. This command differs on different UNIX variants, but will usually print out information including the start and end address of a function, from which the size of a function can be trivially computed.

MS-DOS users may be able to find out about executable size by examining the output produced by some C compilers at the link stage (although not all compilers will produce such output). Alternatively, the MS-DOS link command with the /map option can be used. To use the link command, the object files are linked using a command such as:

```
link /map *.obj
```

2.7 Measuring heap usage

The measurement of dynamic memory usage involving the stack and heap is far more difficult than measuring code size because of its dynamic nature. The amount of memory used will depend on the program's execution; that is, it will depend on the program's inputs.

Measurement of the amount of heap space used can be achieved by adding extra code to keep track of any calls to `malloc`, `calloc`, `realloc` and `free`, or any uses of the C++ `new` and `delete` operators. The programmer can either add extra code to the program in any place that memory allocation is used, or else write a library of allocation functions similar to those in Section 6.8. As a very simple method, the following macros may be useful:

```
#define malloc(n)     ((mem_used += n), malloc(n))
#define calloc(n,m)   ((mem_used += n * m), calloc(n,m))
```

These macros are dangerous in that they may evaluate any side effects to their arguments twice, but they are still useful. Note that these macros are self-referential, which are legal in ANSI C, but may cause infinite loops with older preprocessors.

Unfortunately, it is difficult to decrement `mem_used` for each call to `free`, because the size of the block is not passed to `free`. If it was known how `malloc` encoded the size in the block header, the `free` function could possibly be implemented as something like:

```
#define free(p) \
            (mem_used -= *((int*)p - 1), free(p))   /* CORRECT? */
```

However, this uses machine-dependent knowledge, is non-portable and may not work for a particular implementation of `malloc`.

Although I can think of no useful preprocessor hack for the C++ `new` and `delete` operators, the memory allocation requirements for a particular class can be monitored by overloading the `new` and `delete` for that class. For example, the overloaded operators could be implemented as:

```
void *Object::operator new(size_t n)
{
    mem_used += n;
    return ::new Object;   // Call global new operator
}

void Object::operator delete(void *p)
{
    mem_used -= sizeof(Object);
    ::delete p;       // Call global delete operator
}
```

2.8 Measuring stack usage

Measuring the size of the program stack is very difficult. In many cases, the stack is totally beyond the programmer's control. However, some compilers for personal computers provide options such as enabling run-time stack checking and setting the maximum stack size. Run-time checking is a useful way to determine whether or not the worst case will run short of stack space, simply by executing the program. If stack checking does not report an error when the program is executed with its worst case inputs, the program is not using too much stack space.

If the actual amount of stack space used must be known, it can be found by repeatedly running the program on worst case inputs and progressively reducing the allowed stack size. The smallest stack size for which the program does not fail is the amount of stack space being used.

This approach is very slow, and what is really needed is a software tool that examines all possible sequences of function calls in the C source code, determines the maximum number of functions in scope at any one time, and then adds up the sizes of their local variables and parameters. Although this may appear to be a theoretical impossibility, the *maximum* stack depth can be found by a depth-first-search of the function call graph (in the absence of recursion). This does not solve the Halting Problem, which would require the resolution of whether this maximum stack depth is attained at run-time. Unfortunately, the author is not aware of such a software tool.

2.9 Estimating time and space requirements

Although estimating the efficiency of a proposed project is important in ascertaining its feasibility, it is difficult to find anything concrete to say about arriving at these estimates. Producing advance estimates is more of an art than a science.

Experience is probably the best source of methods for producing an accurate estimate. Hence it is wise to seek out others who have implemented a similar project, or to perform a literature search for relevant papers and books. Unfortunately, neither of these methods is guaranteed to succeed and the implementor may be forced to go it alone.

The only other realistic means of estimation relies on a good understanding of the various data structures and algorithms that will be used by the program. Making realistic assumptions about the input can provide some means of examining the performance of a data structure. How a data structure performs under worst case assumptions may also be of great importance.

An alternative to these methods of plucking estimates out of the air is to code up a prototype version of the program, which implements only the most important parts of the project (especially those which will have the biggest impact). The efficiency of the prototype can then be measured by using the various techniques outlined earlier in this chapter. Even if the prototype is too inefficient, at least the problem has been identified early in the development cycle, when the investment in the project is relatively low.

2.10 Summary

- A profiler is an important tool for identifying "hot spots" in code.
- If no profiler is available, the programmer can "instrument" the program, but this requires a good deal of effort.
- The `clock` ANSI C library function can be used to time code, but care is needed because even the fine resolution of the `clock` function will be much larger than the time for a single instruction.
- Benchmarks should time a large number of operations, with all variables declared as `volatile`.

- If the compiler has an option to produce an assembly listing, this can be examined to see what the compiler is doing and thereby fine-tune efficiency methods.
- Executable size and static storage can be examined by using the UNIX `size` and `nm` commands, or the `link /map` command in MS-DOS.
- Heap usage can be monitored by redefining `malloc` and `free` in C, or `new` and `delete` in C++.
- Run-time stack overflow checking can be used to measure stack usage.
- Advance estimates of either time or space-efficiency are very difficult.

2.11 Further reading

Plum and Brodie's book *Efficient C* gives good coverage of the issues of measurement and estimation of space and time-efficiency. It contains chapters on time measurement and space measurement, and also a discussion of time and space estimation in two other chapters.

PLUM, Thomas, and BRODIE, Jim, *Efficient C*, Plum Hall Inc., 1985.

2.12 Exercises

1. Consider the method of timing loop overhead in Section 2.4 which timed a loop containing the statement x=1. Why does this fail if the compiler implements this assignment statement as a special set-to-one instruction? How can the benchmark timing method be improved to avoid this (rare) pitfall?

2. Why does the instrumenting library call `clock` at the end of `start_clock`, but at the beginning of `stop_clock`? Modify the program instrumenting library in Section 2.3 to use macros that call the `clock` function after calling `start_clock` and before calling `stop_clock`. This avoids including the overhead of calling these functions as part of the time. *Hint:* You may need to use global variables.

3. Modify the `"instrument.h"` header file to remove calls to `start_clock`, `stop_clock` and `clock_report` (by #define'ing them to expand to nothing) if a particular macro name is defined, say, `NO_INSTRUMENT`. This allows instrumenting code to be removed by conditional compilation.

4. [advanced] Modify the instrumenting library to avoid measuring the same time twice on different clocks. This has the advantage that a clock at the start and end of a function will truly indicate how much time the program spent inside the function body. *Hint:* Implementing the better library will involve stopping the (single) clock that is on (if any) in a call to `start_clock`, and restarting this stopped clock when the new clock is itself turned off.

5.   [advanced] Estimation is easier when the completed program is already available. Why is estimation still needed in this situation? Investigate the methods of estimating the following quantities from the source code:

        a) Executable size.
        b) Static data size.
        c) Stack usage.
        d) Heap usage.
        e) Run-time efficiency.

Chapter 3

Algorithm improvements

Changing the underlying algorithms used by the program is often the only real way to gain a large speed increase. In particular, the data structures used can often be modified to give a significant speed increase. Is there a better way to do what your program does? Is it doing too much unnecessary calculation? Although much depends on the ingenuity of the programmer there are some common techniques for improving the performance of algorithms and their data structures.

3.1 Augmenting data structures

Instead of recalculating data every time you need it, a faster way is to store the data in the data structure. This saves the time of recalculation, which need be done only once. If the data ever changes, the calculations must be redone and stored again. Hence this method works best where data is unchanging.

As an example of augmentation, consider a `struct` defined to represent a line segment. The `struct` contains four fields, for the x and y coordinates of the start and end points:

```
struct line_segment {
    int x1, y1;              /* Start point */
    int x2, y2;              /* End point */
};
```

If the computation of the length of the line segment, using:

```
len = sqrt((y2 - y1) * (y2 - y1) + (x2 - x1) * (x2 - x1));
```

is a common calculation, it can be beneficial to store the length of the line segment as an extra field in the `struct`:

25

```
struct line_segment {
    int x1, y1;                 /* Start point */
    int x2, y2;                 /* End point */
    double length;              /* Length of line segment */
};
```

Whenever this length is needed during calculation it is immediately available as a field member. However, it is important to be careful that there is no consistency problem (where the `length` field is not the true length of the line segment). The main danger is that the `length` field won't be recalculated every time one of the other fields change.

3.2 Storing precomputed results: table lookup

This method aims to replace frequently-called costly function evaluations with table lookup (i.e. array references). For example, when calculating the square root of integers, it is possible to precalculate a table of square roots of integers from 1 to 100. In the main calculations, a call to the `sqrt` function is replaced by a table lookup. The use of precomputation of the `sqrt` function (applied to integers) is shown below:

```
#define NUM  100                    /* Precalculate to 100 */

double sqrt_table[NUM + 1];     /* Table of values */

void precalculate(void)
{
    int i;

    for (i = 0; i < NUM; i++)
        sqrt_table[i] = sqrt((double)i);   /* Use real sqrt */
}

double square_root(int n)
{
    return sqrt_table[n];
}
```

The precalculation uses two separate functions: one to perform the precalculation, and another to calculate the values. The `precalculate` function must be called once by `main`. Alternatively, every call to the `square_root` function could check a `static` boolean flag indicating whether the values have been precalculated yet, and call the `precalculate` function if not. Note that this use of precalculation is only worthwhile if some calculations are repeated (i.e. computing the same result).

A common example of precalculation is boolean functions on characters (e.g. `isupper`). To improve performance, it is possible to precompute an array of 256 bytes with 0 if `isupper` is false, and 1 if `isupper` is true. Then `isupper` is evaluated by indexing the character into the precomputed table:

```
#define isupper(ch)    precomputed_array[ch]
```

This is faster, safer and more portable than the use of a boolean expression such as:

```
#define isupper(ch)    ((ch) >= 'A' && (ch) <= 'Z')
```

which has the danger of side effects in the macro argument, and will fail for a non-ASCII character set.

In fact, many systems implement this function and the other functions in <ctype.h> as a table lookup over the 256 characters (plus an extra one for EOF), with precalculated one *bit* per function — that is, a bit indicating isupper, another bit for islower, etc.

3.3 Lazy evaluation

This method is a slight amendment to precalculation or data structure augmentation. Instead of precalculating every result, results are calculated only as needed. To use this method, it is necessary to indicate somehow whether a result is already in the table. When seeking a result, it is necessary to check if the required value is already present. If it is, table lookup is used to get the result. If not, the value must be calculated, stored in the table and that entry marked as present.

The precomputation of sqrt in the previous section can be modified to become lazy evaluation by adding another array of boolean flags, indicating which of the square roots have been computed. When calculating a square root, the function checks if it has been computed, and calculates it if not.

```
#define NUM_PREC  100          /* Precalculate to 100 */

double square_root(int n)
{
    static double sqrt_table[NUM_PREC+1];   /* Table of values */
    static int precalc[NUM_PREC+1];         /* Array of flags */

    if (!precalc[n]) {                       /* precalculated? */
        sqrt_table[n] = sqrt((double)n);    /* Use real sqrt() */
        precalc[n] = TRUE;                   /* Mark as computed */
    }
    return sqrt_table[n];
}
```

The use of lazy evaluation is slower than complete precalculation if all of the values are eventually calculated (because of the overhead of checking whether calculation is needed). However, it can make the program faster overall if not all calculations are needed. Any unnecessary calculations are avoided.

3.4 Compile-time initialization and precomputation

The examples of the precomputation of square roots in the previous two sections are not particularly efficient because they must still call the sqrt function a number of times. A far more efficient alternative is to use C's compile-time initialization of arrays to set up the precomputed sqrt_table array. Hence, the square_root function becomes a simple lookup into an array variable as follows. Note that the array is declared as static so that the initialization occurs at compile-time. Automatic array initialization is legal in ANSI C so it is important not to omit the static keyword; otherwise the initialization will occur every time the function is entered.

```
#define NUM  100                    /* Precalculate to 100 */

double square_root(int n)
{
    static double sqrt_table[] = {
    0.000000, 1.000000, 1.414214, 1.732051, 2.000000,
    2.236068, 2.449490, 2.645751, 2.828427, 3.000000,
    3.162278, 3.316625, 3.464102, 3.605551, 3.741657,
    3.872983, 4.000000, 4.123106, 4.242641, 4.358899,
    4.472136, 4.582576, 4.690416, 4.795832, 4.898979,
    5.000000, 5.099020, 5.196152, 5.291503, 5.385165,
    5.477226, 5.567764, 5.656854, 5.744563, 5.830952,
    5.916080, 6.000000, 6.082763, 6.164414, 6.244998,
    6.324555, 6.403124, 6.480741, 6.557439, 6.633250,
    6.708204, 6.782330, 6.855655, 6.928203, 7.000000,
    7.071068, 7.141428, 7.211103, 7.280110, 7.348469,
    7.416198, 7.483315, 7.549834, 7.615773, 7.681146,
    7.745967, 7.810250, 7.874008, 7.937254, 8.000000,
    8.062258, 8.124038, 8.185353, 8.246211, 8.306624,
    8.366600, 8.426150, 8.485281, 8.544004, 8.602325,
    8.660254, 8.717798, 8.774964, 8.831761, 8.888194,
    8.944272, 9.000000, 9.055385, 9.110434, 9.165151,
    9.219544, 9.273618, 9.327379, 9.380832, 9.433981,
    9.486833, 9.539392, 9.591663, 9.643651, 9.695360,
    9.746794, 9.797959, 9.848858, 9.899495, 9.949874
    };

    return sqrt_table[n];
}
```

The simplest way to produce the values for the precomputed array is to write another program to produce them. Once the values are produced, this program can be discarded. The following program was used to produce the declaration of sqrt_table used in the square_root function given above. The output from the following program was redirected into the source code for the program above.

```
/*-------------------------------------------------------------*/
/*   Produce C declaration for square root table           */
/*-------------------------------------------------------------*/

#include <stdio.h>
#include <stdlib.h>
#include <math.h>

#define NUM  100                    /* Precalculate to 100 */

int main()
{
    int i;

    puts("static double sqrt_table[] = {");
    for(i = 0; i < NUM; i++) {
        printf("%f", sqrt((double)i));
        if(i + 1 < NUM)
            printf(", ");      /* comma after all but last */
        if(i % 5 == 4 && i + 1 < NUM)
            printf("\n");      /* newline every 5 lines */
    }
    printf("\n};\n");      /* finish off C declaration */
}
```

Compile-time precomputation should always be more efficient than lazy evaluation and run-time precomputation. However, compile-time precomputation is only applicable when the function can be computed at compile-time. If the computation involves any variables whose values are known only at run-time, either lazy evaluation or run-time precomputation may be useful.

3.5 Special solution of simple cases

When solving a problem, simple cases can often be solved by specially designed fast functions. These "special solutions" can involve the table lookup of precalculated values (e.g. storing the first ten factorials in an array) or just a fast algorithm for small cases (e.g. sorting less than five numbers quickly).

In general, the special solution of simple cases will give some speed increase if the simple cases are fairly common. The advantage of simple case precalculation over full precalculation is flexibility — it is not limited to those values that can be stored in a fixed size table.

The use of table lookup for simple cases for the `factorial` function is shown below. The method here gives speed increase for all cases, not just the simple ones, because the recursive definition of `factorial` eventually breaks the problem down to a simple case.

```
#define NUM_PRECALCULATED  5       /* How many precalculated */

int factorial(int n)
{
    static precalc[NUM_PRECALCULATED+1] = {1, 1, 2, 6, 24, 120};

    if (n <= NUM_PRECALCULATED)
        return precalc[n];
    else
        return n * factorial(n - 1);
}
```

3.6 Incremental algorithms

It is often easier to modify what has already been done than to start from scratch. This idea can be used to write faster algorithms. Unfortunately, changing an existing algorithm to use incremental calculations will usually require total redesign of the algorithm.

A simple example of an incremental algorithm is counting the number of symbols in a symbol table. The non-incremental way to count them is to traverse the symbol table, counting the number of entries. The incremental method is to keep a running count — increment it when a symbol is inserted; decrement it when a symbol is deleted. The incremental method is better if the count will be required most times. If the count is not required, there has been some unnecessary overhead.

Another good example appears in graphics animation. When displaying a new screen it is usually more efficient to change the existing screen than to redraw the whole screen. The idea is to set only those pixels that need to be changed.

In a chess-playing program using a game tree and the minimax algorithm (see Chapter 9), the static evaluation function usually analyses the material balance (i.e. how many pieces each side has). A simple but inefficient method of computing the material value of a position is to add the values of each piece on the 64 squares. The efficient incremental algorithm is to subtract the value of the piece from a running count whenever it is captured by the opponent.

3.7 Using simple tests to avoid expensive tests

Many algorithms can be improved by pruning off the alternatives by using a fast test that is often successful. This is only worthwhile when avoiding the complicated test is highly probable; if avoiding it is unlikely, the extra simple test reduces efficiency because it adds (slightly) to the run-time cost.

For example, to implement a ray tracing algorithm for graphical image rendering, it is necessary to determine whether a ray strikes an object. Since the objects are often complex and more often than not the ray will miss an object by a large amount of space, a simple test can be used to quickly identify rays that are close enough to the object to intersect with it. A good simple test is to determine if the ray intersects with the *bounding sphere* of an object, as it is relatively efficient to determine this. If the ray does intersect the sphere, the more expensive tests are applied to determine if the ray intersects with the object. If the ray does not intersect with the sphere, the cost of the more expensive tests has been avoided. Interestingly, the simplicity of testing the intersection of a ray with a sphere helps explain why there are so many ray-traced images of spherical objects.

The similar idea of a *bounding rectangle* is useful for collision detection in arcade games. Collision detection usually involves testing many pairs of objects in a two-dimensional setting, and the tests are complicated because of the different shapes of the objects. The more complicated tests can be avoided by examining whether the bounding rectangles of each object are intersecting. If they do intersect, then a closer examination of whether the objects have pixels that overlap is carried out.

For yet another example of using a simple test to avoid complicated tests, consider the problem of a graphical drawing program, where the user can select a vertex (e.g. the end of a line segment) by clicking "close" to the vertex. In other words, the user must click the mouse within a specified radius of the point. Hence, when the mouse is clicked, the program must compare the mouse location with all the currently active vertices. The obvious method is to use the distance formula for two points and apply the following test on the x and y coordinates of the mouse and all points:

$$\sqrt{(x_{Point} - x_{Mouse})^2 + (y_{Point} - y_{Mouse})^2} \leq DISTANCE$$

The efficiency of this test can be improved by avoiding the calculation of the square root. Squaring both sides of the equation gives the equivalent test:

$$(x_{Point} - x_{Mouse})^2 + (y_{Point} - y_{Mouse})^2 \leq DISTANCE^2$$

However, the multiplications involved in computing the squares of the two sub-expressions on the left are quite expensive, although the square on the right-hand side will be a compile-time constant. A simple test can be used to avoid the multiplications in most cases. If the difference between either the x or the y coordinates is greater than DISTANCE, then the points cannot be close enough. Although the cost of these tests is quite high because the absolute value of the difference must be found, it should still cost less than two multiplications, and will be more efficient if there are many widely spaced points to be tested. The code using this idea is:

```
int check_point(int x_mouse, int y_mouse, int x_point, int y_point)
{
    int x_diff, y_diff;

    x_diff = x_point >= x_mouse ? x_point - x_mouse : x_mouse - x_point;
    if (x_diff > DISTANCE)
        return FALSE;
    y_diff = y_point >= y_mouse ? y_point - y_mouse : y_mouse - y_point;
    if (y_diff > DISTANCE)
        return FALSE;
    return x_diff * x_diff + y_diff * y_diff <= DISTANCE * DISTANCE;
}
```

Of course, the best way of improving the efficiency of this program is to avoid the need for multiplications entirely, by changing the program specifications (!) so that the definition of clicking "close enough" refers to clicking within a *square* around the point, instead of a circle.

3.8 Sentinels

Sentinels refer to a value placed at the beginning or the end of a list or array to indicate a special condition. Sentinels are most commonly used to indicate the end of data to be processed (e.g. the character zero at the end of character strings is a sentinel). This way, the program can test for the presence of the sentinel in the input data, which is faster in many situations than testing for the presence of more data. For example, a program using a buffer can use an end-of-buffer marker as a sentinel instead of checking how many characters are left in the buffer each time; the program merely checks each time that the character returned is not the sentinel.

A clever example of the use of sentinels can be found in the sequential search algorithm applied to arrays. The simplest form of sequential search is:

```
int search(int a[], int key, int n)
{
    int i;

    for (i = 0; i < n; i++) {
        if (key == a[i])
            return i;     /* Found it */
    }
    return -1;        /* Not found */
}
```

The test for whether the whole array has been checked (i.e. i<n) can be eliminated by placing a sentinel at the end of the array. The sentinel's key value is set equal to the key being searched for so that when the search reaches the last element, it will find the correct

key. In other words, the sentinel fakes a successful search. After the search, the algorithm must check whether the value found was the sentinel, or a real success. Setting up the sentinel is the only overhead and this compares favorably with removing the test inside the loop.

```
int search(int a[], int key, int n)
{
    int i;

    a[n] = key;                    /* add sentinel to end of array */
    for (i = 0; key != a[i]; i++)
        ;               /* empty loop */
    if (i == n)
        return -1;     /* Not found. Found sentinel only */
    return i;          /* Found the key */
}
```

Unfortunately, this use of the sentinel introduces a potential problem: the array is modified by the search function. This modification will be dangerous if the function is used to search a subarray. The danger can be removed by saving and restoring the value of a[n].

Sentinels can be applied to a number of algorithms. For example, they can be used for searching linked lists or binary trees. Instead of having NULL pointers at the end of the list (or at the leaves of the tree), these pointers point to a global node. Setting this node's key equal to the search key before beginning the search will avoid testing for NULL pointers during the search. A binary tree implementation using sentinels is discussed in Section 8.13.

3.9 Reducing recursion

Recursion is an elegant method of problem solution, but often incurs unnecessary function call overhead. Where possible, recursion should be replaced with a non-recursive algorithm, particularly if recursion can be removed without using an explicit stack data structure.

With a little insight, many recursive algorithms can be coded without recursion. For example, the Fibonacci number sequence (1,1,2,3,5,8,13,...) is defined by the following recursive rules:

$$F_0 = 1$$
$$F_1 = 1$$
$$F_n = F_{n-1} + F_{n-2}$$

This has the obvious recursive implementation:

```
int fibonacci(int n)
{
    if (n <= 1 )
        return 1;
    else
        return fibonacci(n - 1) + fibonacci(n - 2);
}
```

However, there is no need to use recursion here, and a short loop is adequate. A non-recursive computation of the Fibonacci numbers is shown below:

```
int fibonacci(int n)
{
    int small, large, temp;

    small = large = 1;          /* F0 = F1 = 1 */
    while (n > 1) {
        temp = small + large;   /* Fn = Fn-1 + Fn-2 */
        small = large;
        large = temp;
        n--;
        }
    return large;
}
```

There are many examples of common algorithms that are unnecessarily coded using recursion. Almost all linked list algorithms can be coded without recursion, as can the most common binary search tree operations: search, insertion and deletion. For example, the recursive implementation of tree insertion is:

```
void insert(Tree *root, Tree new_node)
{
    if (*root == NULL)        /* Found bottom of tree */
        *root = new_node;     /* So insert here */
    else {
        if (new_node->data <= (*root)->data)
            insert(&(*root)->left, new_node);
        else
            insert(&(*root)->right, new_node);
    }
}
```

whereas the non-recursive version of tree insertion is given below. It is somewhat less elegant, uses a few more variables, but should be more efficient.

```
void insert(Tree *root, Tree new_node)
{
    Tree temp = *root;
    if (temp == NULL)      /* empty tree is special case */
        *root = new_node;
    else {
        for (;;) {
            if (new_node->data <= temp->data) { /* go left? */
                if (temp->left == NULL) {       /* leaf? */
                    temp->left = new_node;      /* insert it */
                    return;                     /* finished */
                }
                else
                    temp = temp->left;          /* go left */
            }
            else {  /* going right */
                if (temp->right == NULL) {      /* leaf? */
                    temp->right = new_node;     /* insert it */
                    return;                     /* finished */
                }
                else
                    temp = temp->right;         /* go right */
            }
        }
    }
}
```

3.9.1 Tail recursion elimination

An example of recursion elimination without a stack is the elimination of tail recursion. Tail recursion occurs when the last action of the recursive procedure is to call itself. The simple modification changes this last recursive call to become a loop back to the top of the current invocation. For example, consider the preorder traversal of a binary tree. The simplest recursive algorithm is:

```
void preorder(node_ptr root)
{
    if (root != NULL) {
        visit(root);
        preorder(root->left);
        preorder(root->right);      /* Tail recursion here */
    }
}
```

Tail recursion can be eliminated by replacing the `if` statement with a `while` loop. The transformation reduces recursion by half (on average), as the second recursive call is eliminated. This reduction in recursion is achieved with virtually no extra overhead!

```
void preorder(node_ptr root)
{
    while (root != NULL) {          /* while loop replaces if */
        visit(root);
        preorder(root->left);
        root = root->right;         /* Move to right subtree */
    }
}
```

Tail recursion removal can be applied to many kinds of recursive algorithms: quicksort, preorder and inorder traversals (but not postorder).

3.9.2 Replacing recursion with a stack

Some recursive algorithms cannot be easily replaced by non-recursive equivalents. For example, in the binary tree traversal in Section 3.9.1, we were unable to remove both of the recursive calls. In these situations recursion can be replaced with an algorithm using a stack data structure. All recursive algorithms can be replaced by a stack because recursive algorithms are actually using an implicit stack (the program stack of function calls).

Whether use of a stack will be more efficient than a recursive algorithm depends on a number of factors. The choice of a stack over recursion is machine-dependent. In particular, it is quite likely that the program stack is supported by efficient low-level instructions and that (recursive) function calls are executed very efficiently. However, recursion requires that much information be stored on the stack (i.e. parameters, automatic local variables, machine registers), whereas an algorithm making use of an explicit stack will usually only need to store a few items, making it potentially faster than the function call stack. If the maximum size of the required stack is known beforehand, a stack can be quite efficiently implemented as an array (using a linked list will usually be more costly because of the cost of memory allocation). A number of stack implementations are discussed in Chapter 8.

The following shows the preorder traversal with tail recursion elimination removing one recursive call and an explicit stack replacing the other. In this case, the explicit stack need only store pointers. The function is an implementation of an algorithm given in [Standish, 1980, p75].

```
void preorder(node_ptr root)
{
    stack_type S;

    init_stack(S);                    /* set to empty stack */
    while (root != NULL || !is_empty_stack(S)) {
        if (root != NULL) {
            visit(root);              /* visit a tree node */
            push(S, root->right);   /* save right subtree */
            root = root->left;      /* go to left subtree */
        }
        else
            root = pop(S);          /* get node from stack */
    }
}
```

3.9.3 Moving the base case higher

In the simple implementation of the preorder traversal given in Section 3.9.1, the recursive base case is `root==NULL`. If this occurs, the function call does nothing. One method of avoiding these unnecessary function calls is to test for the base case *before* the recursive call. The new function becomes:

```
void preorder(node_ptr root)
{
    while (root != NULL) {
        visit(root);
        if (root->left != NULL)      /* Test moved up */
            preorder(root->left);
        root = root->right;
    }
}
```

3.9.4 Collapsing recursive calls

The method of function call collapsing can be applied to recursive functions in a limited sense. Obviously, it isn't possible to collapse a recursive function call completely into inline code, but it is possible to collapse a few levels of recursive calls into inline code, reducing the total number of recursive calls by a constant factor. This way, the function does much more work each time, and makes recursive calls less frequently. For example, the preorder traversal can be rewritten so that the current node *and its two children* are handled by the function, and then recursive calls are made for any of the children's children:

```
void preorder(node_ptr root)
{
    if (root != NULL) {
        visit(root);
        if (root->left != NULL) {   /* do left child */
                visit(root->left);
                preorder(root->left->left);
                preorder(root->left->right);
        }
        if (root->right != NULL) {  /* do right child */
                visit(root->right);
                preorder(root->right->left);
                preorder(root->right->right);
        }
    }
}
```

3.10 Integer arithmetic

Real arithmetic is slow compared to integer arithmetic. Hence it is favorable to replace real arithmetic by equivalent integer arithmetic. Real arithmetic can be replaced by integer arithmetic when only limited precision is required (e.g. 1-3 decimal places). To do this, work in integer units that are 10, 100 or 1000 times larger (for 1, 2 and 3 decimal places) so that the decimal places appear as the lower digits of the integers.

To convert the integer into its true integer and fractional parts is quite simple. To get at the fractional part, calculate the number modulo 10, 100 or 1000 (using the % operator). To get the true integer part, divide by 10 or 100 or 1000 — remember that integer division truncates the fractional part.

A good example is: when working in dollars and cents, do all calculations in terms of cents (an integer). Then when printing it out, convert to dollars and cents using:

```
cents   = value % 100;
dollars = value / 100;
```

3.11 Approximations

If precision of results is not important, it may sometimes be possible to use approximations to mathematical functions. For example, in computer graphics, the precision of floating point values is often unimportant because the end result will be an integer pixel. An approximation can be used, for example, in the matrix for 2-D rotation when the rotation angle is small. The general matrix equation is:

$$\begin{bmatrix} x2 \\ y2 \end{bmatrix} = \begin{bmatrix} \cos\theta & \sin\theta \\ -\sin\theta & \cos\theta \end{bmatrix} \begin{bmatrix} x1 \\ y1 \end{bmatrix}$$

It is easy to implement this rotation matrix in C, using the sin and cos library functions:

```
x2 = cos(theta) * x1 + sin(theta) * y1;
y2 = - sin(theta) * x1 + cos(theta) * y1;
```

For efficiency, we should avoid computing `sin` and `cos` twice by computing the values once and storing them in temporary variables (this is an example of common sub-expression elimination). However, if the angle, θ, is small enough, we can do much better than this by using the approximations:

$$\cos \theta \equiv 1$$
$$\sin \theta \equiv \theta$$

Hence, we can completely avoid the cost of the computation of `sin` and `cos`:

```
x2 = x1 + theta * y1;
y2 = - theta * x1 + y1;
```

3.12 Avoid busy waiting for input

Humans are very slow compared to computers. In particular, a computer can do much work in the background, even when handling the (slow) interactive input of a human. Hence, one method of improving efficiency is to perform background processing while awaiting input, instead of using blocking input that waits for a keypress before doing anything.

A common example of this idea is chess-playing programs that "think" during their opponent's time. The computer performs a game tree analysis while waiting for the player to press a key. At some regular interval, perhaps before each node of the game tree is analyzed, the program determines if a key has been pressed (e.g. by using the `kbhit` function in Turbo C on an IBM PC). If a key has been pressed, the chess program stores information about its current analysis, and processes the key. Unless the key press completes the user's move, the background analysis can continue after processing the key.

Background processing can be achieved by polling the keyboard regularly or by the clever use of interrupts, but neither method is portable. The ANSI C standard provides no facility for non-blocking input, mainly because of C's UNIX ancestry. It is difficult to poll the keyboard for a traditional UNIX line terminal.

3.13 Reducing disk I/O

The cost of performing I/O on disk files can make up a large proportion of the run-time cost of some programs. For reducing the amount of data to be read from or written to the disk, the main methods are:

- Use smaller records.
- Cache frequently used records.
- Buffer multiple reads or writes.
- Compress data.
- Use better data structures.

A very simple method of reducing disk I/O is to reduce the size of records being read or written. This can be achieved using many of the methods discussed in Chapter 7, such as the use of unions, bit-fields, packing or smaller data types.

Caching is useful if some records are being read more often than others. It is a very general idea and there are many possible implementations. It may be possible to keep all of the most frequently used records in main memory, writing them to disk only at the end of the program (even caching records in memory and writing them to disk for *every* modification will still avoid the cost of multiple disk *reads*). If this method cannot be used, try using several memory locations for record I/O, and whenever a read operation is required, examine these in-memory records first. If any of them is the required record, the cost of a disk read is avoided. Caching always has a slight overhead, and may increase run-time slightly if the desired records are rarely in memory; however, it will never increase the amount of disk I/O and the computational overhead is likely to be small compared to the cost of reading a record from disk.

When reading or writing multiple contiguous records, disk I/O can be speeded up by reading in a number of records each time. The advantage is that buffering multiple operations reduces the number of disk seek operations. This can be achieved by manipulating the buffering of `<stdio.h>` functions using the `setbuf` and `setvbuf` functions.

Another alternative is to use other I/O functions, such as the UNIX `open`, `read` and `write` functions. However, this method reduces portability as these functions are not part of the ANSI standard library.

When the amounts of data being read are quite massive, the level of disk I/O can be reduced by *compressing* the data in the file. Read and write operations then have the overhead of uncompressing or compressing the data, but the cost of this computation may well be less than that of the disk I/O (or it might also be more; be careful!). However, methods of compressing data are beyond the scope of this book.

The use of a different data structure for data in disk files is often worthwhile. In particular, if the disk file is being searched, then many of the search algorithms in Chapter 8 are applicable. For example, binary search can be performed on a direct access file if the data is sorted. However, even binary search is inefficient for large disk files, and data structures specifically intended for disk data should be used. The B-tree is a commonly used data structure, and hashing is another possibility. Unfortunately, these algorithms are highly advanced and again beyond the scope of this book.

3.14 Summary

- Precalculation, especially when combined with compile-time initialization, yields very efficient code.
- For small problem sizes a specialized routine will be more efficient than the most general algorithm.
- Incremental algorithms avoid doing a large amount of work at one time by doing a small amount of work many times.
- Expensive tests can often be avoided by using simpler tests for common cases.
- Sentinels provide a useful coding trick to remove tests from a loop.
- Recursion is inefficient and can be reduced in many ways.

- When the full precision of floating point computations is unnecessary, efficiency can be improved by using approximations or integer arithmetic.
- Computers are much faster than humans and can do background work while accepting human input. Unfortunately, there is no portable method of doing this in C.
- Disk I/O is expensive and can be reduced by techniques such as using smaller records or caching commonly used records.

3.15 Further reading

A good discussion of efficient methods of binary tree traversal is given in the book by Standish. Many of the methods covered here are also examined in Jon Bentley's book, and extra examples of applying the methods can be found there.

BENTLEY, Jon Louis, *Writing Efficient Programs*, Prentice Hall, 1982.

STANDISH, T. A., *Data Structure Techniques*, Addison-Wesley, 1980.

3.16 Exercises

1.   Find an example problem where compile-time precomputation is not applicable, but lazy evaluation or run-time precomputation are.

2.   A chess program displays the chess board on a graphics screen. After each move it re-displays the whole board. How can an incremental algorithm be used to reduce the time spent displaying the new board? How much improvement can be expected?

3.   Implement an `isvowel` function by precalculating a table of 256 bytes, similar to that often used for the `<ctype.h>` character testing functions. It should evaluate to true for letters that are vowels.

4.   Section 3.5 gives a recursive implementation of the factorial function as an example of the special solution of special cases. Improve this function to use a loop instead of recursion, but retain the efficiency of the special solution of simple cases.

5.   Combine tail recursion elimination and collapsing recursive calls for the preorder traversal of Section 3.9.1 to produce a faster preorder traversal function.

Chapter 4

Code transformations

There are several methods of directly improving the efficiency of a program just by changing the source code slightly. These methods are quite general, and apply to many programming languages. The techniques covered are only some of the huge number of general transformations that can be applied to a program to make it slightly more efficient without changing its meaning. The area is a research field in itself. The main techniques have been covered in this chapter, but there are always more.

Some of the methods covered below come from the theory of compiler optimization (e.g. code motion, strength reduction on induction variables, sub-expression elimination). Hence, the compiler will often automatically perform these types of optimizations (when the optimizer is invoked). To some extent, this makes these transformations redundant. Even so, it is good programming practice to avoid situations where these optimizations are needed on a large scale. The compiler does not look at the program as a whole and can miss some "obvious" optimizations.

4.1 Loop transformations

Loops are an obvious place to begin improving the efficiency of a program because the code inside the loop body is likely to be executed a number of times. Hence, any improvement to this code will improve efficiency by a larger factor.

4.1.1 Moving code out of loops

Because loops are frequently executed, they should be as fast as possible. There are several ways to make loops smaller and hence faster. The overall aim is to move as much code as possible out of the loop. Any expressions that are constant during a loop can be calculated before the loop, rather than recalculating inside the loop every time through. For example, the computation of `pi*2.0` in the code:

```
for (i = 0; i < 10; i++)
    a[i] *= pi * 2.0;
```

is the same in each iteration because `pi` does not change. Moving this computation out of the loop makes the code more efficient:

```
scale = pi * 2.0;            /* move multiplication outside loop */
for (i = 0; i < 10; i++)
    a[i] *= scale;
```

A common example occurs with the condition of a `for` loop. The conditional expression in a `for` loop is evaluated at each iteration. Any constant contained in this condition should be evaluated outside the loop. For example, consider the code fragment:

```
for (i = 0; i < strlen(key); i++)
    hash += key[i];
```

The computation of the length of the string using `strlen` does not change, but is calculated at each iteration of the loop (each time the loop condition is tested). Efficiency can be improved by moving the computation of `strlen` outside the loop:

```
len = strlen(key);
for (i = 0; i < len; i++)
    hash += key[i];
```

One danger of moving code out of loops is that the transformation can *increase* the execution time if the loop body is executed zero times. Fortunately, this isn't a danger in either of the examples above — the first loop never executes zero times; the second example must compute `strlen` as the loop test even if it executes zero times. Whenever the danger does exist, the loop can be recoded to prevent the calculation of the expression until after the first loop test. For example, the loop:

```
while(condition) {
    x = 2 * pi;
    ...              /* computation not changing x */
    }
```

could be rewritten as:

```
if(condition) {
    x = 2 * pi;
    do {
    ...              /* computation not changing x */
    } while(condition);
}
```

4.1.2 Loop unrolling

One way to make loops more efficient is to reduce the number of times they are executed. This method does not actually reduce the amount of work done by the loop body, but decreases the number of variable tests in controlling the loop (i.e. reduces loop condition evaluations). Loops can be unrolled to any level. The extreme is when the loop is totally replaced by in-line code. This is the most efficient the loop can get (the loop variable is totally eliminated). For example, the loop:

```
for (i = 0; i < 5; i++)
    a[i] = 0;
```

can be replaced by five assignment statements:

```
a[0] = 0; a[1] = 0;  a[2] = 0;  a[3] = 0;  a[4] = 0;
```

In fact, this can be changed to reuse assigned values:

```
a[0] = a[1] = a[2] = a[3] = a[4] = 0;
```

which may be more efficient in some environments, but might be less efficient in others. Reusing assigned values is discussed in Section 4.3.7.

Even if the total number of iterations is not known at compile-time, loop unrolling can still be achieved by repeating the code inside the loop twice (and modifying the header of the loop). This causes the loop to be executed half as many times, and gains efficiency by eliminating some branch instructions and some control variable manipulations. For example:

```
for (i = 0; i < MAX; i++)
    a[i] = 0;
```

becomes:

```
for (i = 0; i < MAX; ) {
    a[i++] = 0;              /* Unrolled by a factor of 2 */
    a[i++] = 0;
}
```

In the example above, the array a will always be accessed an even number of times, because each iteration of the for loop accesses the array a twice. If MAX is an odd number, the second array reference in the last iteration will access an illegal array element. For example, if MAX is 3, the first iteration will access elements a[0] and a[1], the second (final) iteration will access element a[2] and then attempt to access element a[3]. However, the array contains only three elements, a[0], a[1] and a[2], and thus a[3] is an illegal array reference. A solution to the problem is to declare the array a to have an even size. One way to ensure that the array contains at least an even number of elements is to declare one extra dummy element:

```
int a[MAX + 1];
```

If MAX is odd this extra element prevents a bad array reference; if MAX is even the extra element is just wasted space.

Loops can be unrolled more than twice. The problem of odd-sized arrays is more general, and can be eliminated by declaring the array to contain a number of extra dummy elements. However, it becomes impractical to overcome the problem of odd sizes by declaring arrays larger than necessary. An alternative is to use a short non-unrolled loop to handle the odd cases. For example, the code below uses a loop that is unrolled *eight* times to do most of the work and then use a short loop to catch the extra cases. The unrolled loop can only set elements from zero up to, but not including, the highest multiple of 8 (why?), and the non-unrolled loop is used for the rest. The highest multiple of 8 can be computed easily using bitwise arithmetic because 8 is a power of 2. If the desired unrolling factor is not a power of 2, the less efficient % operator could be used.

```
void clear_array(int a[], int n)
{
    int i, max = n & ~ 07;        /* Highest multiple of 8 */

    for (i = 0; i < max; ) {
        a[i++] = 0;               /* Main loop */
        a[i++] = 0;               /* Unrolled 8 times */
        a[i++] = 0;
        a[i++] = 0;
        a[i++] = 0;
        a[i++] = 0;
        a[i++] = 0;
        a[i++] = 0;
    }

    for (; i < n; i++)            /* Do the odd cases */
        a[i] = 0;
}
```

Note that this general form of loop unrolling is efficient only if n is large, allowing a number of unrolled iterations. If n is too small, the overhead of setting up the loops becomes too costly.

4.1.3 Strength reduction on induction variables

Strength reduction refers to replacing a multiplication by an addition or by a shift. More generally, it refers to replacing an expensive operation with a less expensive one. This is discussed in more detail in Section 4.3.3. This section examines the application of strength reduction techniques to a particular type of variable.

An *induction variable* is a variable that changes in an arithmetic progression during a loop. In other words, it is increased by a fixed number each iteration. The control variable of a for loop is often an induction variable incrementing by one each time.

If there is more than one induction variable in a loop, efficiency can be gained by removing all but one of them. Any constant multiple of an induction variable is also an induction variable. The aim is to replace this multiplication with an addition. Instead of the multiplication, the induction variable is initialized alongside the initialization of the original induction variable, and then incremented each loop iteration. For example, both i and x are induction variables in the loop below:

```
for (i = 1; i <= 10; i++) {
    x = i * 4;                        /* x = 4,8,...*/
    ...
}
```

It is possible to remove the multiplication operation, because x is actually increasing by a fixed amount each iteration.

```
for (i = 1, x = 4; i <= 10; i++, x += 4) {      /* x = 4,8,...*/
    ...
}
```

For the example above, we see that this optimization makes the code almost impossible to read. Hence, the use of strength reduction is recommended only when speed is very important. This improvement is commonly performed automatically by the optimizer.

4.1.4 Looping down to zero

On many machines, testing for zero is more efficient than any other test. This leads to a number of minor optimizations (such as placing the most frequently used enumerated constant first in its declaration), and a quite important improvement involving loops. Loops that start at zero and go upwards to a particular value are quite common in the use of arrays. Any such loops where the order is unimportant (e.g. zeroing an array, computing the maximum/minimum of an array, adding elements of an array, etc), can be transformed to start at the top value and loop down to zero. The only danger is if the loop index variable is used after the loop, because it will have a different value to that after the original loop. For example:

```
for (i = 0; i < N; i++) a[i] = 0;
```

can be rewritten as:

```
for (i = N - 1; i >= 0; i--) a[i] = 0;
```

This method can also be applied to loops that start at 1 and increase, or loops that start at 0 or −1 and decrease.

4.1.5 Nested loops

When two or more loops are nested, the innermost loop should be the one with the *larger* number of iterations. For example, consider the nested loops to initialize a multidimensional array:

```
for (i = 0; i < 10; i++)
    for (j = 0; j < 100; j++)
        a[i][j] = 0;
```

This will be more efficient than having the inner loop iterate 10 times and the outer loop 100 times. The difference in speed is not due to a change in the number of array assignments, but due to the reduction in the number of initializations of the inner variable, j, and increments of the outer variable (i.e. i++).

4.1.6 Loop fusion

Another technique for speed improvement is *loop fusion*. This refers to the merging of similar loops so as to avoid loop overhead. The saving gained is that the total number of operations on the loop variables is reduced. For example, this technique can be used to improve the following code fragment:

```
for (i = 1; i < MAX; i++)
    a[i] = 0;
for (i = 0; i < MAX; i++)
    b[i] = 0;
```

Merging both these almost identical loops is simple, except that care must be taken to handle boundary cases correctly:

```
b[0] = 0;                          /* Boundary case */
for (i = 1; i < MAX; i++)          /* Fuse two loops together */
    a[i] = b[i] = 0;
```

4.1.7 Exit loops early

The use of both `break` and `continue` are efficient, as no more of a loop is executed than is necessary. For example, the inefficient method is to use a boolean variable to indicate the end of the loop, as in:

```
done = FALSE;
while (!done) {
    ch = get_user_choice();
    if (ch == 'q')
        done = TRUE;
    else
        ...      /* rest of loop */
}
```

The efficient method is to use a `break` statement to exit the loop immediately:

```
while (1) {                    /* Infinite loop */
    ch = get_user_choice();
    if (ch == 'q')
        break;                 /* Exit early! */
    else
        ...      /* rest of loop */
}
```

Unfortunately, the overuse of jump statements such as `break` and `continue` can make the control flow of a program unclear.

4.1.8 Correct choice of loop

Although the choice of loop is largely a matter of style, there is an important difference between the post-tested `do` loop, and the pre-tested `for` and `while` loops. The loop condition of a `do` loop is not evaluated on the first iteration and a `do` loop is always executed at least once. However, a `for` or `while` loop condition is evaluated before the first iteration and the loop body need not be executed at all. A common form of inefficiency is declaring loops that are always executed the first time, such as:

```
done = FALSE;
while(!done) {
    ....
}
```

It is more efficient to use the do loop, which avoids a single evaluation of the loop condition:

```
done = FALSE;
do {
    ....
} while(!done);
```

To allow the compiler to generate efficient code for an infinite loop, you should make it easy for the compiler to recognize the loop as infinite, by using a common form: either for(;;), while(1), or do..while(1). A small point is that on some (deficient) compilers, only the form for(;;) is recognized as an infinite loop, and the other forms generate redundant comparisons with the constant 1.

4.1.9 Pointer traversals of arrays

When stepping through an array of elements, it can be faster to use pointer variables. The calculation of the address of an array element, arr[i], from the array name and an integer index can be quite slow. The index must be multiplied by the size of an array element and then added to the address of the array. The direct use of pointers removes the need for this calculation, as the address is just the value stored in the pointer variable (i.e. *ptr). For example, to move through a one-dimensional array of size MAX setting all elements to zero:

```
for (i = 0; i < MAX; i++)
    arr[i] = 0;
```

becomes:

```
for (ptr = arr; ptr < arr + MAX; ptr++)
    *ptr = 0;
```

Note that the expression &arr[MAX] is equivalent to arr+MAX and could also be used in the second for loop.

Although the addition of MAX to arr in the for loop condition should be recognized by the compiler as a constant expression and evaluated at compile-time, some compilers may not do so. In this case, it may be more efficient to use an integer variable to count the number of iterations of the loop:

```
n = MAX;
for (ptr = arr; n != 0; n--, ptr++)
    *ptr = 0;
```

Pointers can also be used for traversing multi-dimensional arrays. The method is the same regardless of the dimension of the array. The expression arr+X_MAX (where X_MAX is the number of elements in the first dimension) always calculates the address of the first byte *not* in the array. For example, the two-dimensional case is:

```
int arr[X_MAX][Y_MAX];

for (ptr = arr; ptr < arr + X_MAX; ptr++)
    *ptr = 0;
```

Note that because of how arrays are stored, the order in which the elements are visited is equivalent to two nested `for` loops shown below. Note also that the `for` loop above will work for arrays of dimension greater than two (assuming X_MAX to be the size of the first dimension).

```
for (i = 0; i < X_MAX; i++)
    for (j = 0; j < Y_MAX; j++)
        arr[i][j] = 0;
```

4.2 Control flow transformations

C and C++ have a number of control statements, including loops, `if` statements and `switch` statements. Although greater speed improvement can be achieved through improving loops, there is also room for improvement in the use of `if` and `switch` statements.

4.2.1 Common case first

When testing for a number of different conditions, it is best to test the most common case first. If it is true, the other tests are not executed. When using multiple `if-else-if` statements, place the common case first. For example, consider the binary search function:

```
if (key > a[i])
    ...
else if (key < a[i])
    ...
else
    ...            /* equality */
```

Equality is the least likely of all three conditions, and hence it goes last. Greater-than and less-than are more common, so they go first.

The idea of common case first also appears in boolean expressions using `&&` or `||`. The short-circuiting of these operators makes them very efficient when the common case is first. For `||`, the most likely condition should be placed first (i.e. most likely to be true). For `&&`, the most unlikely condition should be placed first (i.e. most likely to be false).

4.2.2 Simple case first

This method is similar to common case first and involves testing the *simplest* condition first. More complicated (and more time-consuming) computations can be avoided if the first test succeeds (or fails, depending on the context). The opportunity to use this method appears in two main situations: the `if-if` construct (nested `if` statements), and with the logical operators (`&&` and `||`). The simplest test should be the first of a pair of nested `if` statements and should also be the first operand of a `&&` or `||` operator. In the examples below, the sub-expression `x!=0` is evaluated first because it is the simplest and hence the least expensive to evaluate.

```
if (x != 0)
    if (expensive_fn(x) != 0)
        ...

if (x != 0 && expensive_fn(x) != 0)
    ...
```

4.2.3 switch versus else-if sequences

When performing a multiway branch based on the comparison of a *single* expression with a number of *constant* values, there are two possibilities: the `switch` statement or a sequence of `if-else-if` statements. For example, the `switch` statement:

```
switch(c)   {
    case 'a':   ...
                break;
    case 'b':   ...
                break;
    case 'd':   ...
                break;
    default:    ...
                break;
}
```

can also be written as:

```
if (c == 'a')    ...
else if (c == 'b')    ...
else if (c == 'd')    ...
else      ...  /* default statements */
```

Generally speaking, the `switch` statement will be more efficient. Although the method used by a compiler to implement a `switch` statement will vary between implementations, it is reasonable to assume that the compiler will generate quite efficient code. There are a few main methods by which the compiler implements a `switch` statement:

1. Jump table for non-sparse values.
2. Value-address pair table for sparse values.
3. `if-else-if` sequences.

If the case values are not sparse, it can be worthwhile to construct a jump table of addresses. For example, the code above is perfectly compact, and the `switch` statement will probably be implemented in a manner similar to the "pseudo-C" code below:

```
jump_table[] = {
    ADDRESS1,       /* address of code for 'a' */
    ADDRESS2,       /* address of code for 'b' */
    DEFAULT_ADDR    /* address of default code */
    ADDRESS3        /* address of code for 'd' */
};

i = c - 'a';                /* compute index into table */
if (i < 0 || i > 2)         /* check for default case */
    goto DEFAULT_ADDR;
goto jump_table[i];
```

This is quite efficient, and will actually be more efficient if the number of case labels is larger. Note that the jump table has one wasted entry for the 'c' case, which must jump to the code for the default label. The jump table becomes space inefficient if the case values are sparse (say 1, 10, 100 and 1000), because the jump table becomes filled with entries that jump to the default code. Hence, for sparse values it is more space-efficient, but slightly less time efficient, to use a table of value-address pairs, and search this table (using linear or binary search), as shown in the pseudo-C code below:

```
pair_table[] = {
    1,    ADDRESS1,   /* code for 1 */
    10,   ADDRESS2,   /* code for 10 */
    100,  ADDRESS3,   /* code for 100 */
    1000, ADDRESS4    /* code for 1000 */
};

        /* linear search of pair_table */
i = 0;
while (i < 4) {
    if (c == pair_table[i].value)       /* found it? */
        goto pair_table[i].address;
    i++;
}
goto DEFAULT_ADDR;   /* not found; goto default label */
```

If the set of case values has a mixture of compact ranges and sparse values, the compiler may implement a mix of the two methods above. For example, if the values are 1, 10, 100, 1000, 'a'..'z' and '0'..'9', the compiler might test the switch value to determine if it is in the range 'a'..'z' or '0'..'9' using a jump table in each case, and then test for the other sparse values.

Yet another method of implementing the switch statement would be to actually use the machine language equivalent of a sequence of if-else-if statements if there are only a few cases. In the examples above, because the switch was based on only 3 or 4 values, it might in fact be faster to compare each in turn. Nevertheless, this does *not* imply that if-else-if statements be used when the number of cases is small (unless your compiler is hopeless), because a good compiler will determine which method of implementation will be better for a particular set of values. Converting to if-else-if statements will prevent a good compiler from optimizing the switch statement.

There is one situation where it is worthwhile to use if-else-if statements instead of a switch statement to implement the *common case first* optimization. This occurs when the programmer has knowledge that the compiler does not, such as the expected distribution of frequencies of each case. For example, if in a switch statement there is one normal value and all others are exceptional conditions, it will usually be more efficient to test for the normal condition using an if statement, and then test for the other conditions using a switch, as below:

```
if (value == NORMAL) ...
else
switch(value) {
        case EXCEPTION1:   ....
        case EXCEPTION2:   ....
        ... /* etc */
};
```

If the normal condition occurs 99% of the time, then the `if` test will succeed 99% of the time and the `switch` will not be executed. A single conditional test of an `if` statement is likely to be a single machine language instruction, whereas if NORMAL was another case value in the `switch`, any of the implementation methods would involve a number of instructions. By using an `if` statement followed by a `switch` statement, the cost of a common case has been reduced, but the cost of the less common cases is increased very slightly.

4.3 Expressions

With C's large variety of operators and data types, it isn't surprising that there are many ways to increase the speed with which an expression is evaluated. Carefully coding an expression can increase its speed quite noticeably, and this can be very important in programs that perform much computation.

4.3.1 Algebraic identities

The calculations in some complicated expressions can be reduced by transforming the expression into another equivalent form. The aim when using algebraic identities is to group the operations differently, to reduce the total number of arithmetic operations. Care must be taken to ensure that the new expression has equivalent meaning. For example, the short-circuiting of the logical operators can cause differences. Some useful arithmetic identities are:

```
2 * x == x + x == x << 1
a * x + a * y ==  a * (x + y)
 -x + -y   ==   -(x + y)
```

There are also some identities that can be used to improve the efficiency of boolean expressions. The distributive laws of `&&` and `||` can occasionally be used to avoid evaluating a condition twice, provided the condition does not contain any side effects:

```
(a && b) || (a && c) == a && (b || c)
(a || b) && (a || c) == a || (b && c)
```

There are also two identities involving the `!` operator, called De Morgan's laws when used in mathematical texts. In source code notation, they are:

```
!a && !b == !(a || b)
!a || !b == !(a && b)
```

These identities can be used in almost all situations as they preserve the expression's semantics, regardless of whether the sub-expressions contain side effects. Using the identities from left to right will reduce the number of `!` operations by one. When the sub-expressions involve relational operators, using these identities from right to left can improve efficiency. For example:

```
! (x == y || y < z)
```

is more efficient when transformed to:

```
! (x == y) && ! (y < z)
```

because it can then be reduced to:

```
(x != y) && (y >= z)
```

and the ! operation in the original expression has been removed.

4.3.2 Eliminating common sub-expressions

In a complicated expression, there are often repeated sub-expressions. These are inefficient as they require the computer to calculate the same value twice or more. To save time, calculate the sub-expression first and store it in a temporary variable. Then replace the sub-expression with the temporary variable. For example:

```
x = (i * i) + (i * i);
```

becomes:

```
temp = i * i;
x = temp + temp;
```

Note that:

```
x = (temp = i * i) + temp;          /* WRONG */
```

may fail because of its reliance on the order of evaluation of the + operator.

Common sub-expressions do not occur only in single statements. It often happens that a program computes the same thing in subsequent statements. For example, in the code sequence:

```
if (x > y && x > 10)
    ...
if (x > y && y > 10)
    ...
```

the boolean condition x>y need be calculated only once:

```
temp = (x > y);
if (temp &&  x > 10)
    ...
if (temp &&  y > 10)
    ...
```

A common example involves the strcmp library function. Consider the following code sequence:

```
if (strcmp(s1, s2) == 0)
        printf("equal");
else if (strcmp(s1, s2) < 0)
        printf("less than");
else
        printf("greater than");
```

The call to `strcmp` is a common sub-expression that should be removed. Because it involves a function call it is unlikely that the optimizer will improve this automatically. The more efficient code uses an extra `int` variable:

```
ret = strcmp(s1, s2);
if (ret == 0)
        printf("equal");
else if (ret < 0)
        printf("less than");
else
        printf("greater than");
```

4.3.3 Good operator use

C's operators are usually implemented in the most efficient way possible. Hence, it makes good sense to use them where possible. The increment and decrement operators are often especially efficient, as they correspond exactly to low-level assembly language increment and decrement operations. The extended assignment operators are very efficient — never use x=x+2 because x+=2 is more efficient (it evaluates the address of x only once).

4.3.3.1 Replacing multiplication and division with bit shifts

The shift operators are often more efficient than multiplication and division. One optimization is to replace multiplication or division by a power of 2 with a bit shift. Unfortunately, this optimization is only possible for integer multiplication and division, because shift operators do not work with `float` or `double` operands. Left shift corresponds to integer multiplication and right shift corresponds to integer division (for positive numbers only, as discussed below). For example:

```
a *= 2;
```

can be replaced by:

```
a <<= 1;
```

It is important to be careful when making this modification. The operator precedence of << is different to that of *, so that changing:

```
x = a + b * 2;
```

to use the << operator, as in:

```
x = a + b << 1;
```

is incorrect. It is accidentally equivalent to:

```
x = (a + b) << 1;
```

The solution is to bracket the expression, and take no chances. Note also that multiplication by 2 is equivalent to shift by 1. The change above requires a different integer operand as well as the change of operator.

Caution is also required when replacing division with >> when dealing with negative integers. Although >> is fine for positive integers, it has undefined behavior on negative integers. Some machines will sign extend which means that the value of the sign bit is propagated right but remains the same and this is equivalent to division. Some other machines will pad the leftmost bits with zero which yields a positive integer and >> applied to negative integers is not equivalent to division. Even if it is correct on your machine, making use of this feature compromises portability.

4.3.3.2 Replacing % with &

Bitwise-and may be more efficient than the % operator, because % will implicitly perform a division. When finding the remainder from division by a power of 2, a bit mask can be equivalent. For example:

```
y = x % 16;
```

is equivalent to:

```
y = x & 0xF;
```

The operand to apply to the bitwise-and operator is one less than the operand to the % operator — 0xF is hexadecimal for 15 (use of hexadecimal constants is good style as it emphasizes that bitwise arithmetic is being used).

Another example is the test whether a number is even or odd. A portable test is:

```
#define ODD(x)   (x % 2 != 0)    /* Portable */
```

This macro will work for positive and negative values, whereas a similar macro:

```
#define ODD(x)   (x % 2 == 1)    /* Non-portable */
```

is not portable and may fail for negative values of x because it is undefined (even in ANSI C) whether the sign of the result of % on negative operands is positive or negative. Hence, the expression −5 % 2 may return either 1 or −1.

A more efficient version of ODD using bitwise-and can be written, but more care must be taken with portability. The obvious macro:

```
#define ODD(x)   ((x & 1) == 1)    /* Non-portable */
```

will fail for negative values on machines that use the 1's complement representation. However, the efficient macro can be used if the program is only using positive values. Alternatively, this efficient macro can be used in a more portable manner as follows:

```
#if (-1 & 1) == 1         /* will the fast macro work? */
#    define ODD(x)  ((x & 1) == 1)    /* Fast macro */
#else
#    define ODD(x)  (x % 2 != 0)      /* Robust macro */
#endif
```

Conditional compilation will cause the efficient macro to be used on machines for which it will not fail; otherwise the more portable version is used. Unfortunately, this can fail for cross-compilers where the preprocessor may be using arithmetic that differs from the arithmetic used by the run-time machine.

4.3.3.3 Avoiding %

One common use of the remainder operator is the use of modulo arithmetic, such as the wraparound array implementation of a queue abstract data type, where the value of a variable is cyclically counted from 0 up to N−1, and then back to 0. The most common method of coding this is:

```
x = (x + 1) % N;
```

However, the % operator is expensive, and in this case it is not really needed. The following code sequence performs the same task more efficiently:

```
if (x == N - 1)
    x = 0;
else
    x++;
```

which can also be written more concisely, but not necessarily more efficiently, as:

```
(x == N - 1) ? (x = 0) : (x++)
```

Another example of a clever avoidance of % is when the operand is similar to the usual byte or word size. For example:

```
x % 256
```

can be more efficiently coded as:

```
x & 255
```

but can be even more efficiently coded as:

```
(unsigned char) x
```

because the conversion to this type will be efficiently implemented by grabbing a byte out of a word. Unfortunately, this method is not portable to all systems, as it relies on unsigned char containing 8 bits.

4.3.3.4 Replacing division with multiplication

Multiplication is often slightly faster than division, and in some cases a division can be replaced by a multiplication using the reciprocal. A case in point is floating point division by a constant. For example, the division:

```
x = y / 100.0;
```

can be replaced by the multiplication:

```
x = y * 0.01;
```

If the divisor is a symbolic constant, it is possible to replace the symbolic constant with a hard-coded constant (or another symbolic constant). However, it is more convenient to replace the constant with an explicit reciprocal calculation. For example:

```
x = y / DIVISOR;
```

can be rewritten as:

```
x = y * (1.0 / DIVISOR);
```

and the compiler will (usually) calculate the reciprocal of the constant at compile-time. However, be warned that some compilers will defer the computation to run-time and the transformation will increase execution time. Also note that the brackets around the division expression are necessary; otherwise, an ANSI conforming compiler is forced to calculate the expression left to right in compliance with associativity rules.

There appears little to be done to replace *integer* division with multiplication. Multiplying by the reciprocal will change an integer operation to a floating point operation and will probably increase execution time.

4.3.3.5 Increment versus assignment

On some computers the ++ operator is faster than assignment. This fact can be useful for setting boolean flags to "true". Rather than assign the value 1 to the boolean variable, use the fact that it is actually an `int` or `char` variable and increment it instead (assuming an earlier initialization to zero). This efficiency improvement was often used in software tools with boolean flags to indicate what command line options were set. All flags were initially zeroed (by declaring them as global variables), and when a command-line option was detected, the appropriate flag was incremented (i.e. set to true). This method had the slight danger that if a user specified the same option 256 times, the flag would be incremented back to zero, but the problem is rather unlikely!

On machines that have a very fast increment machine language instruction it can be worthwhile to change addition of small constants to use the increment operator. For example:

```
x += 2;
```

could be rewritten as:

```
x++; x++;
```

However, this will reduce efficiency on machines with no special increment instruction.

4.3.3.6 The conditional operator versus if statements

There is no reason to suppose that the conditional operator will be better than the corresponding `if` statement. Both will be implemented as efficiently as possible, and might well produce identical code. However, some compilers will handle them differently, and it may be useful to determine which will be faster for your particular compiler. There is no general rule on which to choose.

On some compilers it may be more efficient to leave the conditional operator's return value unused. For example, instead of:

```
max = x > y ? x : y;
```

a slightly more efficient version may be:

```
x > y ? (max = x) : (max = y);
```

4.3.4 Boolean flags

Because C has no boolean type, the value from a conditional test (0 or 1) can be used in an expression. Boolean conditions can be stored in integer variables. For example, depending on your compiler, the code below:

```
if (x > y)
    flag = TRUE;
else
    flag = FALSE;
```

may be less efficient than the single assignment statement:

```
flag = (x > y);
```

However, in the `if` statement, the > operator need not actually evaluate to 0 or 1 (the compiler will just compare x and y and branch appropriately). In the second form, x>y must actually be evaluated as 0 or 1 and this restriction may well mean that the code is not more efficient.

Overuse of this idea may well lead to code that is very inefficient. For example:

```
if (x < 0)
    y = 5;
else
    y = 0;
```

could be rewritten as a single assignment statement:

```
y = 5 * (x < 0);
```

but this is likely to be much less efficient than the first form because it uses the expensive multiplication operator.

4.3.5 Parallel arrays versus arrays of struct

The replacement of arrays of `struct` with a number of "parallel" arrays (i.e. one array per `struct` field name) can reduce the cost of accessing a data value. However, such a change to the program will often be bad style, and will prevent related data values being manipulated via a single `struct` variable. For example, the two alternatives are shown for the storage of a person's name and age:

```
struct node {           /* Array of struct */
    int age;
    char * name;
} s[10];

int age_array[10];      /* Two parallel arrays */
char * name_array[10];
```

Using the array of `struct`, the `name` field must be accessed using:

```
s[i].name
```

which involves an internal integral computation similar to:

```
s + i * sizeof(struct node) + offsetof(name)
```

Using parallel arrays avoids having to add the field's offset. The equivalent code would be:

```
name_array[i];
```

which would be calculated internally as:

```
name_array + i * sizeof(char*)
```

The main disadvantage of parallel arrays is stylistic, in that separating related data values makes the code unreadable. An efficiency disadvantage of parallel arrays is that aggregate `struct` assignments cannot be used to swap all of the data fields. Hence, if structure assignment is one of the most common operations on an array of structures, converting to parallel arrays may lead to inefficiency.

4.3.6 Register variables

Declaring variables as `register` is a method of improving the speed of programs without sacrificing clarity. By placing the word `register` before variable declarations, the compiler is advised to store the variables in hardware registers, if possible. The compiler is free to ignore this advice if there are no available registers. The idea is that the programmer can indicate to the compiler which variables are most used. In the absence of any `register` variables, the compiler makes its own decisions which may or may not be good decisions — it depends on the heuristics used.

This method may cause some speedup, but if the compiler is clever it would have already chosen the most often used variables to store in registers, and there will be no difference. No harm is done, and it can be worthwhile. A good habit to get into is declaring loop variables and pointers as `register` immediately (rather than going back later to change them). For example:

```
register int i, j;
```

Despite the advantages, do not declare too many variables as `register`. Declare only those that really are used most frequently as `register`. If too many variables are declared as `register`, the compiler cannot know which are the most frequently used.

4.3.7 Reusing assigned values

Improving efficiency by reusing the value of the assignment operator is a common but perhaps misguided technique. It is not likely to yield anything but a very minor improvement, if any, and in fact it might even increase the cost. A reasonably intelligent compiler should perform most of the optimizations automatically.

The assignment operator returns a value that can be used. It returns the value of its right operand (i.e. the value that was being assigned) but with the type of the left operand. On some machines it is worth using the return value of the assignment operator. For example, when setting two variables to the same value, both can be set in one statement. The two statements:

```
i = VALUE;
j = VALUE;
```

can be abbreviated to:

```
i = j = VALUE;
```

Both variables are set to VALUE. The assignment operator is right-associative, so that the above statement is equivalent to "i=(j=VALUE);", so that j is set to VALUE, and then i is set to the result of the assignment (i.e. VALUE). This idea can be generalized to any number of variables, if they are all to be set to the same value and any expression can be used on the right-hand side.

Be warned, however, that on some compilers, reusing the value of the assignment operator may cause *inefficiency*. In particular, using a common initialization statement such as:

```
x = y = 0;
```

may well be less efficient than using two assignment statements. The use of the result of the assignment operator makes the expression more complicated than usual and may require the compiler to add extra instructions. In addition, if the machine has a fast set-to-zero instruction, the reuse of the result of the assignment operator makes it less obvious to the compiler that the statement is setting x to 0, and it might not use the faster instruction.

Nevertheless, using the assigned value inside an if statement or loop condition is quite a common method of improving efficiency slightly. It is efficient as the value returned from the assignment is used directly in the condition, instead of having to be accessed again. For example:

```
f = fopen(filename, "r");
if (f != NULL)
    ...         /* etc */
```

becomes:

```
if ((f = fopen(filename, "r")) != NULL)
    ...         /* etc */
```

Another form of this method is to avoid recalculating values by passing a function result directly to another function. For example, consider the code below which allocates memory for a string and then concatenates two strings into the location.

```
s3 = malloc(MAX);      /* Allocate memory */
strcpy(s3, s1);        /* Copy first string there */
strcat(s3, s2);        /* Append second string to first */
```

Although not used in the code above, the strcpy and strcat standard library functions both return a pointer to the newly modified string. Hence, the three lines above can be combined into a single statement:

```
s3 = strcat(strcpy(malloc(MAX), s1), s2);
```

The advantage is that the calculation of the address of s3 need not be duplicated.

4.3.8 Removing tests for zero

Tests of equality with zero are redundant because the compiler always tests a conditional expression with zero. Zero is assumed to be false, and any non-zero value is true. This means that comparisons with zero as in the expressions:

```
if (x != 0)
if (x == 0)
if (ptr != NULL)
if (ch != '\0')
```

are redundant and can be replaced by `if(x)`, `if(!x)`, `if(ptr)` and `if(ch)`. However, these comparisons do represent good style and the optimizer will often remove the comparisons for you automatically. Any improvement in speed due to this method is likely to be negligible.

4.3.9 Packing boolean flags into integers

If several boolean flags must be checked at once it can be worth storing them all as bits of an `int`. It is then easy to check if any are true by comparing the `int` to zero. If the `int` is non-zero, the individual bits can be examined using bit masks. Accessing individual bits becomes more time-consuming, so this method is only worthwhile if individual bits are rarely examined (e.g. the bits indicate rare error conditions).

4.3.10 Most used struct field first

References to the first field of a structure can often be more efficient than references to other fields because there is no need to add an offset. Hence, the most used `struct` field should be placed first in the declaration. For example, when declaring a `struct` for a linked list, it is probably most efficient to place the `next` field first, as follows:

```
struct list_node {
    struct list_node *next;   /* Most used field first */
    data_type data;           /* Other fields */
};
```

4.4 Avoiding type conversions

One fairly common cost in expressions is the cost of converting between different data types, either explicitly requested by the programmer or performed automatically by the compiler. With some care, many of these conversions can be avoided, thus improving the speed of computing expressions.

4.4.1 Correct type of constants

The use of the correct type of arithmetic constants can avoid the cost of some type conversions. For example, it is important to always use explicit `float` constants in any `float` computations. For example, if x and y are of type `float`, the code:

```
y = x * 3.14;
```

will actually cause `double` multiplication (even though ANSI allows single precision arithmetic) because 3.14 has type `double`, thus promoting the other argument, x, to `double` and invoking `double` multiplication. To get the benefit of ANSI's single precision `float` arithmetic, the constant must be given the suffix f to indicate that it has type `float`. Another try is `(float) 3.14`, but some deficient compilers may generate a run-time conversion for the type cast.

For similar reasons, it is important to use the correct suffix for `long` constants and `long double` constants. However, these are less of a problem because the compiler may well promote their types "upwards" at compile-time.

4.4.2 int only, double only

Mixing different types can make implicit type conversion necessary (e.g. mixing `int`, `short` and `char`). These type conversions take up valuable execution time and can be eliminated by using only `int` variables, possibly leading to a small speed improvement.

In older non-ANSI compilers, all floating point arithmetic is carried out in double precision. This can necessitate type conversions from `float` to `double`, even if all variables are declared of type `float`! Using only `double` variables (and no `float` variables) can make a slight improvement. The brute-force way to achieve this is:

```
#define float  double      /* All floats become doubles */
```

The use of `float` values should also be avoided when using the standard library functions. All functions in `<math.h>` have `double` arguments and `double` return values, and using `float` will cause many conversions. Similarly, printing a `float` value using `printf` will require a conversion to `double`, because `printf` is a variable-argument list function and the non-prototyping conversions are applied (i.e. `float` to `double`, `char` and `short` to `int`).

4.4.3 Avoiding unsigned arithmetic

The basic type, `int`, usually corresponds with the machine's word size, and `int` computations are often particularly fast. This is not necessarily true of `unsigned` arithmetic, where ANSI's strict requirements for proper behavior on overflow and underflow may mean that the compiler has to generate special slower sequences of machine instructions. However, note that most machines use 2's complement arithmetic, and in this case `unsigned` arithmetic will be no slower because the ANSI requirements are identical to what will happen in this case. Thus, the use of `unsigned` integers can slow the program down on some machines, but will cause no difference for most.

4.4.4 Avoiding bit-fields

Bit-fields are designed to reduce space in a structure, often at the cost of extra run-time overhead on any accesses to these fields. For improved efficiency, at the cost of space wastage, change all bit-fields to `signed int` or `unsigned int`. For example, to improve the efficiency of accesses to the `visited` field in the `struct` below, simply remove the `:1` qualification (and the `unsigned` qualifier).

```
struct node {
    unsigned int visited :1;   /* bit-field */
};
```

It may also be beneficial to convert the type of `visited` to a smaller data type such as `char`, rather than `int`.

4.5 Compile-time initialization

C's syntax for initializing variables is not only very convenient, but also very efficient when applied to global or local `static` variables. For this type of variable, initialization takes place at compile-time rather than at run-time, and has only minimal run-time cost (the data must be initialized somehow, so there will be the cost of loading the initialized data from the executable, if nothing else). Hence, an efficiency improvement is to change automatic initialized variables to `static`. This change is applicable when a variable need not be re-initialized each time the function is entered (e.g. the variable is never changed by the function). The change is most effective when applied to aggregate variables (arrays, structures and unions), where the initialization costs are higher.

In some cases it is possible to alter the design of an algorithm to make use of compile-time initialization. For example, this was achieved in the use of precomputation in Section 3.5, and also in the tic-tac-toe game in Chapter 9.

4.5.1 #define versus const

The following discussion is relevant to C, but not to C++. `const` and `#define` are effectively identical for symbolic constants in C++, and use of `const` is far better style.

The definition of symbolic constants using `#define` is likely to be more efficient than the use of `const` variables. `const` variables are not really constants, and the compiler cannot include them in C's restricted constant expressions (i.e. efficiency is not the only reason to avoid `const` variables). Whenever both `#define` and `const` are allowed, `#define` is often more efficient because the compiler can perform "constant folding" (i.e. compile-time evaluation of a constant expression), whereas most compilers will generate code to access a `const` variable (although a sophisticated optimizer could apply constant folding to `const` variables). For example, in the expression:

```
MAX + 1
```

if `MAX` is `#define`'d as `30`, the compiler will replace the expression `30+1` with `31`, but if `MAX` is a `const` variable, the compiler will (usually) generate a sequence of instructions to load `MAX` and add 1 to it.

4.5.2 Constant folding

The compiler will attempt to evaluate any constant expressions that it can, and this process is called "constant folding". Hence, a programmer can slightly improve efficiency by making it "easier" for the compiler to recognize constant expressions. For example, if `x` is a variable and not a constant, the expression:

```
2 * x * 3.14
```

should be replaced by:

```
(2 * 3.14) * x
```

because then the compiler can compute `2*3.14` at compile-time, whereas the first expression cannot be optimized because ANSI requires that the associativity of operators be honored. Some compilers might perform this type of optimization for integers, but are unlikely to do so for floating point numbers.

It is important to ensure that the constants are placed together so that they can be obviously joined, without disregarding associativity. For example, in the code below:

```
x = c + ( 'A' - 'a' );
```

the brackets surrounding the two character constants are important because they allow the compiler to compute the constant expression. Brackets were not strictly necessary in the first example because the associativity of `*` is left-to-right, causing `2*3.14` to be evaluated first, but using brackets is a habit that promotes efficiency.

4.6 Functions

Several optimizations can be applied to improve the performance of functions. Function calls have a reasonable amount of overhead, and any reduction in this overhead is quite worthwhile.

4.6.1 Prototypes

ANSI C's introduction of prototypes improves efficiency by allowing the compiler to use more efficient calling sequences. Hence, a program that uses prototypes may run faster than one that doesn't use them. One of the main advantages of prototyping is that `char`, `short` and `float` arguments need not be promoted, but can be passed directly to the (prototyped) function. The cost of conversion is avoided. Further reasons why function prototypes aid the compiler in generating efficient code are explored in Chapter 10.

4.6.2 Passing pointers to structures

All variables except array variables are passed by value in C. This means that when calling a function, a copy of every variable is made and stored in the activation record for the function. Hence, if whole `structs` are passed, whole `structs` must be copied. It is efficient to pass the address of the `struct`, and use a pointer to this `struct` inside the function. This way only one pointer is copied.

The trap is that the safety of call-by-value is lost and changes made to the local variable also appear in the calling function (as passing is now by reference, and not by value). However, the compiler can be used to detect situations that may change the value simply by qualifying the parameter declaration with `const`. For example, the function:

```
void visit(struct node n)
{
    printf("%d\n", n.data);
}
    ....
visit(str);    /* Call the function */
```

can be modified to become:

```
void visit(const struct node *n)    /* const pointer */
{
    printf("%d\n", n->data);         /* change . to -> */
}

....
visit(&str);   /* Call the function using extra & */
```

The C++ language supports reference parameters which are introduced by adding & to the parameter declaration. The use of references does not require any change to calls to the function, nor any changes of "." to "->" in the function body. The function in C++ would be:

```
void visit(const node & n)    // n is reference parameter
{
    printf("%d\n", n.data);   // no need to use "->"
}

....
visit(str);    // Call the function
```

Class objects, structures or unions should be passed by reference when efficiency is important. C++ reference parameters are discussed further in Section 5.2.

4.6.3 Converting functions to macros

If the program has many levels of nested function calls it can often be speeded up by reducing the level of function calls. This is particularly true of frequently called small functions, where the overhead of function call prologue and epilogue can claim a significant proportion of the function's time usage. Efficiency can be improved by replacing the function call with in-line code. This way, the overhead of the function call is eliminated. In C++ the conversion of function calls to inline code can be achieved automatically by adding the `inline` keyword to the function definition (see Section 5.3). In C, the obvious method is to convert the function into a macro.

There are a few dangers in converting a function to a macro. The first is that any side effects in arguments to a call to the function can cause problems. If this happens with a macro call, the results can be plagued with bugs. The second danger is that, if the function changes its parameters, these changes to arguments passed to the function will be passed back to the calling function if the function becomes a macro. The power of call by reference is achieved without pointers, but the safety of call-by-value is lost.

Although the conversion of a function to a macro is more of an art than a process to be mechanized, there are some common steps to follow. First, a few simple textual changes are needed:

- Delete the types of variables in the parameter list.
- Add a backslash at the end of each line.
- Add brackets around parameters in the replacement text.

The backslashes are needed to make a long function into a multi-line macro. The extra brackets around parameters prevent operator precedence problems.

The best functions to convert to macros are very simple ones. For larger functions, there are some major problems to deal with:

- The `return` statement.
- Loops and `if` statements.
- Local variables.

The `return` statement does not work inside a macro. If the `return` statement is left in the macro, the `return` will leave the encompassing function, possibly even `main`!

Converting `void` functions is usually quite straightforward. The braces are left around the statements in the function. Local variables are left unchanged (they are still in a block). If the function uses `return` in the middle of the function, the control structure of the macro must be changed to give the same effect (using `if-else`).

Non-`void` functions present further problems because a result has to be returned. The entire macro must be an expression, as only an expression can return a result. A block cannot return a result. For simple functions the conversion can be quite easy, but for large functions it can be difficult or impossible. The whole structure of the function may have to be modified to overcome problems with local variables and general control structure.

Sequences of statements can be made an expression by using the comma operator (i.e. replace each semicolon with a comma). Any `if-else` statement can be made an expression by using the conditional operator. There is no obvious solution to the removal of a loop or `switch` statement. A function containing a loop should stay as a function!

The problems caused by the `return` statement are larger in non-`void` functions. The control structure must be modified so that the effect of an early `return` is achieved and this is more difficult because of the replacement of `if-else` statements by the conditional operator. Furthermore, if the function contains sequences the returned value must be computed as the last operand of the comma operator. Hence, it is much simpler to convert a non-`void` function if it contains no sequences of statements. For example, the `max` function:

```
int max(int a, int b)
{
    if (a > b)
        return a;
    else
        return b;
}
```

becomes:

```
#define max(a, b)   ((a) > (b) ? (a) : (b))
```

Local variables present a more difficult problem. A block cannot be an expression, so the containing braces of the function must be deleted. Local variable definitions are no longer syntactically legal. One partial solution is to replace every occurrence of a local variable with the expression it evaluated.

4.6.4 Parameters as local variables

Parameters to functions can be used as if they were local variables. Because of call-by-value parameter passing, this does not change the values of any variables not local to the function. This method saves on initialization time, and on stack space. In the example below, to zero an array, the size is counted down, rather than having a local variable counting up.

```
void zero(int a[], register int n)
{
    while (n > 0)
        a[--n] = 0;
}
```

Note that this method cannot be used for array local variables because they are passed by reference, and changes will be passed back.

4.7 Command line arguments

The most efficient method of examining all command line arguments is to combine pointer traversal with use of the sentinel value `argv[argc]==NULL`, as shown in the following program to print out options.

```
main(int argc, char *argv[])
{
for(; *argv !=NULL; argv++)
        printf("Option is %s\n", *argv);
}
```

Note that incrementing the "array" parameter `argv` is legal in ANSI C, because array parameters are immediately converted to pointers. If it is necessary to examine arguments twice, such as to process options and then filenames, it becomes necessary to save the original value of `argv` in a temporary variable.

4.8 IBM PC memory models

A number of compilers for IBM PCs allow the program to be compiled using different *memory models*. These memory models are required by the segmented architecture of the 8086 family of processors. The choice of memory model affects how the compiler translates some statements into machine language instructions, and hence affects efficiency. In particular, pointer operations and function calls are affected by the choice. Memory models can usually be set via a compiler option.

Although the models that are supported vary between compilers, and in fact, some models are given different names, the most common models are:

Small Medium Compact Large Huge

As a general rule, the `small` model is the most efficient, but also the least flexible, whereas the `huge` model is the most flexible, but the least efficient.

Memory models affect how the compiler organizes memory into segments. The models have different organizations for code and data. For example, the `small` model packs all code into a single segment and all data into another segment, whereas the `huge` model gives both code and data multiple segments. The memory organization for each memory model is shown in Table 4.1.

Table 4.1. Memory organization of each memory model

Model	Code segments	Data segments	Data pointers	Code pointers
Small	One	One	16 bits	16 bits
Medium	Many	One	16 bits	32 bits
Compact	One	Many	32 bits	16 bits
Large	Many	Many	32 bits	32 bits
Huge	Many	Many	32 bits	32 bits

All different forms of data are treated in an identical manner. The stack, heap and static data all either have one segment (i.e. they are packed together) or use many segments (allowing them to use separate segments). This occurs because C permits addresses of any of these data spaces to be compared, and it would be difficult to implement pointer operations if different types of data had different size addresses.

As shown in Table 4.1, there is no difference between the `large` and `huge` models in terms of the organization of code and data into segments, using multiple segments for both. The difference between the `large` and `huge` models is related to how pointers to data are treated, and becomes apparent only when a single object becomes larger than 64K. A pointer in the `large` model is incremented by operating on its lower 16 bits only, and the upper 16 bits (the segment) are ignored. Hence, the pointer will always operate within a single 64K segment, and any pointer arithmetic "wraps around" (e.g. when its value is `0x0000FFFF`, incrementing it by one byte will give it a new value of `0x00000000`, thus staying within segment `0000`). This is not useful when trying to iterate through the memory for an object larger than a single segment (e.g. if trying to examine all of the extended RAM memory). The `huge` model forces the compiler to use extra instructions to perform pointer arithmetic in a more general form. Hence, the `huge` model is more flexible, but less efficient.

Table 4.1 also shows the size of pointers to data and the size of function addresses. The general rule is that if the code/data is in one segment, the appropriate segment register can be "set and forgotten", and pointers use their 16 bit value plus the segment register to get their full address. If the code/data is in multiple segments, the pointers must be 32 bits to contain a 16 bit segment address and a 16 bit offset. Any access through a data pointer or a function call to an address sets the segment register using the first 16 bits, and then the other 16 bits are an offset to the segment register. With multiple segments, every pointer access or function call must set the segment register, thus requiring an extra machine instruction and reducing efficiency.

Table 4.1 can be used to guide the choice of memory model. If the program is small, with its executable code occupying less than 64K, only one segment is needed for code and either the `small` or `compact` model should be chosen. If the amount of total memory used by the stack, heap and static data is less than 64K, either the `small` or `medium` model is suitable. If both code and data each require more than 64K then either the `large` or `huge` model is needed. The `huge` model should not be used unless the size of a single object, such as a large array, is greater than 64K. Even in this case, there is a useful alternative to using the inefficient `huge` model, and this is discussed in Section 4.8.1.

4.8.1 The near, far, and huge qualifiers

Most modern compilers for IBM PCs support the `near`, `far` and `huge` non-ANSI type qualifiers. These qualifiers can be used by the programmer to override the current memory model for a particular operation. The qualifiers can be applied either to pointer variables or to functions.

```
huge void *p;                   /* huge pointer */
near int max(int x,int y)       /* near function */
{
   ...
}
```

Applying one of these qualifiers to a pointer will affect the efficiency of a dereference or a comparison of a pointer. `near` pointers are rarely used, `far` pointers can be used to access data that is not part of the program's data segment (e.g. the screen memory, interrupt ports), and `huge` pointers are used for accessing an object larger than 64K.

Applying a qualifier to a function will affect the cost of a call to that function. Usually only `near` functions are useful for reducing the cost of a function call; `far` functions can occasionally be useful for accessing ROM functions.

In some cases, the move to a less efficient model can be avoided by using the `far` and `huge` type qualifiers. For example, the addition of a single object larger than 64K (e.g. a very large array) to a program necessitates movement to the `huge` model, but this can be avoided by qualifying the declaration of any pointers accessing the object with the `huge` qualifier. The program will use less efficient instructions for operations involving `huge`-qualified pointer variables only, whereas a move to the `huge` model would use the inefficient instructions for all pointer operations. For example, to add all values of RAM for a checksum starting at zero (where memory is effectively a data object larger than 64K), the `huge` qualifier should be applied to the pointer:

```
#define MAX      (640*1024)        /* 640 K */

unsigned int checksum(void)
{
    huge unsigned char *p;    /* Huge pointer needed */
    unsigned long sum = 0;

    for (p = 0; p < MAX; p++)
        sum +=  *p;
    return sum;
}
```

There is a trap in using qualifiers when they are not actually needed: it can lead to inefficiency. For example, using the `huge` qualifier when an object is less than 64K is needlessly inefficient. The effect of the various qualifiers on programs using the various models is shown in Table 4.2.

Table 4.2. Effect of qualifiers on pointer accesses and function calls

Memory model	near	far	huge
Small	No effect	Both slower	Both slower
Medium	Functions faster	Pointers slower	Pointers slower
Compact	Pointers faster	Functions slower	Functions slower
Large	Both faster	No effect	Pointers slower
Huge	Both faster	Both faster	No effect

Another possible efficiency improvement is to declare a function as `near`. This is particularly worthwhile for a recursive function because most of the calls to it will occur "nearby" (from statements in its own body). Declaring a function as `near` allows the compiler to use fewer instructions in the function call sequence, thus improving time-efficiency and reducing code size. A function declared as `near` should also be declared as `static` so that only the functions in that same file can access it. There is little point declaring a function that is used in many files as `near`, because it cannot be declared as `static`, and function calls in a different source file must use the usual less-efficient call mechanism.

4.9 Exercises

1. Examine the claim made about nested loops in Section 4.1.5 by converting the two `for` loops into `while` loops, and by examining how many times each operation occurs. Compare it with the code that results if the loops are reversed.

2. How can the idea of "code motion" be used to improve the efficiency of the following loop?

    ```
                    /* Compute either maximum or minimum */
    result = a[0];
    for(i = 1; i < n; i++) {
        if(maximizing)
            result = a[i] > result ? a[i] : result;
        else
            result = a[i] < result ? a[i] : result;
    }
    ```

3. How can the conditional operation in the previous exercise be more efficiently coded?

    ```
    result = a[i] > result ? a[i] : result;
    ```

4. Consider the well-known mathematical computation of the roots of a quadratic equation. How can this be efficiently implemented, assuming that the roots will never be complex (i.e. $b^2 - 4ac \geq 0$)?

    $$r_1, r_2 = \frac{-b \pm \sqrt{b^2 - 4ac}}{2a}$$

5. What minor change may marginally improve the efficiency of the following code fragment?

```
enum { ERR1, ERR2, NO_ERROR} x;
....
while(x != NO_ERROR)
        process(&x);
```

6. Fix the following function so that the multiplication in the `return` statement is replaced by more efficient code:

```
int my_atoi(char *s)
{
    int value, sign;

    if (*s == '-') {
        sign = -1;
        s++;             /* skip over the '-' */
    }
    else
        sign = 1;

    for (value = 0; isdigit(*s); s++)
        value = 10 * value + *s - '0';

    return value * sign;          /* MULTIPLICATION!? */
}
```

7. Consider the following code fragment that sets a flag only if the flag is not already set. Under what conditions is this code more efficient than the assignment statement alone?

```
if (!flag)
    flag = TRUE;
```

8. One method of improving C++ programs is to declare variables as close to their first use as practicable. Does this apply to C variable declarations?

9. On some machines multiplications are hugely expensive compared to shift operations. How can the following multiplication be coded using shift instead of multiplication?

```
x * 17
```

10. Some machines have a very fast post-increment assembly language addressing mode where the value at an address is fetched and the address in the register is then incremented. There is usually also a corresponding pre-decrement mode. What implications does this have for efficiency?

11. Apply the loop optimization method of "pointer traversals of arrays" to a loop that processes the same field of each structure in an array of structures, as follows:

```
for (i = 0; i < n; i++)
    process(arr[i].field);
```

12. What is the most efficient method of implementing a macro `is_power2` which determines whether a non-negative integer is a power of 2?

13. The zoom routine in a graphics program needs to expand the low-end nibble (4 bits) of a byte into 8 bits, such that each 1 bit becomes two 1 bits in the result, and similar for 0 bits. For example, the nibble 1010 must become the byte 11001100. The following code is currently used to achieve this:

```
#define  nibble_extend(x)    \
        (( (x & 8) << 4) | ( (x & 8) << 3) |    \
         ( (x & 4) << 3) | ( (x & 4) << 2) |    \
         ( (x & 2) << 2) | ( (x & 2) << 1) |    \
         ( (x & 1) << 1) | ( (x & 1)) )
```

How can the efficiency of this routine be improved?

Chapter 5

C++ Techniques

Because C++ is a superset of the C language, most of the methods already covered in previous chapters also apply to C++. However, C++'s extensions make it possible to use several new techniques for efficiency improvement. This chapter discusses techniques that apply to C++ but not to C.

5.1 C++ versus C

It is a misconception to believe that a C++ program will run more slowly than its corresponding C program. C++ was designed to retain the run-time efficiency of C and almost all of C++'s extra enhancements come at no extra run-time cost. In particular, most of the C++ class structure does not slow down the program at run-time, but only costs the compiler more at compile-time. The compiler performs the extra type-checking, inheritance and encapsulation checks as it compiles the program and no run-time code is produced.

The one single exception to this is `virtual` functions (discussed in Section 5.5), but even a C++ program using `virtual` functions is not necessarily slower than the corresponding C program. `virtual` functions are very powerful, and may be faster than the C code necessary for the same effect.

5.2 Passing parameters by reference

The C++ language provides a very convenient method of achieving pass-by-reference, by simply using & in the parameter declaration. This efficiency technique is similar to the use of pointers to structures in C (see Section 4.6.2), but in C++ no & is needed on an argument to the function, as is required when using pointers to achieve pass-by-reference in C.

One method of improving efficiency is to pass objects to functions as reference parameters. This avoids not only the cost of copying the object onto the stack, but also

71

the cost of the (copy) constructor and destructor for the object within the function (i.e. the parameter is a separate object when passed by value).

A function can be changed to use pass-by-reference parameters only if it does not change the object. Fortunately, modifications to parameters can be detected simply by qualifying the parameter declaration with `const`, thus forcing the compiler to warn about any modifications to the object within the function. An example of the use of reference parameters in the definition of a `Complex` object is shown below:

```
class Complex {
        double r, i;
    public:
        Complex & operator += (const Complex & c);

            // c is passed by reference for efficiency
            // The return type is also a reference
};

Complex & Complex::operator += (const Complex & c)
{
    r += c.r;       // add to both data fields
    i += c.i;
    return *this;  // return reference to updated object
}
```

Passing the argument by reference improves efficiency, as does making the return value a reference, because the `return` statement does not invoke the copy constructor. Note that a returned reference is necessary only if the user of the `Complex` class uses complicated expressions such as x+=y+=z. If such expressions are not required, efficiency can be improved by making the return value `void`.

Pointers could also be used instead of references, with a similar gain in efficiency, but there is a notational disadvantage in that any arguments would need to be prefixed with an `&`, and any references within the function body using the "." operator would have to be changed to "->". The speed improvement of both methods would be similar because pointers are used behind the scenes to implement references.

The use of references is best limited to class objects and to structures and unions. Arrays are already passed by reference in C and C++ and hence there is no need to change them. The use of references for scalar types (integers and pointers) is unlikely to give much improvement, if any. However, if pointers (used by the compiler to implement references) were smaller than, say, `double` values there might be some improvement. Another disadvantage of using reference parameters for scalar types is the inefficiency caused if a constant value is passed as an argument (i.e. not a variable). Paradoxically, passing a constant argument to a reference parameter is not an error in C++, but instead a new object with this type is created automatically by the compiler and its address passed.

Note that the object to which a member function is applied is already passed by reference (using the implicit `this` parameter). Hence, the replacement of the member function call:

```
int MyClass::fn()               // member function
{
    return x;
}
```

with a non-member (friend) function call using an explicit reference parameter, as follows, will not be more efficient (and is probably less efficient):

```
int fn(MyClass & object)        // friend function
{
    return object.x;
}
```

5.3 inline functions

The C++ language allows a programmer to inform the compiler that certain functions are small enough for it to be more efficient to generate inline code than to generate a function call sequence. The programmer simply declares the function by using the `inline` specifier. For example:

```
inline int max(int a,int b)
{
    return (a > b) ? a : b;
}
```

The `inline` specifier is a "hint" to the compiler, much like the `register` qualifier, and the compiler can ignore the request for inlining a function. In principle, a good optimizing compiler could ignore `inline` and choose for itself which functions to inline. However, few (if any) modern C++ compilers are as sophisticated as this.

All C++ functions can be specified as `inline`, including member and non-member functions. However, the `inline` specifier should not be used without restraint. As a general rule, `inline` should be used only for "small" functions, where the number of executable statements is quite small. In this case, the overhead of a function call will be a significant proportion of the total cost of the function call, and inlining will probably increase efficiency. Note that the notion of "small" function refers to the number of statements executed at run-time, not the actual number of statements in the source code, although the two measures will usually be similar.

Do not use the `inline` specifier for "large" functions. Although the execution time may improve marginally, the size of the executable code will increase greatly because every call to the `inline` function will be replaced by all the statements in the function's body. Hence, the use of larger `inline` functions is a trade-off between speed of execution and code size.

The use of `inline` on very small functions can sometimes *decrease* the size of the executable. For example, if the function simply returns a value, as in:

```
inline int MyClass::get_a() { return a; }
```

any occurrence of the function call may well be replaced by a direct reference to the variable being returned. For example, a call to the above function, as in:

```
b = my_object.get_a();
```

might be equivalent to the direct reference (in the compiler's internal representation):

```
b = my_object.a;
```

This simple reference will require fewer machine language instructions than a function call, thus becoming faster and smaller. Note that there is no problem with encapsulation violation because this change is being performed internally by the compiler and the scope has already been checked.

A very important point to note about `inline` functions is that the `inline` specifier, by itself, is not enough to guarantee that inline code will be generated. The other requirement is that the compiler must know the function body code, where the function is called. An `inline` function prototype declaration is not enough. The executable statements inside the function's definition (i.e the function body) must be available. Otherwise, how is the compiler to know what inline code to expand a function call into? This requirement imposes two restrictions on the use of `inline` functions:

1. Member functions declared as `inline` should include the function body inside the *same header file* as the class declaration. This can be achieved by placing the function body of a member function inside the class declaration. For a more readable style when there are many `inline` member functions, the class declaration can declare the `inline` function prototypes, and then provide the `inline` function definitions immediately after it, in the same header file. This restriction ensures that whenever the class declaration is included as a header file, the member function body is available for inlining.

2. Non-member `inline` functions must be defined before they are used within a source file, preferably by placing the `inline` functions in a header file. Placing `inline` functions at the top of a source file allows the inlining of any function calls later in the same source file, but calls to the functions from a different source file cannot be inlined by the compiler unless the `inline` function definition is placed in a header file.

Some functions declared as `inline` will not be expanded into inline code by the compiler, simply because they are too complicated for the compiler to handle. In this case, the `inline` specifier is ignored and the function is treated like any other function. The sophistication of the inline code generation depends on the implementor.

Even if a compiler can inline a function, the compiler is sometimes still forced to generate a "real" function. There are two reasons for this:

1. The name of an `inline` function is used as a pointer-to-function constant.
2. A call to the `inline` function from within another source file.

When an `inline` function is called from a source file, where the function body has not been made available, the compiler generates a real function call (simply because it cannot inline the function). Hence the real function must exist and be linked like any other function. Fortunately, the placement of `inline` functions in header files as discussed above will avoid this for any function the compiler decides to inline.

5.4 friend functions

If a class declaration has a good deal of private data, it is common C++ style to declare an interface of public member functions to access private data. Although the class interface can be quite efficient if member functions are declared as `inline`, the need to call a function to access a data value can still make it inefficient in some cases. The use of `friend` functions and `friend` classes can be efficient because this bypasses the class interface. For example, a member function to set a data member may perform some range checking on the value, but if we can be sure that a particular function will not use incorrect data, a `friend` function can be used to bypass this checking.

`friend` functions (or classes) should not be considered unless the function needs very fast access to data members, and the member functions to access the data perform other computations. Note that a member function, with its special privileges, also bypasses the class interface (because it is part of it), and `friend` functions should not be used where member functions would be more appropriate. Programming style is the consideration here, as they would both have similar efficiency.

A good example of `friend` function efficiency occurs when an operator function operates on two different classes, such as when an operator multiplies a `Matrix` object by a `Vector` object to yield a new `Vector`. Assume that both classes have member functions to access individual elements of the `Vector` or `Matrix`. Consider the declaration of the `multiply` function as neither a class member nor a `friend` function, as in:

```
const int N = 10;     // Number of elements in vector/matrix

class Vector {
        double data[N];
    public:
        double get_element(int i) const { return data[i]; }
        void set_element(int i, double value) { data[i] = value; }
};

class Matrix {
    double data[N][N];
    public:
    double get_element(int i, int j) const { return data[i][i]; }
};

Vector operator * (const Matrix & m, const Vector & v)
{
    Vector temp;
                                // multiply matrix by vector
    for (int i = 0; i < N; i++) { // for each row
        double sum = 0.0;             // sum of N multiplications
        for (int j = 0; j < N; j++) {
            sum += m.get_element(i, j) * v.get_element(j);
        }
        temp.set_element(i, sum); // store new vector element
    }
    return temp;                 // return new vector
}
```

This will be inefficient because the `operator*()` function must go through both class interfaces to access elements. Although it isn't necessarily any less efficient here, if range checking of the array index i were present in the member functions to set or access the elements, this would cause inefficiency. Note that if the `Vector` class overloaded the [] operator instead of using a `get_element` member function, this would make no difference to efficiency — notational convenience is gained but the `operator[]` function has the same cost as any other function.

One alternative to consider is to make the `operator*` function a member of the `Vector` class, but this will still mean using the interface for the `Matrix` class. A more efficient solution is to make the `operator*` function a `friend` of both `Matrix` and `Vector` classes, thus allowing it direct access to their individual data elements, bypassing any range checking on array indices. The more efficient version, using a `friend` function, is:

```
const int N = 10;    // Number of elements in vector/matrix

class Matrix;

class Vector {
        double data[N];
    public:
        friend Vector operator * ( const Matrix & m, const Vector & v);
};

class Matrix {
    double data[N][N];
    public:
    friend Vector operator * ( const Matrix & m, const Vector & v);
};

Vector operator * ( const Matrix & m, const Vector & v)
{
    Vector temp;
                                    // multiply matrix by vector
    for (int i = 0; i < N; i++) { // for each row
        double sum = 0.0;            // sum of N multiplications
        for (int j = 0; j < N; j++) {
            sum += m.data[i][j] * v.data[j];   // access data directly
        }
        temp.data[i] = sum;        // store new vector element
    }
    return temp;                   // return new vector
}
```

The disadvantage of using `friend` functions is that they make use of hidden information, and any change to the class requires a change to the definition of the `friend` function, whereas in the first version of the `operator*` function the use of the `get_element` member functions of both `Vector` and `Matrix` meant that it would need no changes, provided the `get_element` functions were changed correctly.

5.5 virtual functions — good or bad?

Are `virtual` functions inefficient? This section will attempt to answer this question. The main reason to suspect `virtual` functions of inefficiency is that they use "late binding" of a function call to a machine address. The binding takes place at run-time and thus affects the speed of execution. However, as we will see, `virtual` functions have many advantages to counter-balance this cost.

5.5.1 How compilers implement virtual functions

Although different implementations might choose different methods of handling `virtual` functions, thus making some of the observations in this section incorrect, the method examined in this section is prevalent. In fact, I know of no compilers that implement `virtual` functions differently.

Let us examine the details of a call to a `virtual` function. In situations where the compiler cannot determine what type of object for which a `virtual` function is being invoked, the compiler must add a few run-time instructions to test the type of object (using a special hidden data field stored in any object of a class that uses a `virtual` function). In this case, a call to a `virtual` function will cause the following steps:

1. The pointer data member in the object is accessed.
2. An index is added to the pointer value (to find the pointer to the correct function).
3. A call to a pointer-to-function is performed.

whereas an ordinary (non-`virtual`) function call will cost only the time to call a function directly (often similar to the cost of calling a pointer to a function), and avoids completely the first two steps.

However, the extra overhead is not needed on *all* calls to a `virtual` function. In many cases, the compiler can determine the type of the object at compile-time and can translate the `virtual` function call exactly as an ordinary statically-bound function call, with exactly the same run-time cost. The only time the compiler cannot determine the type at compile-time is when *pointers or references* to class objects are used.

It is likely that most `virtual` function calls won't involve pointers or references and will be executed as ordinary function calls.

5.5.2 Space requirements of virtual functions

The extra space required by the use of `virtual` functions is of two types:

• A hidden pointer data member in each object.
• One table of pointers to functions per class.

No matter how many member functions of a class are declared as `virtual`, the amount of extra space in an object will be only a single pointer field. Naturally, if there are no `virtual` functions at all, the extra data member is not needed. Each class has a table of pointers to functions of a size equal to the number of `virtual` member functions. Although a large number of `virtual` functions doesn't increase object size, it does increase executable size because of some extra tables of pointers to functions.

5.5.3 Attempting to improve on virtual functions

Let us examine how the programmer might try to avoid using `virtual` functions. First, note that the only time that `virtual` functions are potentially inefficient involves pointers or references to objects. For example, one such situation would be traversing a (heterogeneous) linked list of objects of varying types (although all must be derived from the one base type). To handle the situation without `virtual` functions, we will still need some way of identifying the type of object (possibly an integral flag). Testing this flag will involve a selection statement (i.e. `if` or `switch`) and this would probably be less efficient than the very fast method used by `virtual` functions.

Hand-coding is better than `virtual` functions in some cases. For example, if it is possible to determine an object's type without extra information, the space wastage of a hidden pointer member can be avoided.

5.5.4 Unnecessary use of virtual functions

The use of `virtual` functions, when they are not needed, is obviously inefficient. `virtual` functions are needed only when dealing with pointers or references to objects of unknown type. If the program never uses pointers or references to objects, or if it does not have any derived classes, no function needs to be `virtual` and the use of `virtual` wastes space. In addition, because `virtual` functions relate only to the use of derived classes, declaring any functions as `virtual` in a class that has no derived classes is also unnecessarily inefficient.

One common situation where `virtual` may appear necessary, but need not be, occurs with redefining a member function in a derived class. This does not necessarily mean that the function must be defined as `virtual` in the base class (nor in the derived class — the `virtual` keyword is never needed in the derived class). Of course, if the program starts using pointers or references to these classes, the functions may need to be `virtual`, in which case it may be better style to declare the member function as `virtual`.

A call to a `virtual` function need not always be a "real" `virtual` call. For example, passing an object by reference (either as a reference or as a pointer type) can occur when changing functions to pass-by-reference for efficiency improvement. Any calls to `virtual` functions inside that (not necessarily `virtual`) function will be such that the compiler cannot know that an ordinary function call to the member function would suffice. It does not perform any global analysis to determine that all arguments to the function are base objects, and not derived objects. For example, in the following code, it isn't clear that the call to the (`virtual`) `print` function could be replaced by an ordinary call:

```
void print_base_object( Base & object)
{
    object.print();
}
```

The overhead of `virtual` function calls can be removed whenever the programmer can be sure that only one type of pointer/reference to an object is being used. In particular, whenever a programmer can be sure that a pointer/reference to a base class object points to a particular object, the qualified member function name can be used. For example, instead of:

```
p->print();
```

the more efficient code is:

```
p->Base::print();
```

An example of extra information making this change possible occurs when a program uses a number of different (homogeneous) linked lists, with each linked list containing the same type of object (one with base objects, one with derived objects). When implementing a `print_list` function to print out a linked list, you can write it generally to call a `virtual print_object` function:

```
void LinkedList::print_list()
{
    for (Base *temp = head; temp != NULL; temp = temp->next())
        temp->print_object();
}
```

This means that each call to `print_object` has the run-time overhead of a `virtual` function call. A more efficient alternative is to make use of the knowledge that each list must contain the same type of object, and have two different `print_list` functions (i.e. use a `virtual` function to do the dirty work of printing the objects).

```
void Base::print_list_hidden()
{
    for (Base *temp = this; temp != NULL; temp = temp->next())
        temp->Base::print_object();
}
void Derived::print_list_hidden()
{
    for (Derived *temp = this; temp != NULL;
                        temp = (Derived*)temp->next())
        temp->Derived::print_object();
}
void LinkedList::print_list()
{
    if (head != NULL)
        head->print_list_hidden();    // call virtual function
}
```

With this approach, all calls to `print_object` can be bound at compile-time and the only `virtual` call is the call to `print_list_hidden`. Hence, by using our knowledge about the linked lists, we have reduced the number of run-time `virtual` function calls.

5.5.5 Conclusions on virtual functions

It appears that `virtual` functions, when used properly, are no less efficient than any equivalent code, are probably more efficient and are certainly much more convenient. In most cases, a `virtual` function call is translated by the compiler into an ordinary function call, and even when the "virtualness" of the function is used by a call involving a pointer or reference to an object, the extra overhead instructions generated by the compiler are likely to be more efficient than anything the programmer could substitute for it. Of course, `virtual` functions can become inefficient if they are used improperly, and the programmer should learn to avoid such situations.

5.6 Overloading new and delete

C++ improves on C's dynamic memory allocation facilities by adding two new operators
to the language: new and delete. This means that the (rather hacked) method of
making allocation more efficient in C (see Section 6.8) can be performed more gracefully
in C++ by overloading these operators. This allows the memory allocation to be easily
taken over for a particular class.

An example of the method is shown below, where a dummy class is declared so that it
allocates memory for itself by using large chunks, thus cutting down the calls to the
memory allocator used by the default new operator (probably malloc):

```
#include <stdlib.h>        // declare malloc()
#include <stddef.h>        // declare size_t
#include <assert.h>        // declare assert()

#define NUM_OBJECTS_PER_BLOCK  20  // how many objects
                                   // in each large block

class Object {
    static Object *free_list;      // free list of blocks
                                   // one per class
    union {                 // anonymous union
        Object *next_ptr;          // linked list next ptr
        int data;                  // other object data
    };
        // ... possibly more private data
    public:
        void *operator new(size_t n);
        void operator delete(void *p);
        // ... rest of the public interface
};

Object *Object::free_list = NULL;       // initialize static member

void *Object::operator new(size_t n)
{
    Object *memory_block;   // large block of memory
    Object *ptr;

    assert(n == sizeof(Object));  // check correct object
    if (free_list == NULL) {
        memory_block = malloc(NUM_OBJECTS_PER_BLOCK * sizeof(Object));

                // Thread blocks onto the free list (linked list)

        for (int i = 1; i < NUM_OBJECTS_PER_BLOCK - 1; i++)
            memory_block[i].free_list = &memory_block[i + 1];
        memory_block[i].free_list = NULL;
        ptr = memory_block;             // take one block
        free_list = memory_block + 1;  // rest on free list
    }
    else {              // delete from front of linked list
        ptr = free_list;                    // take front block
        free_list = free_list->next_ptr;  // update head of list
    }
    return ptr;
}

void Object::operator delete(void *p)
{
    Object *p2 = p;         // get pointer of correct type

    p2->next_ptr = free_list;   // add to front of linked list
    free_list = p2;             // update head of list
}
```

Overloading the `new` and `delete` operators has some restrictions and there are many nitty-gritty issues in this implementation, including:

1. The `size_t` parameter to `operator new`.
2. The assertion involving the parameter to `operator new`.
3. The `void*` parameter to `operator delete`.
4. The `static` data member `free_list`.
5. The anonymous `union` holding `next_ptr`.
6. The use of `malloc`.
7. Restrictions on the allocation of arrays of objects.

The `operator new` function is supplied the size of its object as a parameter of type `size_t`, which is a type name defined in `<stddef.h>` (usually `int` or `unsigned int`). Although the size may seem unnecessary, because it will always be the size of the object, the size is needed when another class is derived from this class. As implemented above, the assertion in the program will fail with a run-time error if this is the case. If it is desirable to handle derived classes correctly, a call to `malloc` with the correct number of bytes could be used if the size differs from the size of the object.

An annoying feature of `operator delete` is that its parameter type must be `void*`, and cannot be `Object*`, hence the need for the extra variable, `p2`.

The `free_list` pointer is declared as a `static` data member because there is only one free list for the class. Alternatively, `free_list` could have been a global variable.

An anonymous `union` is used inside the object to overlay the next pointer of the free list (which is used when the memory is free), and an actual data member of the object (which is used when the memory is in use). This method is far neater than using type casting to access bytes in an `Object`, such as:

```
*(Object **)&memory_block[i] = &memory_block[i+1];
```

The `malloc` function is used to create the large block of bytes. Alternatively, the `new` operator could be used, provided its argument was not of type `Object`. For example, an alternative statement would be:

```
memory_block = new char[NUM_OBJECTS_PER_BLOCK * sizeof(Object)];
```

As another alternative, the global `new` operator could be used, as in:

```
memory_block = ::new Object[NUM_OBJECTS_PER_BLOCK];
```

Finally, note that the allocation and deletion of arrays of objects cannot be handled by the overloaded `new` and `delete` operators. Statements such as:

```
Object *p = new Object[10];
delete [10] p;
```

will call the default `new` and `delete` operators, and not the overloaded operators. If it is important to have all allocation handled by the overloaded operators, arrays of objects must be avoided.

Because the overloading of the `new` and `delete` operators is possible only when they are applied to classes, it is still difficult to replace the low-level allocation requests, such as the allocation of bytes for the fundamental types (i.e. `int`, `char`, etc.). For example, there is no easy way to implement the `char_malloc` function in Section 6.8, unless we decide to implement strings as a class (which is better style anyway).

Overloading the `new` and `delete` operators is not available in early versions of C++ (before version 2.0). In these early versions, memory allocation for classes could be controlled by examination of and assignment to the `this` implicit parameter inside a constructor. This is an obsolete feature of C++ and its use is not recommended.

5.7 Specializing functions with default arguments

Default arguments to functions are not a source of inefficiency in themselves, and cost no more than using a fixed-argument function and passing some constants explicitly. However, the use of default arguments indicates the possibility of improving efficiency by replacing a single function with a number of specialized functions. This specialization will often make other optimization techniques possible, thus improving overall efficiency at the cost of some duplication of executable code. Nor is there any need to change any other code because the compiler will still make the correct choice of function to call. However, default arguments are certainly convenient and the slight increase in efficiency should be balanced against the loss of good programming style.

As an example of the possibilities that can exist, consider the function with default arguments:

```
void indent(int n = 4)       // default argument n=4
{
    for (int i = 0; i < n; i++)
        cout.put(' ');
}
```

Rewriting this single function as one general function and one specialized function leads to opportunities for optimization in the specialized function. In this case, loop unrolling can be employed:

```
void indent()      // Specialized function
{
    cout.put(' ');       // Loop completely unrolled
    cout.put(' ');
    cout.put(' ');
    cout.put(' ');
}

void indent(int n)      // General function
{
    for (int i = 0; i < n; i++)
        cout.put(' ');
}
```

5.8 Specializing inherited member functions

In an inheritance hierarchy, the derived class is a specialized version of the base class. This means that member functions inherited from the base class can often be rewritten more efficiently to make use of the form of the derived class.

For example, consider the class UTMatrix (upper triangular matrix) which is derived from Matrix and represents matrices where all elements below the diagonal are zero. The general matrix addition function of the Matrix class is inherited by the UTMatrix class, and it will work correctly. However, this inherited function is inefficient and it is more efficient to add a new member function to the UTMatrix class to add two upper triangular matrices avoiding all additions involving elements below the diagonal. In fact, it is also more efficient to write special functions to add ordinary matrices to upper triangular matrices. The computation of the determinant of a triangular matrix is also more efficient than that for a general square matrix, so this member function should be rewritten in the UTMatrix class.

As another example, consider a class Imaginary (imaginary numbers) derived from another class Complex (complex numbers). For all operations involving Imaginary objects, it is certain that the real part of the complex number is zero. Hence, it is more efficient to rewrite all inherited operations that use the real part of a Complex object, such as: addition, multiplication, norm, etc.

The main disadvantage of specializing member functions is that the code reuse advantage of inheritance is negated; more programmer time must be spent on recoding the specialized member functions. Other disadvantages are the increased probability of error, and an increase in executable code size.

5.9 Initializing base and member objects

When a class declaration contains a class object as one of its members it is important to use the correct method of initialization to retain efficiency. Consider the declaration of a class B containing a member object from class A:

```
class A {
    private:
        int val;
    public:
        A() { val = 0; }
        A(int x) { val = x; }
        void operator = (int i) { val = i; }
};

class B {
    private:
        A a;   // member is itself an object
    public:
        B() { a = 1; }        // INEFFICIENT
};
```

Declaring an object of type B will cause the default constructor for the member object of type A to be invoked immediately before the default constructor for B. Then the = operator for class A is used to set the member object, a. Hence, the constructor for B involves a call to A's default constructor and a call to the assignment operator. The call to A's default constructor is redundant and should be avoided.

Fortunately, C++ provides a convenient syntax for passing arguments to constructors of member objects. The default constructor for B should be recoded as:

```
B() : a(1) { }                // EFFICIENT
```

This initialization syntax causes the constant 1 to be passed to the constructor for the member object, a (the constructor accepting the int parameter is called, instead of the default constructor). Thus instead of calling the default constructor *and* the assignment operator for A, only the int constructor for A is called.

This initialization method is efficient whenever calling the default constructor for a member object is not appropriate, for instance, when the member object is initialized by a call to the assignment operator within the main object's constructor (as above, where B's constructor assigned to its member of type A). This form of initialization can be used for any type of data member (i.e. not only class objects), although it will be neither more nor less efficient than assignment for built-in types. The special initialization syntax should be used wherever it is applicable, since it can never be less efficient than assignment to the data members within the constructor, and will often be more efficient.

Similar efficiency considerations apply to constructors in derived classes, since the data member(s) in the base class act like an object member. The constructor for the base class is always called when a derived class object is constructed. When the default constructor for the base class is of no use to a derived class object, it is more efficient to pass arguments directly to a non-default base class constructor, using the special initialization syntax. The same syntax applies as for data member initialization, except that the type name of the base class is used instead of the name of a data member. A contrived example of this form of initialization is:

```
class Derived : public Base {
   public:
       Derived() : Base(0) { }  // Call Base(int) constructor
};
```

5.10 Avoiding temporary objects

In the same way that temporary integer variables are used to compute an integer expression, so too are temporary objects used in non-trivial expressions involving class objects. For example, if the Complex class has defined the + and = operators, the expression:

```
Complex c1,c2,c3;

c1 = c2 + c3;
```

is likely to create a temporary Complex object as the result of the addition, and this temporary object is then passed as an operand to the = operator. In other words, the expression is actually evaluated as:

```
operator=( c1, operator+(c2,c3));
```

and a temporary object must be used to store the sub-expression computed for the second argument to =. Whether the operands to `operator=` are passed by reference or by value has no effect on whether a temporary is created in this situation (although it does affect the creation of new objects *inside* the `operator=` function).

One (rather hacked) method of avoiding this creation of temporaries is to create a specialized function to handle it:

```
void AssignThree(Complex &c1, Complex &c2, Complex & c3);
  ...
AssignThree(c1,c2,c3);          // c1 = c2 + c3;
```

The function should probably be a friend function to allow efficient access to the data members of the three complex objects.

The problems with this solution are its very poor style (because the neatness of the use of overloaded operators is lost), and also its non-general character. More complicated expressions will still generate temporaries, unless more special functions are added as friends, leading to even worse style. This "cure" is far worse than its disease.

5.10.1 Avoiding temporaries via extra member functions

There are situations where the removal of temporaries does not lead to poor style. Consider the following definition of a minimal `Complex` class:

```
class complex {
    private:
        double re;      // real part
        double im;      // imaginary part
    public:
                        // Constructors
        complex()        {   re = 0.0; im = 0.0; }
        complex(double r) {   re = r; im = 0.0; }
        complex(double r, double i) { re = r; im = i; }
                        // Copy constructor
        complex(complex &c) {  re = c.re; im = c.im; }

                        // Overloaded assignment operator
        void operator = (complex & d) { re = d.re; im = d.im; }

                        // Overloaded + operator
        friend complex operator + (complex &c1, complex &c2);
};

inline complex operator + (complex &c1, complex &c2)
{
return complex(c1.re + c2.re, c1.im + c2.im);
}
```

When this class definition is used for the following code sequence:

```
complex c1, c2;

c1 = 2.0;
c2 = c1 + 3.0;
```

the effect is identical to:

```
c1 = complex(2.0);      // invoke 'double' constructor for 2.0
c2 = c1 + complex(3.0); // invoke 'double' constructor for 3.0
```

The C++ compiler automatically creates two temporary objects from the `double` constants, and calls the `double` constructor to do so. The inefficiency of the creation of a temporary object and the call to the constructor can be avoided by adding a few more functions to the class declaration:

```
void operator = (double d) { re = d; im = 0.0; }
friend complex operator + (double d, complex &c2);
friend complex operator + (complex &c1, double d);
```

If these functions are present, then the `double` constants are passed directly to the `double` parameters of these functions. No temporary object is created, and hence the constructor is not called. Note that two symmetric versions of `operator+` are required because the C++ compiler cannot assume that the commutativity of + holds for user-defined class objects.

By making the "interface" efficient for mixing `complex` and `double` variables, the creation of temporaries has been reduced. This can be generalized: it is better to provide member or friend functions to class X for a specific parameter type Y, than to provide only a constructor to create new X's from Y's.

5.11 Declaration close to use

The C++ language allows variable declarations to appear almost anywhere within a program. Although the placement of variable declarations may seem unrelated to efficiency, it can have some effect when objects with non-trivial constructors are declared. For efficiency reasons, an object must be declared as close to its first use as possible. In particular, the C style of declaring all variables at the top of a function is often inefficient. Consider the C++ code below:

```
void dummy(...)
{
    complex c;                // create object
    if (... ) {
        ....    // use c
    }
}
```

The `complex` object is not used if the condition in the `if` statement is false — the constructor and destructor for the unused object are called needlessly.

Another consideration is that objects should not be declared until there is enough information to construct them fully. For example, given a user-defined class `complex`, the following code:

```
complex c;          // construct c
    ....
c = 1.0;            // initialize c
```

is less efficient than calling the correct constructor directly by using:

```
complex c(1.0);    // construct and initialize c
```

The first code sequence involves a call to the default constructor and the overloaded = operator, whereas the second declaration calls only the (double) constructor for the complex class.

Unfortunately, there are practical limits to the extent to which objects can be declared near their first use. If the first use of an object is inside a compound statement, and this object must also be used outside the compound statement, the scope resolution rules prevent the declaration from being placed inside the compound statement. For example, in the code below:

```
double d;
complex c;

while(....) {
    cin >> d;       // get double value from user
    c = d;          // set complex number
}
cout << c;          // print the complex number
```

it would be more efficient to declare c inside the loop block using the direct call to a double constructor:

```
complex c(d);
```

However, this would prevent the use of c outside the scope of the braces. This limitation is an unfortunate consequence of the programming language design choice to make braces both the method of grouping statements *and* the scoping mechanism in C++ (but there are many more important advantages supporting this decision). Unfortunately, it is not even possible to remove the braces in the above example, using the comma operator as by:

```
while(....)
    cin >> d, complex c(d);      // FAILS: compilation error
```

because C++ syntax prevents a declaration from being an operand of the comma operator. Overcoming this limitation by using dynamically allocated objects is examined in the exercises.

5.12 <iostream.h> versus <stdio.h>

The early version of the C++ I/O library was called <stream.h> but this was superseded in C++ 2.0 by <iostream.h>. This section examines <iostream.h>, but the same considerations apply to <stream.h>.

Although the relative efficiency of the <iostream.h> and <stdio.h> libraries depends on their respective implementors (and may vary between implementations), there are a few reasons to expect <iostream.h> to be marginally more efficient. Although the putchar, getchar, puts and gets <stdio.h> functions are likely to be very efficient, the printf and scanf functions are slightly inefficient because they must parse their format string argument. Thus, the C code:

```
printf("%d", x);
```

requires the analysis of the string argument "%d" at run-time, before printf knows to call an inner function to print an integer. However, in the C++ code:

```
cout << x;
```

the type of x is examined at compile-time, and the << notation is converted to a call to the correct function to print out an integer. The cost of parsing the format string is avoided and the correct output function is chosen at compile-time, not run-time.

Another reason that the functions in <stdio.h> may be less efficient is that few of them are macros (because defining safe macros is difficult), whereas most of the common methods in <iostream.h> are efficient inline functions. The printf and scanf functions in <stdio.h> are a case in point, since they are variable-argument functions and *cannot* be implemented efficiently as macros because variable-argument macros do not exist.

5.13 Reference counts

Reference counts refers to a general programming technique for keeping track of dynamically allocated objects. This technique is not actually part of the C++ language, as such, but is a commonly used programming technique that is well supported by the C++ class structure. As with any general programming technique, reference counts could in theory be used in C, but it is far more difficult to do so elegantly.

Reference counts improve the efficiency of objects where the cost of copying the object, either by the copy constructor or the assignment operator, is prohibitive. This is most often true of objects which allocate dynamic memory, in which case both the copy constructor and assignment operator must allocate memory, and the assignment operator may have to deallocate memory.

The advantage of reference counts is that the copy constructor and assignment operator, instead of creating a new object, simply set a pointer to the original object. The cost of copying an entire object, including any memory allocation or deallocation, is replaced by the cost of a pointer assignment.

Reference counts appear to suffer the disadvantage that extra space is used in each object to store the integer count, and also the extra pointer. However, the total amount of space used by the program may actually decrease if there are many objects pointing to a single allocated memory block. In addition, there is some extra run-time overhead involved in maintaining the reference counts, and this reduces efficiency if the advantage gained from avoiding copying complex objects is not sufficient (e.g. if the program does not either copy or assign these objects).

As an example of the addition of reference counts to a class, we will use a dynamic array implementation of a stack. Since it allocates memory within its constructor and assignment operator, it is a good candidate for improving efficiency by adding reference counts. Admittedly, stacks may seldom be assigned to each other or copied, which is where reference counts gain efficiency, but let us assume that the Stack class is being used in a large project where this does occur frequently. Here is the code for the Stack class before reference counts are added:

```
//------------------------------------------------------------
// Dynamic Array Implementation of Stack
//------------------------------------------------------------

#include <iostream.h>
#include <stdlib.h>
#include <string.h>

typedef int data_type;          // Type of data is int

class Stack {
    private:
        data_type *arr;         // Dynamic array holding the stack
        int sp;                 // Stack pointer
        int size;               // Maximum size of the stack
    public:
        Stack(int sz);                         // Ordinary constructor
        Stack(const Stack &s);                 // Copy constructor
        void operator =(const Stack &s);       // Assignment operator
        ~Stack()   {   delete arr; }           // Destructor
        int is_empty() { return sp == 0; }
        void push(data_type data);
        data_type pop();
        data_type top();
};

//------------------------------------------------------------------
// Ordinary constructor
//------------------------------------------------------------------

inline Stack::Stack(int sz)
{
    size = sz;
    sp = 0;
    arr = new data_type[sz];
}

//------------------------------------------------------------------
// Copy constructor
//------------------------------------------------------------------

inline Stack::Stack(const Stack &s)
{
    arr = new data_type[s.size];
    sp = s.sp;
    size = s.size;
    memcpy(arr, s.arr, size * sizeof(data_type));  // Copy data
}

//------------------------------------------------------------------
// Assignment operator
//------------------------------------------------------------------

inline void Stack::operator =(const Stack &s)
{
    delete arr;                      // delete old stack memory
    size = s.size;
    sp = s.sp;
    arr = new data_type[size];       // make room for new data
    memcpy(arr, s.arr, size * sizeof(data_type));  // Copy data
}

//------------------------------------------------------------------
//    PUSH:  Push an element on the top of the stack
//------------------------------------------------------------------

inline void Stack::push(data_type data )
{
    if (sp >= size) {        // Already too many?
        cerr << "Overflow error\n";
```

```
        exit(1);
    }
    arr[sp++] = data;          // Push onto end of array
}
//------------------------------------------------------------------
//   POP():   Take element from the top of the stack
//------------------------------------------------------------------
inline data_type Stack::pop()
{
    if (sp == 0) {             // No elements ?
        cerr << "Underflow error\n";
        exit(1);
    }
    return (arr[--sp]);        // Pop from end of array
}
//------------------------------------------------------------------
//   TOP():   Return element on the top of the stack
//------------------------------------------------------------------
inline data_type Stack::top()
{
    if (sp == 0) {             // No elements ?
        cerr << "Underflow error\n";
        exit(1);
    }
    return (arr[sp - 1]);      // Return top element
}
```

Experienced C++ programmers will recognize a common class idiom in the code above, as discussed in James Coplien's book (see the references in Section 5.16). Note that this idiom is recommended for *all* C++ classes, and has no specific relationship with reference counting (except that a proper implementation of reference counting must use this idiom with greater care). This idiom requires that a class contain the following methods:

1. Ordinary constructor(s).
2. Destructor.
3. Copy constructor.
4. Overloaded assignment operator (=).

It is important to note that both the copy constructor and = operator allocate memory for a new stack, and copy the old stack into it. If either the copy constructor or = operator were missing, the delete operation in the destructor would be in danger of clobbering allocated memory (i.e. de-allocating the same location twice) in some circumstances. This problem occurs because allowing either the assignment operator or the copy constructor to default to memberwise copying (or bitwise copying in early C++ versions) will cause the pointer data members to simply be copied. The objects they point to are not copied by memberwise copying. Hence any use of the assignment operator on the class, or use of the copy constructor (e.g. via argument passing, or return values) will cause two objects to have pointer data members pointing at the same address. Since both objects will have their destructor called, the address will be de-allocated twice by the delete operator in the destructor.

The addition of reference counts to Stack objects requires a number of changes. A new class, which we have called StackData, must be created and it subsumes many of the operations that were originally part of the Stack class. In particular, all of the data members that were part of the `Stack` class are moved to the `StackData` class, and the only data member in the `Stack` class is a pointer to a `StackData` object. An extra integer data field is added to the `StackData` class to store the reference count.

The constructors, assignment operator and destructor for class `Stack` change markedly, and perform most of the manipulation of the reference counts (which are actually stored in the `StackData` objects). The ordinary constructor simply sets its pointer to point to a new `StackData` object, whose reference count is set to one, because there is only this newly created `Stack` object pointing at it.

The copy constructor is changed to increment the reference count of the `StackData` object pointed to by the `Stack` parameter. The newly created `Stack` object is then set to point at this same `StackData` object.

The destructor tests whether it is the only reference to the `StackData` object. If so, the object is de-allocated. If not, the reference count is decremented, as there is now one less `Stack` object pointing at it.

The assignment operator must do two things. First, it acts in a similar manner to the destructor, and unlinks the `Stack` object that was on the left-hand side of the = operator. If there are no further references to the `StackData` object, it is de-allocated. Second, the object on the left-hand side is set to point to the same object as pointed to by the `Stack` object on the right-hand side of the = operator. This part of the procedure is the same as for the copy constructor.

Finally, all the member functions now must access the data members through an extra level of indirection, as they are now stored in a `StackData` object. In our example, this means that all references to `arr`, `sp` and `size` must be changed to `ptr->arr`, `ptr->sp`, and `ptr->size`. The `Stack` class has been made a friend of the `StackData` class to avoid the need to call interface functions to access private data members.

The code for most of the reference counted version of the `Stack` class is given as follows; the `push` and `pop` member functions have been temporarily omitted because they pose special problems, and they are discussed in Section 5.13.1.

```
//------------------------------------------------------------
// Reference Counted Dynamic Array Implementation of Stack
//------------------------------------------------------------

#include <iostream.h>
#include <stdlib.h>
#include <string.h>

typedef int data_type;           // Type of data is int

//------------------------------------------------------------
// Hidden class that contains the allocated data
//------------------------------------------------------------

class StackData {
private:
        data_type *arr;          // Dynamic array of stack data
        int sp;                  // Stack pointer
        int size;                // Maximum size of the stack
        int count;               // Reference count!

        StackData(int sz);                   // Ordinary constructor
        ~StackData() { delete arr; }     // Destructor
    friend class Stack;
```

```
};
//-----------------------------------------------------------
// Ordinary constructor for StackData
//-----------------------------------------------------------

inline StackData::StackData(int sz)
{
    count = 1;                  // Initially only one reference
    size = sz;
    sp = 0;
    arr = new data_type[sz];
}

//-----------------------------------------------------------
//-----------------------------------------------------------
// This is the main Stack class used by the user
//-----------------------------------------------------------
//-----------------------------------------------------------

class Stack {
    private:
        StackData *ptr;   // Pointer to reference counted object
    public:
        Stack(int sz);                      // Ordinary constructor
        Stack(const Stack &s);              // Copy constructor
        void operator =(const Stack &s);    // Assignment operator
        ~Stack();                           // Destructor
        int is_empty() { return ptr->sp == 0; }
        data_type top();
};

//------------------------------------------------------------------
// Ordinary constructor
//------------------------------------------------------------------

inline Stack::Stack(int sz)
{
    ptr = new StackData(sz);    // Create new hidden object
}

//------------------------------------------------------------------
// Copy constructor
//------------------------------------------------------------------

inline Stack::Stack(const Stack &s)
{
        s.ptr->count++;         // Increment reference count
        ptr = s.ptr;            // Make new object point there too
}

//------------------------------------------------------------------
// Assignment operator
//------------------------------------------------------------------

inline void Stack::operator =(const Stack &s)
{
                                // Unlink the '*this' object
        ptr->count--;           // Decrement reference count
        if(ptr->count == 0) {   // Only reference?
                delete ptr;     // Return allocated memory
        }
        ptr = s.ptr;            // Make this object point there too
        ptr->count++;           // Increment reference count
}

//------------------------------------------------------------------
// Destructor
//------------------------------------------------------------------
```

```
inline Stack::~Stack()
{
    ptr->count--;              // decrement reference count
    if(ptr->count == 0)        // if no other references
        delete ptr;            // destroy hidden data
}

//----------------------------------------------------------------
//    TOP():  Return element on the top of the stack
//----------------------------------------------------------------
inline data_type Stack::top()
{
    if (ptr->sp == 0) {        // No elements ?
        cerr << "Underflow error\n";
        exit(1);
    }
    return (ptr->arr[ptr->sp - 1]);      // Return top element
}
```

5.13.1 Member functions that change objects

You may have noticed the absence of the push and pop member functions from the reference counted implementation of a stack given above. They were not forgotten, but left out on purpose because they *change* the Stack object, and hence have an extra layer of complexity in their implementation. Whereas it was adequate for the is_empty and top member functions simply to add a prefix of "ptr->" to any reference to a data member of the stack object, doing so for push and pop can cause a program failure.

Reference counts complicate the definition of member functions that *change* the object. This problem is a form of *aliasing* that arises from the use of multiple pointers to the same address. Because the allocated memory block may have more than one pointer to it from different objects, any change to that allocated memory will change *all* the objects pointing at it.

The solution is to test the number of references to the object before changing it. If there is more than one reference, it is necessary to create a new object copied from the original, so as to leave the other references pointing at the unchanged object. The member function then changes the newly created object, which now has only the one reference to it.

This may seem to be a very damning limitation on the use of reference counting, because it seems that every member function may be called upon to create a new object. In fact, the only extra overhead is the test of the reference count to determine if the number of references is greater than one, because even if the member function must copy the object, this can only occur because the copying of the object has been *avoided* earlier in the copy constructor or assignment operator. The copying of the object has been delayed until it is actually needed, and the only slight loss in efficiency is the integer test. Hopefully, this small overhead will be overshadowed by the large savings from avoiding copying a reasonable proportion of objects (i.e. we expect that not all objects will be changed between copying/assignment and destruction).

The missing definitions of push and pop for the Stack class are now presented. The unlinking of the object to which they are being applied from any other references and creation of a new object is all handled in a new private function, the unhook function, which must be called at the start of any member function that may change a Stack object. Making the `unhook` function an `inline` function means that the extra over-head is a single integer test in most situations.

```
//-------------------------------------------------------------------
// UNHOOK:   Called by member functions that CHANGE the object
//-------------------------------------------------------------------

inline void Stack::unhook()
{
    if (ptr->count > 1) {      // Other references?
                               // Yes. Create a new object
        StackData *old = ptr;
        ptr = new StackData(old->size);
        memcpy(ptr->arr, old->arr, old->size * sizeof(data_type));
        ptr->sp = old->sp;
        ptr->count = 1;      // One reference to new memory
        old->count--;        // One less reference to old object
    }
}

//-------------------------------------------------------------------
//   PUSH:  Push an element on the top of the stack
//-------------------------------------------------------------------

inline void Stack::push(data_type data)
{
    unhook();
    if (ptr->sp >= ptr->size) {        // Already too many?
        cerr << "Overflow error\n";
        exit(1);
    }
    ptr->arr[ptr->sp++] = data;        // Push onto end of array
}

//-------------------------------------------------------------------
//   POP():  Take element from the top of the stack
//-------------------------------------------------------------------

inline data_type Stack::pop()
{
    unhook();
    if (ptr->sp == 0) {                // No elements ?
        cerr << "Underflow error\n";
        exit(1);
    }
    return (ptr->arr[--ptr->sp]);      // Pop from end of array
}
```

The same aliasing problem is true of any member function that returns either a pointer or reference to part of the allocated memory, because there is now the *potential* to change the object. For example, if a reference counted `String` class overloads the `[]` operator to return a reference to a single character in the string, the string contents may be changed by using `[]` on the left of an assignment statement:

```
char & String::operator [](int index) { ... }

String str;

str[0] = 'A';      // Changes only str ?
```

Exactly the same solution is needed as for member functions that explicitly change the object. Hence, reference counting imposes a slight overhead on any functions that either change an object or provide the user of a class with the possibility of changing it (unless the class designer can guarantee that the objects will not be changed by the class user).

5.14 One-instance classes

In a one-instance class there will only ever be one object defined from it. In this situation the class can be defined very efficiently by making use of compile-time initialization. An example is a hash table implementation of a symbol table in a compiler, where only one symbol table will ever be used (as shown in Section 8.14) and the crucial fragment from this code is:

```
class SymbolTable {
    private:
        Node * table[TABLE_SIZE];    // Hash table - array of pointers
    public:
        SymbolTable();      // constructor
};
//------------------------------------------------------------
// Constructor - initialize the hash table to empty
//------------------------------------------------------------
SymbolTable::SymbolTable()
{
    for (int i = 0; i < TABLE_SIZE; i++)     // all pointers are NULL
        table[i] = NULL;
}
```

If there will only be one hash table, the constructor is needlessly inefficient. A more efficient version declares the hash table as a `static` data member and the implicit initialization to zero will set all the pointers to NULL at compile-time. The efficient code for a one-instance hash table is:

```
class SymbolTable {              // ONE INSTANCE ONLY
    private:
        static Node *table[TABLE_SIZE]; // Compile-time initialization
    public:
        SymbolTable() { }        // constructor does nothing
};
```

5.15 Summary

- C++ is as efficient as C because most of the extra work is performed by the compiler.
- Large objects should be passed by reference.
- Small functions should be `inline` functions.
- `friend` functions can be used to bypass the class interface efficiently.
- `virtual` functions have an undeserved reputation for inefficiency.
- Memory allocation can be controlled for a class by overloading `new` and `delete`.
- Functions with default arguments and inherited member functions each offer opportunities for writing efficient specialized code.
- The syntax for passing arguments to member objects should be used for initialization.
- Temporary objects can be avoided by pass by reference, and defining extra member functions.

- Objects should be declared close to their first use.
- `<iostream.h>` should be more efficient than `<stdio.h>`, although the difference will be minor.
- Reference counts are an advanced technique for improving the efficiency of classes with high copying or assignment cost, particularly those allocating dynamic memory.

5.16 Further reading

Although I am not aware of any book covering C++ efficiency in detail, there are several books that contain sections of interest. They are all good general C++ books, and their coverage of efficiency is part of a more global coverage.

In Jonathan Shapiro's book, *A C++ Toolkit*, the chapter on performance tuning gives a detailed discussion of `inline` functions, `register` variables and pass by reference. There is also a chapter on memory management which discusses overloading `new` and `delete` for efficiency.

The second edition of the classic book *The C++ Programming Language* by Bjarne Stroustrup covers C++ in its entirety and mentions efficiency in a number of places. The topics covered include (but are not limited to): `inline` functions, overloading `new` and `delete`, saving space with unions and `static` data members, and the `register` qualifier.

James Coplien's excellent book on advanced C++ programming techniques devotes several sections to efficiency. On page 58 there is a very useful discussion of reference counting which covers four alternative methods, including a useful method for converting existing classes to reference counting without changing their definition (and even without re-compilation). Memory management issues involving the overloading of `new` and `delete` are also given good coverage on page 72, and the method of rewriting derived class member functions for efficiency is covered on page 91.

COPLIEN, James O., *Advanced C++ Programming Styles and Idioms*, Addison-Wesley, 1992.

SHAPIRO, Jonathan S., *A C++ Toolkit*, Prentice Hall, 1991.

STROUSTRUP, Bjarne, *The C++ Programming Language (2nd edn)*, Addison-Wesley, 1991.

5.17 Exercises

1. My C++ compiler will not produce inline code for an `inline` function containing a loop. Is this a fundamental limitation of the `inline` keyword, or a deficiency in the compiler? What types of functions cannot be properly inlined?

2. Implement a `String` class which dynamically allocates exactly the right number of bytes to store its string of characters. Be sure to define the ordinary constructor(s), copy constructor, destructor and assignment operator correctly. *Hint:* The copy constructor and assignment operator cannot simply copy the pointer to the allocated memory, but must allocate new memory for the characters and copy the characters into this new memory.

3. Modify the `String` implementation of the previous exercise to use reference counts. *Hint:* The changes to the class should be similar to those for the reference counted `Stack` example class given in this chapter.

4. [advanced] The four-function class idiom (default constructor, copy constructor, assignment operator and destructor) was mentioned in the discussion of reference counts. It was indicated that a common error in C++ classes was failing to provide this idiom for classes that allocate memory in the constructor and de-allocate it in the destructor. This causes the destructor to attempt to de-allocate the same memory location more than once. Is this four-function idiom needed when the dynamic memory allocated for an object will never be released? For example, in the `String` class from earlier exercises, is the idiom needed if the memory allocated to contain the characters need not be returned to the heap? Obviously, leaving the `delete` operation out of the destructor will improve efficiency (at the cost of space wastage), but can the cost of memory allocation in the copy constructor and assignment operator also be avoided?

5. [advanced] Consider the problem of declaring an object close to use discussed at the end of Section 5.11, where the scope rules prevent the declaration at the first point of use. How can the `new` operator be used to overcome this limitation? When will this optimization be beneficial?

6. How can a two-instance class make use of compile-time initialization?

7. [advanced] Section 5.10 presented a hacked method of avoiding temporary objects for evaluating the expression:

    ```
    Complex c1,c2,c3;
    c1 = c2 + c3;
    ```

    Why is it not possible to simply make the return value of the overloaded + operator a *reference*? *Hint:* Consider how the `operator+` function would have to be defined.

Chapter 6

The ANSI C standard library

The ANSI C library functions must be used properly when efficient code is required. This applies not only to C programs, but also to C++ programs where the same library functions are used. The first general rule about the library functions is that they should be used whenever possible, unless they show specific evidence of inefficiency. In many cases, the library functions have been highly optimized (perhaps even written in assembly language), and will be more efficient than any equivalent code you might produce. For example, the functions in <ctype.h> are usually much faster than an equivalent expression such as:

```
'a' <= c && c <= 'z'
```

In fact, the use of the macros in <ctype.h> is also more portable and more readable!

A second general rule for library functions is to use them for their intended purpose. For example, printf and scanf are not meant for single character I/O — use putchar and getchar instead.

A third general rule is that many of the more complicated library functions are very general, and hence inefficient. It is often better to replace them with your own specialized code. For example, functions such as malloc, printf, scanf, qsort and bsearch can often be replaced with code that solves the specific problem at hand.

6.1 Character functions in <ctype.h>

As mentioned above, the <ctype.h> functions are very hard to beat. The list of the character-testing functions in <ctype.h> is given in Table 6.1, and the programmer should attempt to use these functions whenever possible.

Table 6.1. Character class functions

Function	Character class
isalpha(c)	Letter
isdigit(c)	Digit
isalnum(c)	Letter or digit
islower(c)	Lower case letter
isupper(c)	Upper case letter
isxdigit(c)	Hexadecimal digit (0-9, a-f, A-F)
isspace(c)	Space, '\f', '\n', '\r', '\t' or '\v'
isprint(c)	Printable character (0x20...0x7E ASCII)
iscntrl(c)	Control character (0...0x1F and 0x7F ASCII)
ispunct(c)	Printable characters except space, letter or digit
isgraph(c)	Printable characters except space

The character-testing functions in <ctype.h> are usually implemented as macros that use the character as an array index for a 256-byte precalculated table and apply a bit test to this byte, as in:

```
#define isupper(ch)    ((_hidden_array + 1) [ch] & 4 )
```

where the "+ 1" is used so that the macro will still work for EOF, which usually has value −1. In other words, the precalculated table's first (zeroth) entry is for EOF. This addition of 1 should have no run-time cost, since it is part of a constant expression which the compiler can evaluate at compile-time.

Each library function has a particular bit to test (i.e. each byte in the table has one bit for isupper, one bit for islower, etc). These functions could be implemented slightly more efficiently, with a 256-byte table for each function, but this would be space inefficient and remove only a single bitwise & operation for each function call.

One area for improvement for some <ctype.h> implementations is the tolower and toupper functions. Although many implementations use efficient accesses into 256-byte tables, some implementations use real function calls. Unfortunately, it is difficult to design macros for these functions without a (hidden) lookup table because of problems with side effects to macros. ANSI requires that these functions return the character unchanged if it is not a letter, and this makes it difficult for a macro to avoid evaluating its argument twice. For example, the definition of a macro for tolower would involve the conditional operator, as in:

```
#define tolower(c)        (isupper(c) ? ((c) - 'A' + 'a') : c)
```

For implementations involving a costly function call for these functions, it can be worthwhile defining new macros for these functions:

```
#define TOLOWER(c)        (isupper(c) ? ((c) - 'A' + 'a') : c)
#define TOUPPER(c)        (islower(c) ? ((c) - 'a' + 'A') : c)
```

If the restriction that `tolower` and `toupper` work correctly for values other than lower (upper) case letters is removed, faster macros can be used so long as the argument is a letter of the correct case:

```
#define TOLOWER(c)        ((c) - 'A' + 'a')
#define TOUPPER(c)        ((c) - 'a' + 'A')
```

On some implementations, fast versions of `tolower` and `toupper` are provided as `_tolower` and `_toupper`, and these macros can be used instead of writing new macros.

Unfortunately, any of these methods sacrifice portability. The `_tolower` and `_toupper` are not part of the ANSI standard library and are hence non-portable. Our own `TOLOWER` and `TOUPPER` macros may also be non-portable to machines that have a non-ASCII character set. The `tolower` and `toupper` ANSI functions are portable to most environments, but may be inefficient in a few cases.

6.2 String functions in <string.h>

There are some methods for efficient use of the ANSI C string functions (defined in `<string.h>`). For example, the test for the empty string:

```
if (strlen(s) == 0)
```

is equivalent to the far more efficient character comparison:

```
if (s[0] == '\0')
```

Some programmers may prefer `if(!*s)` but this is less readable and should cost the same on a good compiler. A sample of the many variations on this theme is presented in Table 6.2.

Table 6.2. String expressions

Expression	Equivalent
`strlen(s) == 1`	`s[0] != 0 && s[1] == 0`
`strlen(s) > 1`	`s[0] != 0 && s[1] != 0`
`strlen(s) < 2`	`s[0] == 0 || s[1] == 0`
`strcpy(s, "");`	`s[0]=0;`
`strcpy(s, "a");`	`s[0]='a'; s[1]=0;`

When comparing strings twice, once for equality and once for ordering, don't call `strcmp` twice, as in:

```
if( strcmp(s1,s2) == 0)
        printf("Strings %s and %s are equal", s1, s2);
else if( strcmp(s1,s2) < 0)
        printf("%s is before %s\n", s1,s2);
else
        printf("%s is before %s\n", s2,s1);
```

Instead, assign the return value of `strcmp` to an `int` variable, and test this variable twice, as below:

```
int ret = strcmp(s1,s2);
if( ret == 0)
        printf("Strings %s and %s are equal", s1, s2);
else if( ret < 0)
        printf("%s is before %s\n", s1,s2);
else
        printf("%s is before %s\n", s2,s1);
```

The idea of "common cases" can be applied to string comparisons. Strings usually differ at the first character, which inspires us to write fast macros for testing string equality, inequality and order which compare the first characters in each string before calling `strcmp`:

```
#define STR_EQUAL(s1,s2)      (*s1 == *s2 && strcmp(s1, s2) == 0)
#define STR_DIFF(s1,s2)       (*s1 != *s2 || strcmp(s1, s2) != 0)
#define LESS_THAN(s1,s2)      (*s1 < *s2 || strcmp(s1, s2) < 0)
#define GREATER_THAN(s1,s2)   (*s1 > *s2 || strcmp(s1, s2) > 0)
```

Another common inefficiency is passing a string constant to `strlen`. The result could have been calculated at compile-time, but is actually calculated at run-time. This can occur when a string is defined by a macro, such as:

```
#define TITLE        "Efficient C and C++"
#define TITLE_LEN    strlen(TITLE)
```

Although the second macro is convenient in that it need not be changed if the title changes, it is more efficient to count the characters and hard-code the constant:

```
#define TITLE        "Efficient C and C++"
#define TITLE_LEN    19
```

Another clever solution would be to declare `TITLE` as a variable and use the compile-time `sizeof` operator to determine the length of the string, as in:

```
char TITLE[] = "Efficient C and C++"
#define TITLE_LEN    (sizeof(TITLE) - 1)
```

where the subtraction of 1 is necessary to get the correct string length because `sizeof` also counts the null character.

Avoid using `strlen` in the conditional test of `for` loops. For example, the inefficient way of printing out a string is:

```
for (i = 0; i < strlen(s); i++)
    putchar(s[i]);
```

This calls the `strlen` function for every loop iteration. The efficient method is to test the character for zero:

```
for (i = 0; s[i] != 0; i++)
    putchar(s[i]);
```

6.3 Input/output functions in <stdio.h>

The standard I/O functions in `<stdio.h>` are likely to be implemented more efficiently than you could manage. For example, it is unlikely that you could write a more efficient version of the `getchar` macro. However, there are some methods of improving efficiency. C++ programmers might also consider using the `<iostream.h>` library instead of `<stdio.h>`, as discussed in Section 5.12.

One general method of improving efficiency is to use the simplest function. Replace statements such as:

```
printf("\n");
printf("Hello, world\n");
```

with more efficient versions using simpler functions:

```
putchar('\n');
puts("Hello, world");      /* Note: no newline */
```

In fact, you might find that, say, `printf("abcd")` is less efficient than four calls to `putchar`, because `printf` will usually be a real function call but `putchar` is probably a macro. `puts` is not useful in this case because it will add a newline, but `fputs(stdout,..)` may also be worth considering as it does not append a newline. Try exploring the relative efficiencies of `printf`, `puts` and `putchar`. However, note that the dominating cost will be that of actually displaying the character, and the improvements may be marginal.

You are also unlikely to improve performance by adjusting the level of buffering with `setbuf` or `setvbuf`. However, you could try, just to see how good the implementor of your compiler library really was!

You may be able to improve on `<stdio.h>` functions with the `%d` formats to `printf` and `scanf`. Because these functions are so general, they can be improved upon if the program has no need for special format options such as field width and precision. It can be worthwhile to write your own `print_num` or `scan_num` functions to avoid the overhead of examining the format string (as done by both `printf` and `scanf`). This is especially true if you know the maximum size of the integers to be handled (i.e. how many digits) because this may mean that loops in the conversion algorithm can be unrolled. For example, if you are sure that the numbers will always be positive and less than 1000, the following version of `print_num` may be more efficient than `printf`'s `%d` format.

```
void print_num(int n)          /* n = 0..999 */
{
    if (n >= 100) {
        putchar( (n / 100) + '0');
        n %= 100;
    }
    if (n >= 10) {
        putchar( (n / 10) + '0');
        n %= 10;
    }
    putchar(n + '0');
}
```

Avoid the use of `float`, `char` or `short` arguments to `printf` because of the non-prototyping type conversions that are applied to such arguments. The consistent use of `int` and `double` will remove this slight overhead.

6.4 Mathematical functions in <math.h>

Avoid `float` variables when using the `<math.h>` library. All the arguments and return values of functions in `<math.h>` are `double`, and `float` values will cause many conversions.

Besides noting the specific techniques in the next few sections, it may be worth considering writing your own versions of the mathematical functions if less precision than provided by the `<math.h>` functions is required. In particular, for an ANSI prototype-supporting compiler, a library of mathematical functions accepting arguments of type `float` would be worthwhile (unfortunately, there are no such functions provided by the ANSI standard).

Another improvement gained by coding your own mathematical functions is the removal of code to test if the argument values are within the valid domain of the function (assuming you are certain that the program uses the functions correctly). Unfortunately, writing mathematical functions is far from simple, and only a few simpler functions are examined in this chapter.

6.4.1 fabs and abs

It may be more efficient to write your own macro version of the `fabs` function (and also the `abs` function in `<stdlib.h>`), since many libraries will implement it as a real function. There are difficulties in writing macros for these functions since ANSI requires that a side effect in an argument to these macros must be evaluated exactly once. This restriction can be dispensed with when writing our own macros and makes it simple to write fast macros. The macro equivalents of `abs` and `fabs` can both have similar replacement text:

```
#define ABS(x)    ((x) >= 0 ? (x) : -(x))
#define FABS(x)   ((x) >= 0.0? (x) : -(x))
```

It is good style to use capital letters to avoid clashes with the existing library functions. The apparent overuse of brackets is necessary to avoid precedence problems, although they do not avoid side effect problems and uses such as `ABS(i++)` must be avoided.

On the other hand, the library functions `abs` and `fabs` in `<math.h>` might be implemented efficiently using machine-specific knowledge of the internal representations of integers and floating point numbers, making them faster than the macros above. In fact, the overhead of a real function call may not actually occur in some implementations as an advanced optimizer might generate inline code for the function call during its code generation phase (even though the function is not a macro in the header file). This method is known as compiler *intrinsics*, and is discussed further in Chapter 10. You should use the measurement techniques in Chapter 2 to determine if the macros really are faster than the library functions.

The `fabs` function in `<math.h>` may be able to handle obscure values such as +Inf, -Inf and NaN (not a number). Note that these values are not mentioned by the ANSI standard, and are hence non-portable. The efficient macros should be used only if these special values are not important.

6.4.2 floor and ceil

For positive values, the `floor` function is often equivalent to simple type casting to `int`, which may be more efficient. Similarly, the `ceil` function may be equivalent to a simple macro involving type casting. Possible macros for `floor` and `ceil`, on non-negative values only, are:

```
#define FLOOR(x)    ((int)(x))
#define CEIL(x)     ((int)((x) + 0.999999999))
```

These macros are especially efficient if an `int` value is needed, and not a `double` as returned by `floor` and `ceil`. However, they are non-portable, as implementations differ in how they handle conversions from `double` to `int`.

6.4.3 Integral powers: pow

The standard library contains the `pow` library function to compute powers: `pow(x,y)` computes x^y. However, because the `pow` function must handle general exponents, it is not as efficient as it could be in special cases. For example, `pow(x,0.5)` will probably be more efficiently coded as `sqrt(x)`. Another special case occurs when `y` is an integer. Thus calls such as:

```
pow(x, 3.0);    /* x cubed */
```

are most likely more efficient if they call a special function to handle integer powers (the above statement might be even faster as `x*x*x`). A simple function to compute integer powers is:

```
double intpow(double x, int n)     /* compute x^n */
{
    double result;

    for (result = 1.0; n != 0; n--)      /* n-1 iterations */
        result *= x;
    return result;
}
```

However, it is not too difficult to write a more efficient version which uses fewer than $n-1$ multiplications. For example, the computation of x^7 can be written as:

$$x^7 = x^4 * x^2 * x^1$$

which can be written out as the following code which uses only four multiplications:

```
x2 = x * x;
x4 = x2 * x2;
x7 = x4 * x2 * x;
```

An improved algorithm has reduced six multiplications to four, and the improvement is even greater for larger powers — in fact, the number of multiplications reduces from $O(n)$ to $O(\log n)$. This idea can be implemented as a general algorithm, which uses the fact that x^n can be broken down into multiplications of values that are all of the form x^i, where i is a power of 2. For example:

$$x^7 = x^4 * x^2 * x^1$$
$$x^6 = x^4 * x^2$$
$$x^5 = x^4 * x^1$$

A careful examination of the pattern reveals that each bit that is 1 in the binary representation of the exponent, n, indicates that a corresponding power of x should be used in the multiplication to create the final result. In the following implementation, `bitmask` steps through all the binary bits of n, while the statement `x*=x` creates a power of x with an exponent that is a power of 2.

```
double intpow(double x, int n)      /* compute x^n */
{
    int bitmask;
    double result = 1.0;

    for(bitmask = 1; bitmask <= n; bitmask <<= 1) {
        if ((n & bitmask) != 0)          /* bit set? */
            result *= x;                 /* use x in the result */
        x *= x;                          /* make next power */
    }
    return result;
}
```

Note that this function is not valid for very large values of n (i.e. close to `INT_MAX` declared in `<limits.h>`), as it will loop infinitely if the expression `n<<1` is an overflow (why?).

As a final caveat, note that the mathematical standard library functions may have hardware support on some large machines. On one machine I tried, the `pow` standard library function ran faster than the better version of `intpow`, particularly for large powers.

6.5 Avoiding qsort and bsearch

It is usually more efficient to write your own specialized sorting and searching routines than to use the general library functions `qsort` and `bsearch`. This is because both library functions have the relatively high overhead of a call to the user-supplied function for every comparison (i.e. a call to the pointer-to-function argument). `qsort` and `bsearch` must call this comparison function even to compare two integers. Obviously, it will be more efficient to write your own special integer sorting and searching routines. This is discussed in Chapter 8.

Another reason to avoid `qsort` is its $O(n^2)$ worst-case performance on certain sets of data (which depend on the specific variant of quicksort used) — for example, when the data is sorted in reverse order.

The quicksort algorithm is not the best algorithm to use for a small number of elements. It has some initial overhead, and some simpler algorithms such as bubble sort or insertion sort may do better when the number of elements is small.

In addition, if the data is already partially sorted, it may be more efficient to use a different sorting algorithm, such as insertion sort or even the notoriously inefficient bubble sort, because these algorithms will perform well on data that is almost sorted. The various sorting algorithms are compared in Chapter 8.

6.6 Random numbers: rand

The `rand` function may be more general than what you require. A faster pseudo-random number generator might be a better alternative if the numbers needn't be as "random" (i.e. if the period of the sequence need not be particularly high, or if the distribution need not be uniform). It can even be worthwhile to use code for a sophisticated generator with good mathematical properties — access to the code makes it possible to write the random number generator out as in-line code and avoid the function call overhead of `rand`. A common method of generating large pseudo-random integers is the linear congruential method, which uses the following formula for the sequence of random numbers:

$$R_{i+1} = (A R_i + B) \bmod C$$

where A and B are large prime numbers, and C is usually 2^n, where n is the number of bits in a word (the *mod* operation effectively prevents the random number from overflowing the limits of an `int`). Fortunately, the *mod* operation can be implemented efficiently as a bit mask because C is a power of two. The linear congruential method is often used to implement the `rand` function. It does suffer problems in that the lower order bits are non-random (e.g. `rand()%2` may produce the non-random sequence 0,1,0,1... on some implementations), but the high-order bits have reasonable properties.

Note that since many implementations use this algorithm, programmers should avoid expressions such as:

```
value = rand() & 01;     /* DANGEROUS */
```

to generate a random sequence of 0's and 1's; on many implementations the generated values will be the not-so-random sequence: 0,1,0,1,.... A better solution is to use the higher-order bits, as in the following code for a 32-bit `int` machine:

```
value = ((unsigned int) rand() >> 16 ) & 01;
```

If a particular application needs only small random numbers, a simple version of the linear congruential method can be used, although the generated values will not have good mathematical properties. For example, when generating random values to give random motion to creatures in an arcade game, a very limited random number generator will probably be satisfactory because small random integers are adequate. A simple implementation of the linear congruential method generating numbers in the range 0..127 is:

```
value = (value * 41 + 1) & 127;
```

The small prime values of 41 and 1 are adequate here because the range is small (i.e. C is small). If C is large, the values of A and B must also be large.

The bitwise & operation can be removed by using one of C's builtin types. The use of `unsigned char` is equivalent to performing arithmetic modulo 256, and is usually implemented efficiently by grabbing the first byte of a word. The following code will generate numbers in the range 0..255:

```
unsigned char value = 0;
   .....
value = (value * 41 + 1);
```

A reasonably efficient method of generating a reasonably random sequence of 0's and 1's is to grab the *highest* bit of this value:

```
unsigned char value = 0;
   .....
value = (value * 41 + 1);
bit = (value & 128) >> 7;
```

One limitation of these efficient methods using small numbers is that the pattern will repeat frequently. In general, the pattern will repeat after C values, and the value of C has been 128 and 256 in the above code fragments.

There are a very many non-portable methods of generating random numbers. There may be an easy way to get a random number from the most random element in the system — the human. For example, the program could examine the mouse position (if the user is frequently moving the mouse), or by measuring the number of clock ticks between user keypresses. Another hardware-specific solution is to grab groups of bits from a particular memory block (e.g. ROM code).

6.7 Removing assertions

When considering this optimization, note that it may be far better to leave assertions in production code. The ungraceful termination of the `assert` macro is often preferable to the unpredictable behavior from the program. An alternative worth considering is to define your own `assert` macro to exhibit more graceful behavior. Nevertheless, removing assertions is one method of extracting the last drop of speed from your code.

The removal of assertions is an optimization that is commonly forgotten and the program does not run as fast as it could. These should be removed by defining NDEBUG before including <assert.h>:

```
#define NDEBUG
#include <assert.h>
```

Other types of debugging checks should also be removed. In particular, any debugging statements that produce output should be removed as unnecessary output will waste much processor time. If debugging code is properly placed in the program by using conditional compilation (i.e. #if DEBUG), this is a minor change to the definition of a preprocessor symbol.

6.8 Writing your own malloc function

The standard library functions declared in `<stdlib.h>` for dynamic memory allocation
are very general, and hence, very slow. The `malloc` and `calloc` functions must be
general to accommodate varying requests for differing size blocks and must return
addresses satisfying the most stringent alignment requirements. This generality makes it
difficult for the allocation functions to be efficient. Writing your own allocation
functions can improve the efficiency of your program. Alternatively, C++ programmers
can overload the `new` and `delete` operators as discussed in Section 5.6.

The `malloc` and `calloc` functions must store information in each block so that the
`free` and `realloc` functions know how large the block is (this is stored in a header
block just before the address passed back to the program). This all takes time, and the
allocator can run faster if the flexibility to reuse blocks of memory is abandoned. Note
that this is a case of wasting space to gain a speed increase.

A good example of this situation is the symbol table in a compiler. The symbol table
must store each of its symbols, of unknown length, in the table. Because the maximum
number of symbols is unknown in advance, it is best to use dynamic memory. Rather
than use `malloc` to allocate memory for the string storing each symbol, a new function
`char_malloc` is used. The source code for this function is shown below:

```
/*--------------------------------------------------------------------*/
/* CHAR_MALLOC.C:  Customized dynamic memory allocator for STRINGS   */
/*--------------------------------------------------------------------*/

#include <stdio.h>
#include <stdlib.h>

#define BIG_BLOCK_SIZE 1024          /* Size of large memory blocks */

char *char_malloc(int size)
{
    static char *address = NULL;     /* Address of remaining memory */
    static int bytes_free;           /* Bytes remaining in block */
    char *temp;

    if (address == NULL || size > bytes_free) {
        address = malloc(BIG_BLOCK_SIZE);      /* Use the real malloc */
        bytes_free = BIG_BLOCK_SIZE;
    }
    temp = address;
    address += size;        /* Move to next free spot for next time */
    bytes_free -= size;     /* Count bytes remaining */
    return temp;            /* Return address of string */
}
```

The `char_malloc` function runs much faster than the `malloc` function because it
performs much less computation. It works by allocating a very large block of memory,
using the real `malloc` function, and then breaking off chunks of this block for each
string. Although the call to `malloc` is slow, it is called infrequently and this does not
greatly slow down the new memory allocator. The main disadvantage of the
`char_malloc` function is that memory for the strings cannot be reused after it is no
longer needed — that is, the strings cannot be freed. It would be possible to implement a
`char_free` function, but for `char_malloc` to reuse the small blocks of memory for
each string it would be necessary to maintain a list of free blocks and their sizes, and
maintaining this free list would defeat the purpose of writing a fast allocator.

The main difficulty with `malloc` and `calloc` is that these functions must operate without knowledge of how many blocks will be requested, or of which different sizes will be requested. The programmer, however, will often know roughly how many blocks of the various sizes will be required, and can use this information to write a more efficient version of the allocation function for the particular program.

A good candidate for such an efficiency optimization is a program that uses dynamic memory for only one type of node, such as a binary tree implementation of a symbol table. The knowledge that only one size block will be required can be applied to write faster node allocation and de-allocation functions. Instead of using `malloc` and `free`, the program can use the new functions, `new_node` and `free_node`:

```
node = new_node();              /* Allocate a node */
free_node(node);                /* De-allocate a node */
```

The disadvantage here is the need for a call to a slow initialization function called `setup_heap`. However, the cost of a call to `setup_heap` should be overshadowed by the efficiency of `new_node` and `free_node` if they are called frequently enough. Assuming the binary tree nodes are of type "`struct node`", the `setup_heap` call looks like:

```
setup_heap(sizeof(struct node), ESTIMATED_NUM_NODES);
```

The improvement gained by this method comes from initially calling `malloc` from `setup_heap` to allocate a large block, and then using the `new_node` function to break off chunks to use as nodes. Because the `malloc` function is not usually called by `new_node`, the `new_node` function can be very fast (indeed, it could be a macro).

The estimate of the number of nodes required by `setup_heap` is quite important; it determines how big a block to allocate in `setup_heap`. If the estimate is too small, `new_node` will occasionally need to call `malloc` to allocate another large block, which is less desirable than a single initial call to `malloc` in `setup_heap`. If the estimate is too large, this wastes space and will also slow down the initial call to `setup_heap`. Hence, the estimate should be large enough to accommodate the most likely requirements of the program, but not a huge worst-case upper bound.

The source code for the new functions is shown as follows. The only non-trivial details of the program are in the creation and maintenance of the free list. The `new_node` function takes the first node off the front of the free list, the `free_node` function adds the node to the front, and the `setup_heap` function initializes the free list with a single loop. The free list is implemented as a linked list, with the "next" pointers stored in the first word of each node. This can cause alignment problems if the size of requested blocks is an irregular number of bytes, but there is usually no problem if the requested size is the size of a `struct` variable because such variables are always of a size that prevents alignment problems. However, if alignment is a problem the free list could be maintained as a separate list in another block of allocated memory.

```
/*------------------------------------------------------------------*/
/*  EFFICIENT_MALLOC.C : fast dynamic allocation functions          */
/*------------------------------------------------------------------*/

#include <stdio.h>
#include <stdlib.h>

static int estimate;        /* estimated number of blocks */
static int block_size;      /* Size of the block */
static void *free_list;     /* Pointer to first free block */

/*------------------------------------------------------------------*/
/* Internal function to allocate big block, and thread the free list */
/*------------------------------------------------------------------*/

static void *allocate_large_block(int size, int number)
{
    char * address, * temp;
    int i;

    address = malloc(size * number);      /* Allocate large block */

            /* Thread linked list of free blocks */

    for (temp = address, i = 0; i < number - 1; i++, temp += size)
        *(void**)temp = temp + size;      /* Store next pointer */
    *(void**)temp = NULL;                 /* NULL on end of list */
    return address;
}

/*------------------------------------------------------------------*/
/* Initialize the heap for an estimated number of nodes             */
/* If more nodes are required, more memory is allocated later       */
/*------------------------------------------------------------------*/

void setup_heap(int size, int estimated_number)
{
    if (size < sizeof(void*)) {          /* room for 'next' pointers? */
        fprintf(stderr, "Block is too small\n");
        exit(1);
    }
    free_list = allocate_large_block(size, estimated_number);
    estimate = estimated_number;         /* Save for use in new_node() */
    block_size = size;                   /* Save the block size too */
}

/*------------------------------------------------------------------*/
/* Allocate new node of size requested earlier                      */
/*------------------------------------------------------------------*/

void *new_node(void)
{
    void *temp;

    if (free_list == NULL)       /* Need another big block? */
        free_list = allocate_large_block(block_size, estimate);
    temp = free_list;                    /* Save the block address */
    free_list = *(void**)temp;   /* Get 'next' pointer in block */
                                 /* Update free list */
    return temp;                 /* Return the block address */
}

/*------------------------------------------------------------------*/
/* Free one of the nodes for re-use by new_node()                   */
/*------------------------------------------------------------------*/

void free_node(void *address)
{
    *(void**)address = free_list;  /* Add node to front of free list */
    free_list = address;
}
```

One minor disadvantage of this implementation is that the memory allocated by `malloc` is never properly de-allocated by the `free` function. To overcome the limitation, it is necessary to maintain a list of the large blocks that are allocated and add another function to free all the large blocks. This function is called when *all* the nodes are no longer needed.

6.9 Memory block functions in <string.h>

There are several efficient "block operation" functions declared in `<string.h>`. These are likely to be efficient as they are often supported by assembly "block move" instructions or similar. The full list of memory block functions is given in Table 6.3.

Table 6.3. Memory block functions

Function	Meaning
int memcmp(s1, s2, n)	Compare first n bytes of s1 and s2
void *memcpy(s1, s2, n)	Copy n bytes from s2 to s1
void *memmove(s1, s2, n)	As for memcpy, but allow overlap
void *memchr(s1, c, n)	Find first occurrence of c in s1
void *memset(s1, c, n)	Set the first n bytes of s1 to c

The `memcpy` function is a highly efficient method of copying arrays. Rather than copy each element of an array, one at a time, in a loop, the `memcpy` standard library function defined in `<string.h>` can be used to copy the entire array in one statement:

```
memcpy(b, a, sizeof(a));                    /* copy array a to b */
```

An alternative method of copying arrays is to make use of the fact that C permits `struct` assignments. This method is not portable, is very unreadable and uses pointers incorrectly by converting between two different pointer types. However, it can be faster than `memcpy` because it makes use of the assignment operator rather than calling a function. To copy an array by this method it is necessary to declare a new dummy `struct` type the same size as the array that is to be copied. Then type-casting is used to fool the compiler into thinking it is copying `struct`s when really it is copying arrays. The method is illustrated below:

```
struct dummy_transfer {    /* The new struct type */
    int a[MAX];            /* This field gives the right size */
};
int a[MAX], b[MAX];        /* The array variables being copied */

*(struct dummy_transfer *)a = *(struct dummy_transfer *)b;
```

The assignment statement first type-casts both a and b to be pointers to the new `struct` type, and then dereferences these pointers so that the compiler believes it is assigning between two `struct`s. Note that the above code does not violate the constraint that a type-cast expression cannot be an l-value. The assignment operator is applied to the result of the `*` operator, which always returns an l-value. The type-cast expression is an operand to `*`, which does not require an l-value as its operand.

memcpy can also be used to copy structures efficiently on non-ANSI compilers. The usual method of copying one struct to another is to use an assignment statement (i.e. "b=a;"). However, some older compilers do not permit the assignment of whole structs. If this is the case, the memcpy standard library function can be used instead of copying fields one-by-one.

```
memcpy(&b, &a, sizeof(a));        /* copy struct a to b */
```

In cases where the memory locations to be copied may overlap, the memmove function must be used, as memcpy gives undefined results. The memmove function will be less efficient than memcpy, but should still be better than the alternatives, such as an initializing loop.

6.10 Summary

- Avoid using general functions when a simpler function will do the same job.
- Functions such as abs and fabs are difficult for compilers to implement as safe macros, and it may be more efficient to define unsafe macros to perform these operations.
- String comparisons can be improved by testing the first character before calling strcmp.
- The %d formats for printf and scanf are very general, and it may be efficient to write specialized print_num and scan_num functions.
- Use only double arguments when using <math.h>.
- qsort and bsearch are inefficient because they call a function for each comparison.
- Using in-line code to generate pseudo-random numbers can be faster than calling the rand library function.
- Memory allocation can be improved by allocating larger blocks of memory.
- The memcpy, memset and memmove functions are efficient.

6.11 Further reading

For further information on the ANSI standard library, the definitive reference is the ANSI standard (refer to the Bibliography for details of how to obtain a copy). An interesting book discussing both use and implementation of the standard library, including full C source code for all library functions, is the book by Plauger:

PLAUGER, P. J., *The Standard C Library*, Prentice Hall, 1991.

6.12 Exercises

1. Fix the function `intpow` in Section 6.4.3 so that it is valid for all values of n, even as large as `INT_MAX`, for which it will currently loop infinitely. *Hint:* Modify the loop so that n is shifted right, instead of `bitmask` being shifted left.

2. Generalize the function `intpow` in Section 6.4.3 so that it handles negative integer exponents. *Hint:* $x^{-n} \equiv 1/x^n$.

3. Modify the `intpow` function to employ "special solution of simple cases" for greater efficiency for small values of n.

4. Write an efficient `scan_num` function to replace the use of `scanf`'s %d format, under the assumption that numbers are in the range 0..999.

5. What sequence of statements can be used instead of `strcat(s, "a")`?

6. What modification should be made to the `TOLOWER` and `TOUPPER` functions in Section 6.1 to ensure that the constants `'A'` and `'a'` are constant folded? *Hint:* see Section 4.5.2.

7. Implement the following functions as efficiently as possible:

    a) `strlen`
    b) `strcpy`
    c) `strcat`

    Ensure that `strcpy` and `strcat` behave properly and return the value of their first argument.

8. The `strcpy` function can be coded as a macro by lifting the requirement that it return a value and then coding it as a `void` function. Design a macro for this modified `strcpy` function. Make sure that the macro is "safe", in that side effects in the arguments are not evaluated twice. *Hint:* The easiest way to avoid side effect problems is to ensure that the macro arguments appear *exactly once* in the replacement text. This can be simply achieved by declaring some temporary variables.

9. Use a fast library function to improve the efficiency of the following array initialization loop:

    ```
    for (i = 0; i < SIZE; i++)
        arr[i] = 0;
    ```

Chapter 7

Space-efficiency

In these days of rapidly declining memory prices, memory reduction techniques are perhaps not as important as those for increasing speed. However, there are certainly situations when reducing space requirements is far more important than increasing the speed of a program. This section discusses a number of techniques for reducing memory requirements. Unfortunately, reducing space requirements can often reduce speed. There is a trade-off between space-efficiency and time-efficiency.

Every C and C++ program uses memory for several different purposes, and each of these areas must be attacked separately. The memory usage of the program can be divided into the following memory sections:

- Executable instructions.
- Static storage.
- Stack storage.
- Heap storage.

The executable instructions for a program are usually stored in one contiguous block of memory. Static storage refers to memory used by global and local `static` variables, string constants and (possibly) floating point constants. Stack storage refers to the dynamic storage of non-`static` local variables. Heap storage refers to the memory that is dynamically allocated by the `malloc` and `calloc` standard library functions, or by the C++ `new` and `delete` operators.

The memory requirements for the executable instructions are largely independent of the other memory areas, whereas the techniques for reducing the memory required for the other three areas are often similar. However, care must be taken that applying a technique to reduce data space does not increase the amount of code too greatly, thus increasing the executable size.

7.1 Reducing executable size

The size of the executable obviously depends on the size of your program. Hence, the obvious way to reduce executable size is to reduce the number of executable statements in your program. This could involve deleting non-crucial functions from the program, although this is not often possible. Compile-time initialization of global and static variables instead of assignment statements can also reduce code size.

Another possibility is that your compiler may support an option that makes the optimizer focus on space reduction; it generates executable instructions that are as compact as possible, rather than as fast as possible. Consult your compiler documentation for information about the optimizer, if it exists.

The size of the executable depends not only on the source code, but also on the extra library functions that are linked by the linker. Although it may seem that the programmer has no control over this, there are some techniques for reducing the amount of linked code. The techniques depend largely on how "smart" your linker is — that is, whether the linker links only the functions you need. For example, a "dumb" linker might link the entire I/O library if one function is used, whereas a smart linker would link only that function (and any extra code it might need). If the linker is dumb, there is little to do except avoid the library functions completely and write your own non-portable machine-specific functions. If the linker is smart, executable size can be reduced by replacing large general-purpose library functions with your own special-purpose versions. For example, the printf and scanf functions are very large because they have to handle a multitude of format specifications (especially real numbers). Executable size can be reduced by writing your own functions to perform I/O, using getchar and putchar as the basic I/O calls. For example, if you are using only %d in printf, you can avoid using printf by writing your own print_num function:

```c
#include <stdio.h>

#define BASE 10        /* decimal numbers */

void print_num(int num)
{
    if (num < 0)
        num = - num, putchar('-');      /* handle negatives */
    if (num < BASE)
        putchar(num + '0');              /* only 1 digit number */
    else {
        print_num(num / BASE);           /* do left digits */
        putchar((num % BASE) + '0');     /* do rightmost digit */
    }
}
```

This function can be used to perform all integer output, and putchar and puts can be used to output characters and strings (they are smaller than printf). Another possibility is writing your own minimal printf function that supports only those format specifications that you actually use.

UNIX programmers can also use the strip utility which strips symbol table information from the executable. However, this is more relevant to the amount of disk space the executable file uses than it is to the amount of memory it uses during execution. In any case, UNIX programmers are rarely short of memory.

When reducing executable size, avoid long macros and large C++ `inline` functions; use functions instead of macros, and remove the `inline` keyword from large functions. Surprisingly, the use of macros and C++ `inline` functions can actually reduce executable code if the macro or `inline` function performs a very small computation (e.g. adding two numbers, or accessing a variable in a class). The instructions generated by the inline code may well be fewer than those generated for a function call. However, if the macro or `inline` function is very large, every call to that function will generate a large number of instructions and executable size will increase.

The choice of IBM PC memory model, as discussed in Section 4.8, can have some effect on executable size. Using some of the "smaller" models can reduce the number of instructions associated with pointer operations and function calls. The `small` and `compact` models cause smaller function call sequences. The `small` or `medium` models use very few instructions for pointer operations; the `compact` and `large` models use more, but less than the number for the `huge` model. The `near` and `far` (non-ANSI) qualifiers can also reduce the code size of particular pointer statements. The declaration of `near` functions, `near` pointers and `far` pointers can reduce code size.

7.1.1 C++ linkage problems

C++ poses some difficult linkage problems for compilers that must use an existing linker, such as many C++ implementations on UNIX-based operating systems. The main areas of difficulty are `inline` functions and the `virtual` function table. Let us examine the problem of `inline` functions.

C++ allows `inline` functions, unlike ordinary functions, to be *defined* multiple times. The main advantage this offers is that a class declaration and its `inline` function definitions can be included as a header file without producing compilation (linkage) errors about multiply defined functions.

Unfortunately, the `inline` function must appear in the object code as a real function, even if the compiler can expand all its calls, because the compiler cannot guarantee that it will always be called in a file where the function body is visible. Hence, the compiler must emit a definition of the function into the object code. However, doing so every time the `inline` function is found will generate the function for every file in which the class declaration is included, which will lead to multiply-defined function errors on most linkers. The simplest solution is to give `inline` functions the equivalent of `static` function linkage to eliminate linkage errors. However, this leads to a huge increase in executable code size. To combat this problem, some compilers use a simple heuristic that allows them to emit the `inline` functions into only one object file. The code for all `inline` member functions is emitted only when the *definition* of the first *non-inline* function is found (i.e. the definition of the non-inline function that appears physically first in the class declaration). If there is no such non-inline function, the inefficient method of emitting the function into every object file must be used. Hence, a simple rule that will reduce executable size for some C++ implementations is:

Always have at least one non-inline member function.

This can be achieved by ensuring one of the member functions is non-inline, or even by creating a small dummy non-inline member function. The few unused bytes of executable code for this dummy function may well be worth the overall saving gained from only linking `inline` functions once.

The implementation of `virtual` functions has exactly the same problem in that the virtual function table must be emitted into exactly one file. Compilers use the same heuristic tricks to do this, and one solution is the rule given above.

Linkage should not be a problem for personal computer C++ compiler packages as the implementor can simply improve the linker. The linker can be made smart enough so that it merges identical `inline` functions and virtual function tables without emitting an error message. In addition, it is reasonable to assume that this linkage problem will gradually disappear, as linkers become smart enough to merge identical functions, or to avoid linking unused (`static`) functions from an object file. Unless executable size is a crucial issue for some reason, it is probably best to ignore the linkage problems in some C++ implementations.

7.2 General techniques for reducing data size

There are many techniques for reducing the size of program data. These techniques apply to all three types of memory — static, stack and heap storage. In some cases, a method may increase the memory storage in one area to decrease the memory usage in another, which is valid only if the total storage requirements decrease.

7.2.1 Different data structures

The program should be examined to determine if a large space reduction can be achieved by changing to different data structures. For example, the program could use arrays instead of linked lists or binary trees, to avoid the extra space due to pointer storage. However, this also wastes more space if the array is not full, and it is even better to use dynamic arrays, which do not waste any storage, as exactly the right amount of memory is allocated. Unfortunately, using different data structures can sometimes reduce the time-efficiency of programs.

7.2.2 Recalculation

This is exactly the opposite of the data structure augmentation, storing precomputed results and lazy evaluation techniques for time-efficiency. The idea is to store as little redundant information as possible. Whatever can be calculated from the existing data is recalculated each time. Naturally, this reduces the time-efficiency of a program.

7.2.3 Unions

When using a lot of structures, space can be reduced by overlaying the data fields. This can only be done if the fields to be overlayed are mutually exclusive (i.e. they never have active data in them at the same time). There is a special data type for this purpose: the `union`. A `union` can be useful, for example, when storing a token from a compiler's lexical analyzer. The `union` declaration below defines a variable that overlays two fields, a character pointer and a `long` value.

```
union token_node {
        int token;
        union {
            char *identifier;    /* name of identifier */
            long constant_value; /* value of constant */
        } un;
};
```

The two fields of the union never contain a value both at the same time. If the token is an identifier, the pointer field points to the identifier string. If the token is a constant (e.g. an integral constant or character constant), the long field contains its value. If the token is some other type, neither field is used.

7.2.4 Reusing space

One way to conserve memory is to reuse the space used by a variable. The union data type is an example of this general idea, and another is reusing variables for different purposes. For example, rather than letting several functions each have a local temporary variable, i, they could all use the same global variable (although this is a very dangerous practice). As another example, if a program uses two similar arrays, examine whether the two arrays can share the same storage (possibly as a union).

7.2.5 Small data types: short, char

Instead of using arrays of ints, use arrays of short, char or unsigned char. There is no problem with this method, provided large integer values are not being stored (e.g. larger than 127 for char, or larger than 255 for unsigned char). This technique is also worthwhile when applied to int fields in structs although alignment restrictions may limit the improvement — use the sizeof operator to determine if the size of the struct has been reduced. Smaller local variables could also be declared as a smaller type, but this may increase the executable size due to type conversions. Note that speed can be compromised by using smaller data types because of the type conversions that often result. Similarly, use float instead of double, where the greater precision of results is not important.

For example, it is needlessly inefficient to store school grades, which are restricted to 0..100 as an int. The type unsigned char is adequate as it allows values from 0..255 and it will only require one byte, compared to two or four bytes for int.

7.2.6 Bit-fields in structs

When storing small integers in structs, there is a way to specify exactly the number of bits required. These types are called bit-fields, and can only be used for fields inside structs or unions. When using bit-fields, small integers or boolean flags are automatically packed into a struct or union. This reduces storage requirements significantly, but reduces speed because it is necessary to pack and unpack bits.

The type of a bit-field can only be int or unsigned int. It cannot be specified as char, short or an enumerated type. Unless the values can be negative, the field should be declared as unsigned int. If not, one of the bits will be used as a sign bit, limiting the values that the field can hold (and possibly causing errors if the integer overflows these limits).

To minimize storage, all the bit-fields should follow one after the other. If not, the compiler may not pack them all into the same word. In the following example three fields are packed into seven bits:

```
struct node {
    unsigned int    active:1;         /* boolean flag (0/1) */
    unsigned int    visited:1;        /* boolean flag (0/1) */
    unsigned int    component:5;      /* 0..31 */
};
```

7.2.7 Parallel arrays versus arrays of struct

Because of alignment restrictions, a structure may have unusable padding bytes. The number of padding bytes can be determined by using the `sizeof` operator, and subtracting the sizes of each individual field from the size of the `struct`. If there are padding bytes, replacing an array of `struct` with a number of "parallel" arrays removes the need for this padding. An example of this change is given in Section 4.3.5. Note that reordering the `struct` fields may also be effective (see Section 7.2.9).

7.2.8 Packing

When dealing with large arrays of small integers, it can be more efficient to pack them together (i.e. more than one value per word), particularly when the information is binary (true or false), because only one bit per value is needed. On some machines it can even be worthwhile to pack arrays of `char` into arrays of `int` — some machines use whole integers for the representation of `char`s.

Note that bit-fields are a form of packing provided by the compiler and are much easier to use. However, bit-fields cannot always be easily used. For example, in the following set implementation, bit-fields are not very useful because efficiently accessing 256 different bit-fields (one per character) is very difficult.

Sets of characters can be packed in arrays of bits. Since each of the 256 characters in a set requires only 1 bit each to indicate membership in the set, a set data structure need contain only 256 bits. For space-efficiency, these bits can be packed into 32 bytes (each byte contains 8 bits).

The `unsigned char` type is used to represent a byte. If the `unsigned` qualifier is omitted, the routines may fail because a `signed char` value might be negative, and bitwise operations on negative values are not well-defined.

Table 7.1. Set operations

Function	Meaning
init_set(set)	Initialize as the empty set
add_member(set, ch)	Add character to set
is_member(set, ch)	Test if character is member of set
remove_member(set, ch)	Remove character from set

The basic functions needed for a set of characters are shown in Table 7.1. An implementation of these set operations is shown below:

```
typedef unsigned char Set[32];     /* set is array of 32 bytes */

void init_set(Set s)
{
    s[0] = s[1] = s[2] = s[3] =
    s[4] = s[5] = s[6] = s[7] = 0;      /* clear 8 bytes */
}

void add_member(Set s, unsigned char ch)
{
    s[(ch & 0xf8) >> 3] |= 1 << (ch & 07);    /* set bit */
}

void remove_member(Set s, unsigned char ch)
{
    s[(ch & 0xf8) >> 3] &= ~ (1 << (ch & 07));   /* clear bit */
}

int is_member(Set s, unsigned char ch)
{
    return (s[(ch & 0xf8) >> 3]
            & (1 << (ch & 07))) != 0;   /* test bit */
}
```

The most complicated part of the implementation is the method by which the value of ch, in the range 0..255, is converted into an array index 0..31 and a bit mask. The array index is found as the topmost 5 bits of ch, shifted down 3 places to give a value in the range 0..31. The lowest 3 bits of ch give a value in the range 0..7 to indicate which bit is to be examined. Shifting a 1 left by that many bits gives a unique bit mask for each of the 8 cases, with exactly one bit set. Thus any character value is mapped to a unique bit, which represents its membership in the set.

7.2.9 Reordering struct fields

Because of the word alignment on some machines, the order of fields in a structure can change the size of a struct. This only applies to structs containing different size fields. A general rule for minimizing the space is to order the fields from largest to smallest. This heuristic may not give the best ordering — examine the size of a few different orderings using the sizeof operator, if space is crucial. This is a machine-dependent optimization, and may not work well on some machines.

7.2.10 Using malloc for character strings

A common space wastage occurs with structures containing strings. These are often declared containing arrays of char, as in:

```
char label[MAX];         /* Array of MAX characters */
```

If the strings are usually less than the maximum length, there is great wastage. A better method is to allocate exactly the right number of characters for each string. When storing the string, malloc is called to allocate the memory as follows:

```
char *label;                        /* Pointer to the string */

label = malloc(strlen(s) + 1);    /* allocate memory */
strcpy(label, s);                  /* store the new label */
```

One disadvantage of this method is that extra complications are caused by strings stored separately to the `structs`. Care must be taken as the labels are now pointers. This complicates operations such as saving and loading to/from a file, as problems with pointers must be resolved.

The method may also actually *increase* space usage (if strings are about MAX characters long) due to the extra memory used by `malloc` for each allocated block. One method of avoiding this is to use the `char_malloc` function as described in Section 6.8, but this will increase executable size.

7.2.11 IBM PC memory models

The choice of memory model on an IBM personal computer can affect the size of pointer variables. The `small` or `compact` memory models will store pointers to data using 16 bits, whereas other memory models will store pointers using 32 bits. Pointers to functions are slightly different: the `small` and `medium` models both store function pointers using 16 bits. The declaration of `near` pointers, to code or data, by using the `near` type qualifier, also reduces pointer size to 16 bits. Memory models are discussed fully in Section 4.8.

7.2.12 C++ static data members

One method of reducing the size of a C++ class object is to declare some of its members as `static`. This change can be applied to any data members that are the same for any object. To declare a `static` data member, the member declaration is simply prefixed with the "`static`" keyword, as below:

```
class Circle {
        static int x_origin, y_origin;  // static data members
        int x_centre, y_centre;
};
```

A `static` data member is effectively a global variable, but with the restriction that it is enclosed in the scope of a class. This is very similar to the single-function scope restriction of `static` local variables inside functions.

The initialization of these `static` data members is slightly difficult. The correct method of initialization is to place an explicit initialization of the `static` members, qualified by the class name, in exactly one file (thus there is exactly one definition). The statements for this are:

```
Circle::x_origin = 0;       // initialize static members
Circle::y_origin = 0;
```

Unfortunately, the compile-time initialization benefits of `static` data members are lost in early versions of C++ (before C++ 2.0) because this syntax is not permitted. In these versions, the only method of initializing `static` members is to use an assignment statement in a member function, and it is often useful to declare a dummy object just to initialize these members:

```
class Circle {
        static int x_origin, y_origin;     // static data members
        int x_centre, y_centre;
        initialize() { x_origin = 0; y_origin = 0; }
};

main()
{
    Circle c;

    c.initialize();
    ....         // rest of program
}
```

In such situations, it can be more efficient to rely upon the implicit initialization to zero of `static` data members (similar to that for global variables). However, this is of little use if initial values of zero are not required.

7.3 Reducing static storage

Static storage refers to the memory for global and local `static` variables, string constants and (possibly) floating point constants. All of the general techniques discussed above can reduce the size of the global and `static` variables.

The space requirements for string constants can be reduced if the compiler has an option to merge identical string constants (which arise quite frequently). Note that this can create problems if string constants are modified, although modifying string constants does defy the ANSI standard and should be avoided.

If there is no such option, or the option does not merge string constants across object files (which is quite likely), merging string constants can be achieved by the programmer, although the method is far from elegant. A global variable can be declared to hold the string constant and the name of this `char` array is used instead of the string constant. For example, instead of using:

```
#define TITLE   "A very long string ... "
```

in a header file, a global array of `char` can be declared to hold the string. As with all C global variables, the initialized definition of the array should appear in only one C source file, and an `extern` declaration of the variable should appear in any header file or other source file that uses the variable.

```
extern char TITLE[];        /* in header file */

char TITLE[] =   "A very long string ... ";  /* in C file */
```

This change is unlikely to reduce the speed of the program, nor does it increase memory requirements even if `TITLE` is used only once (there may seem to be an extra 4 bytes to hold a pointer value pointing at where the string of characters is stored, but this is not so).

If there is a large global or `static` variable, the amount of static storage can be reduced by allocating it on the heap using `malloc` or the `new` operator, or by making it an automatic variable. This is particularly useful if the object has a short "lifetime", in the sense that it is used only briefly (e.g. the array is used as temporary storage inside a function). If the variable is used all the time, this change doesn't reduce the overall space problem, but simply moves the problem to another area.

7.4 Reducing stack usage

Stack storage refers to memory storage used for function calls, and includes non-`static` local variables, function parameters and system information used to keep track of function calls. Hence, the basic methods of reducing stack storage are:

- Using fewer and smaller automatic local variables.
- Using fewer and smaller function parameters.
- Reducing the depth of function call nesting.

The size of parameters and local variables can be reduced using the general techniques discussed above. Another method of reducing the size of parameters is to pass pointers to `struct`s instead of passing whole `struct`s (see Section 4.6.2). In C++ this can be done using reference parameters, which are more elegant than converting a function to the use of pointer arguments (see Section 5.2).

Local variables can be reduced by reusing local variables, although this can introduce bugs if not enough care is taken. Common examples of reusable variables are scratch variables, such as temporaries or `for` loop index variables. For example, if a function uses two different variables for non-nested `for` loops, a single variable can usually be used for both loops.

Parameters can be reduced by using global variables, or by packing some of them into a `struct` and passing a pointer to this `struct`.

Local variables and parameters stored on the stack can be reduced by declaring them as `register`. Any local variable or parameter of integral or pointer type is a candidate for declaration as `register`. If the compiler does actually use a register for the variable, the amount of stack space has been reduced. Note that `register` variables are not helpful if the function is recursive, because the value of any non-`static` variables, including `register` variables, must be stored on the stack.

Another method of reducing local variables is to use parameters as if they were local variables. This is safe in most cases because call-by-value parameter passing prevents the function arguments from being changed. This optimization is examined in Section 4.6.4.

Reducing the depth of function call nesting (especially by avoiding recursion) also reduces stack space requirements. This can be achieved by using preprocessor macros, `inline` functions or explicit inline code, but all these methods will increase code size (unless the function is very small).

Recursion should be avoided as much as possible by using iterative algorithms or tail recursion elimination (see Chapter 3), but whenever recursion does occur, there are some extra considerations for reducing stack usage. The conversion of a recursive algorithm to one using an explicit stack data structure will greatly reduce stack usage, although it will increase other memory usage because of the memory requirements of the stack (see Section 3.9.2).

Since, in a recursive function call, all non-`static` variables are saved on the function call stack, local variables should be specified as `static` if possible. A variable can be made `static` if the value it has before a recursive function call is not used again after the recursive call has returned (i.e. it doesn't matter if the recursive call overwrites its value). Note that making a variable `static` changes the meaning of initialization and will usually require changing the initialization to an explicit assignment statement at the start of the function. As an example, the following `print_tree` function (to print a binary tree using indentation to show its tree structure) has its local variable `i` declared as `static` because its value is not important to the recursive calls:

```
void print_tree(node_ptr tree, int indent)
{
    static int i;        /* ---- static variable! ---- */

    if (tree != NULL) {
        print_tree(tree->left, indent + 4);    /* left subtree */
        for (i = 0; i < indent; i++)           /* indent */
            putchar(' ');
        printf("%d", tree->key_field);         /* print key */
        print_tree(tree->right, indent + 4);   /* right subtree */
    }
}
```

7.5 Reducing heap usage

The amount of heap storage used depends on the size of blocks, the number of blocks and how quickly allocated blocks are freed. The size of blocks can be reduced by the general techniques discussed above (e.g. packing, `union`s). The number of heap blocks affects heap usage in the obvious way (more blocks means more memory) and because of the fixed space overhead of a few hidden bytes to store information about the block (so that `free` can de-allocate it).

When small blocks are used, it can be useful to pack more than one block together to avoid this fixed overhead of a few bytes per block. A good method of doing this is to redefine the C library functions `malloc` and `free` (see Section 6.8), or to overload the C++ `new` and `delete` operators for the class (see Section 5.6).

All allocated memory should be returned to the heap as early as possible, using the `free` function in C, and the `delete` operator in C++. If memory is not freed, unused memory (called garbage) can accumulate and reduce the available memory.

7.6 Alternative methods of data representation

There are many ways to represent data, and all have varying space usage. For example, storing all the primes less than 1000 can be done with a list of integers, a list of the differences between successive primes, or a bit vector, one bit for each integer 1..1000.

Compressing data can reduce space requirements when large amounts of data are involved. For example, a program using a large number of graphical images may find that storing them as pixmaps is impractical. However, if only a small number of pixels are set in each image, only a list of pixels set need be stored. Similarly, if the images are line drawings, lists of start-end points for each line can be stored. There are many other more general methods of image compression, but these are beyond the scope of the book.

Another data representation technique is to use a function to represent the data. For example, consider the storage of several images generated by a fractal algorithm: the simplest method of storing the images is to store them as pixmaps. But a much more space-efficient method is simply to store the values of any arguments passed to the function creating the fractal images. This way, the images can be recreated by calling the function with the correct arguments. The only space used is a small number of values containing the arguments and the instructions for the function. However, the recalculation of an image by this method is extremely time-inefficient.

7.7 Summary

- Executable size can be reduced by avoiding large macros and `inline` functions and by not using the larger library functions.
- Space can be reduced by using `unions`, small data types and C++ `static` data members.
- Packing can be implemented by using bitwise operations or bit-fields.
- Stack usage can be reduced by replacing local variables with global or `static` variables, and by passing objects by reference.
- Heap usage can be reduced by redefining `malloc` and `free` in C, or the `new` and `delete` operators in C++.

7.8 Further reading

A number of methods of trading time for space, such as recalculation, are discussed in Jon Bentley's book. Jonathan Shapiro discusses the problems of linkage in C++ of `inline` functions and the virtual function table.

BENTLEY, Jon Louis, *Writing Efficient Programs*, Prentice Hall, 1982.

SHAPIRO, Jonathan S., *A C++ Toolkit*, Prentice Hall, 1991.

7.9 Exercises

1. Write a more time-efficient non-recursive version of the `print_num` function given in Section 7.1. *Hint:* Generate the digits right-to-left and store them in a temporary array of characters, then print out the characters in reverse order. The size of the temporary array will depend on the maximum value an `int` can hold, which can be found by examining `INT_MAX` in `<limits.h>`.

2. [advanced] Write your own minimal `printf` function supporting only `%d`, `%s` and `%c` using the `<stdarg.h>` macros: `va_start`, `va_end`, `va_arg`. By how much does linking this function, using the name `printf`, reduce the code size?

3. An educational program needs to store the first 1000 Fibonacci numbers. What is the most space-efficient method of storing these numbers?

4.   A program that tests a large data structure generates a list of random numbers to insert (and then later delete). After seeding the random number generator by calling srand, the program repeatedly calls rand to generate a number which is inserted into the data structure. Because the program must later call a delete function with the same sequence of numbers, each random number is also stored in a huge array. Naturally, this involves massive space wastage. How can the huge array variable be dispensed with? *Hint:* The sequence of numbers generated by rand is not truly random and can be reproduced (how?).

5.   When attempting to reduce the size of the executable, why is it usually foolish to replace scanf with a specially written function but still allow calls to sscanf or fscanf?

6.   Will moving local variable declarations into inner blocks reduce stack usage? The following declaration is legal in both C and C++:

```
if (...) {
        int i;   /* declaration in inner block */
}
```

7.   In a certain school grades are given from 0..100, with half marks allowed. Hence, the following are legal grades: 0, 0.5, 1, 1.5, 2.0, etc. What is the most space-efficient method of storing these grades?

Chapter 8

Abstract data types in C++

This chapter examines efficiency at a much higher level than others do. The methods of implementing various abstract data types are examined from the point of view of *choosing* the correct data structure to implement the abstract data type (ADT). In most cases, there are advantages as well as disadvantages in a particular choice of data structure, and this chapter examines the trade-offs involved.

This chapter assumes that the reader is familiar with the most common data structures, such as stacks, arrays, linked lists, binary trees and hashing. The level of knowledge assumed approximates the level gained in a first-year computer science course.

The C language does not specifically support the concept of abstract data types, but the C++ language provides classes as a direct means of implementing abstract data types. For example, the C++ notion of constructors and destructors makes it very simple to initialize a new object. The compile-time warnings about access violations are also useful in guaranteeing that an abstract data type cannot be modified by functions other than its own member functions. Because of the simplicity of coding abstract data types in C++, almost all the examples in this chapter are coded in C++.

8.1 What is an abstract data type?

The concept of an abstract data type is related to modular code and becomes increasingly important in larger programming projects. The aim is to separate the manipulations on a data structure from the code that uses the data structure. To do this, it is necessary to ensure that the data structure is accessed only by special routines and not by direct reference to the underlying representation of the data structure.

It is important to distinguish between an *abstract data type* and a *data structure*. An abstract data type is an abstract entity that is implemented in practice by using a data structure. It is the aggregate of the data structure and the functions operating on the data structure.

8.2 The stack ADT

The classic example of an abstract data type is the stack. The everyday concept of a stack is that things are put on the top, and removed from the top. The stack abstract data type supports the same operations. The most common stack operations are shown in Table 8.1.

Table 8.1. Stack operations

Operation	Meaning
push	Put an element onto the top of the stack
pop	Remove an element from the top of the stack
is_empty	Test if the stack is empty

To implement the stack as a proper abstract data type, these operations should be the only way the data structure implementing the stack is acted upon. These functions create and modify the data structure. The program using the stack abstract data type should use the stack as if it is a *black box* that provides the required functionality — i.e. elements pushed onto the stack can be later popped. Exactly how this black box is implemented should be unimportant. This approach is called *information hiding* or *encapsulation* because the details are hidden in a small part of the program. The program using the stack should not rely upon which data structure the abstract data type is implemented with. For example, it should not use the knowledge that the stack is implemented by a structure containing an array and an integer stack pointer. Using this knowledge to check if the stack is empty with:

```
if (stack.sp == 0)        /* If empty stack */
```

is incorrect practice because at some stage the implementation of the stack abstract data type may change to use some other data structure, such as a linked list. The test should be made with a call to the appropriate abstract data type operation:

```
if (is_empty(stack))      /* If empty stack - C style */
if (stack.is_empty())     /* If empty stack - C++ style */
```

The program should never access the data structure directly. If any operation is required that is not currently supported by the existing abstract operations, a new abstract data type operation should be added.

To the novice programmer, the use of abstract data types may seem totally pointless. Defining an extra function or macro, is_empty, may seem wasteful and inefficient. Why shouldn't the program take advantage of how the stack is implemented? Why call a function just to test an integer?

The advantages are qualities such as increased readability and greater modularity. Modularity refers to the lack of dependence between parts of the program. If a program is modular, it is easier to debug. Once the abstract data type routines are debugged, there should be no need to test their correctness, no matter what program they are used in. With less modular code, a small change to an external routine could ruin the data structure. With proper use of an abstract data type, the consistency of the data structure is ensured once the abstract routines have been debugged.

The objection that the `is_empty` function is inefficient can be overcome by using an `inline` function in C++, or a preprocessor macro in C.

In fact, the declaration of abstract data types can aid efficiency because it is simple to modify the abstract data type to use a different, more efficient data structure. If the stack pointer variable, sp, were allowed to be accessed directly, changing the data structure implementing the stack would involve a search through all the source files for such uses. If the `is_empty` function is used, only its definition need be changed, and any code that *uses* a stack remains unchanged.

8.3 Array implementation of the stack ADT

A simple and efficient implementation of a stack uses an array of elements and an integer (called the *stack pointer*) which is an index into the current top of the stack (in the implementation below it is actually one past the top of the stack). The stack grows up and down in the array, from the zeroth element up to the entry indicated by the stack pointer (actually one less than the stack pointer, as the stack pointer usually points to the next free space). When the stack pointer is zero, this indicates an empty stack. The array implementation is limited in that its size is fixed. The stack can hold no more than some maximum number of elements, leaving the potential for stack overflow.

The stack has been implemented in C++ simply because the declaration of abstract data types is more transparent in C++ than in C. The C++ code for the various routines is shown below:

```
//-------------------------------------------------------------------
// Array Implementation of Stack
//-------------------------------------------------------------------

#include <stdlib.h>
#include <iostream.h>

const int SIZE = 100;          // How many elements in stack
typedef int data_type;         // Type of data is int

class Stack {
    private:
        data_type arr[SIZE];          // Array holding the stack
        int sp;                       // Stack pointer
    public:
        Stack() { sp = 0; }          // constructor
        int is_empty() { return sp == 0; }
        void push(data_type data);
        data_type pop();
};

//-------------------------------------------------------------------
//    PUSH:  Push an element on the top of the stack
//-------------------------------------------------------------------

inline void Stack::push(data_type data )
{
    if (sp == SIZE) {          // Already too many?
        cerr << "Overflow error\n";
        exit(1);
    }
    arr[sp++] = data;          // Push onto end of array
```

```
    }
    //--------------------------------------------------------------------
    //   POP(): Take element from the top of the stack
    //--------------------------------------------------------------------

    inline data_type Stack::pop()
    {
        if (sp == 0) {              // No elements ?
            cerr << "Underflow error\n";
            exit(1);
        }
        return (arr[--sp]);    // Pop from end of array
    }
```

8.4 Linked list implementation of the stack ADT

The main disadvantage of the array implementation of the stack ADT is that stack overflow can occur. Stacks implemented as linked lists can not suffer from overflow (except in the rare case of the system running out of heap memory), and may also be more space-efficient, as only the actual amount of space needed is allocated (this more than balances the extra space needed for the "next" pointers). However, the disadvantage is that they are less time-efficient than array implementations because the linked list nodes require calls to the memory allocator.

Linked list implementations of a stack usually use a singly linked list. Insertions and deletions (push and pop) are performed at the head of the list. For each push, a new element is allocated memory. For each pop, an element is returned to the heap. The C++ code for an implementation of a stack is given below:

```
    //--------------------------------------------------------------------
    // Linked List Implementation of Stack
    //--------------------------------------------------------------------

    #include <iostream.h>
    #include <stdlib.h>

    typedef int data_type;          // Type of data is int

    class Stack;

    struct Node {                   // Node on the linked list
        Node *next;
        data_type data;
        Node(data_type d) { next = NULL; data = d; }
    };

    class Stack {
        private:
            Node *stack;            // Head of linked list of nodes
        public:
            Stack() { stack = NULL; }           // constructor
            int is_empty() { return stack == NULL; }
            void push(data_type data);
            data_type pop();
    };

    //--------------------------------------------------------------------
    //   PUSH: Push an element onto the top of the stack
    //--------------------------------------------------------------------

    void Stack::push(data_type data)
    {
```

```
        Node *new_node = new Node(data);

                    // Add to Front of list

    if (stack == NULL)          // if empty list
        stack = new_node;
    else {                      // Insert at front of list
        new_node->next = stack;
        stack = new_node;
    }
}
//-------------------------------------------------------------------
//   POP():      take element from the top of the stack
//-------------------------------------------------------------------
data_type Stack::pop()
{
    data_type temp;         // Temp storage of fn return value
    Node *temp_ptr;

                // Get from Front of linked list

    if (stack == NULL) {        // if empty stack
        cerr << "Internal error: POP from empty stack \n";
        exit(1);
    }
    else {              // Get from front, then delete first element
        temp = stack->data;
        temp_ptr = stack->next;
        delete stack;           // delete the used node
        stack = temp_ptr;       // store new head of list
    }
    return temp;
}
```

8.5 Hybrid implementation of the stack ADT

The array implementation of a stack is more efficient than the linked list implementation, but has the limitation that stack overflow can occur. A better method that is both efficient and general is to use a *hybrid* implementation, and combine both approaches. If the number of elements on the stack is small, they are stored in an array; if there are too many, a node is allocated and the new element is stored on a linked list. Hence, the first *n* elements of the stack are stored in the array and any extras are placed in a linked list. The code for the hybrid implementation is:

```
//-------------------------------------------------------------------
// Hybrid Implementation of Stack
//-------------------------------------------------------------------

#include <iostream.h>
#include <stdlib.h>

const int SIZE = 100;           // How many elements in array

typedef int data_type;          // Type of data is int

class Stack;

struct Node {                   // Node on the linked list
        Node *next;
        data_type data;
        Node(data_type d) { next = NULL; data = d; }
};
```

```
class Stack {
    private:
        data_type arr[SIZE];    // Array holding the stack
        int sp;                 // Stack pointer
        Node *stack;            // Head of linked list of nodes
    public:
        Stack() { sp = 0; stack = NULL; }          // constructor
        int is_empty() { return sp == 0; }
        void push(data_type data);
        data_type pop();
};

//---------------------------------------------------------------------
//   PUSH:  Push an element onto the top of the stack
//---------------------------------------------------------------------

void Stack::push(data_type data)
{
    if (sp == SIZE) {             // Array is full; use list
        Node *new_node = new Node(data);

                    // Add to Front of list

        if (stack == NULL)        // if empty list
            stack = new_node;
        else {                    // Insert at front of list
            new_node->next = stack; // add new node to front
            stack = new_node;       // update head of list
        }
    }
    else {      // Array not full; add to array
        arr[sp++] = data;
    }
}

//---------------------------------------------------------------------
//   POP():      take element from the top of the stack
//---------------------------------------------------------------------

data_type Stack::pop()
{
    data_type temp;        // Temp storage of fn return value
    Node *temp_ptr;

    if (stack != NULL) {   // Pop from linked list
                           // Take from front,
                           // then delete first element
        temp = stack->data;
        temp_ptr = stack->next;
        delete stack;          // delete unused node
        stack = temp_ptr;      // update head of list
        return temp;
    }
    else {     // Not using linked list;  get from array
        if (sp == 0) {         // if array empty
            cerr << "Internal error: POP from empty stack \n";
            exit(1);
        }
        return arr[--sp];
    }
}
```

8.6 Searching — the symbol table ADT

The symbol table is an abstract data type that supports searching, insertion, and deletion. In its abstract form, the symbol table consists of a number of records, each record containing a number of fields. One special field, called the *key field* or the *symbol*, distinguishes the records. The other fields in a record are the data associated with the key. For example, when implementing a dictionary of words, the key field is the word and the other fields are the word's meaning and pronunciation.

These records must be stored in some data structure. Later sections will examine the implementation of a symbol table as an array, a linked list, a binary tree and a hash table. As the symbol table is an abstract data type, it is necessary to define the operations allowed on a symbol table. The most common operations are given in Table 8.2.

Table 8.2. Symbol table operations

Operation	Meaning
search	Search the symbol table for a key
insert	Add a new key to the symbol table
remove	Delete a key from the symbol table
visit	Examine all keys, not necessarily in order
print_sorted	Print all keys in sorted order

Unfortunately, "delete" is a C++ keyword, otherwise I'd use it as the name of the member function performing deletion.

The visit operation refers to any operation on all the keys that does not require that the data be sorted — for example, printing the unsorted data, or counting the number of stored keys. The visit operation is distinguished from printing the data in a sorted fashion because some data structures support efficient non-ordered visiting, but are inefficient when sorted data is required.

An important decision to be made when implementing a symbol table is whether *duplicates* in the list of records are to be allowed. Duplicates are records where the key fields are equal, but the data fields are not necessarily equal. If duplicates are allowed, some routines must be modified accordingly. For example, the delete function may need to delete more than one record if it is to remove all duplicates. If duplicates are not permitted, what action is to be taken when the insert function tries to insert a key that is already stored in the symbol table? For example, the program could either silently ignore duplicates by preventing the insertion, or terminate with an error message.

8.7 Alternative data structures

Later sections examine the implementation of the symbol table using arrays, linked lists, binary trees and hashing, all of which have various advantages and disadvantages. The choice depends upon which operations are most important.

Search is likely to be fastest using hashing. Sorted arrays give guaranteed fast search; binary trees give good *average* search performance; linked lists and unsorted arrays are not as efficient.

Insertions in sorted arrays and sorted linked lists are slow; insertions into binary trees are not quite as slow; insertions into unsorted linked lists and unsorted arrays are very fast; insertions into a (chained) hash table are quite fast.

Deletions are similar to insertions in terms of cost, except for unsorted arrays and unsorted linked lists which have slow deletions. Note that deletion will always cost at least the same as search, because deletion involves a search operation to find the key being deleted.

Sequential processing is an important consideration. For example, some data structures facilitate the printing of a sorted list of entries in the symbol table. If the entries need not be processed in a sorted order, the array, linked list and binary tree implementations are equivalent; hashing is slightly less efficient because of the traversal of empty locations in the hash table. If entries must be processed in sorted order (e.g. to print a sorted list of entries), some implementations require an explicit sort operation. Unsorted arrays and lists, and hashing all require a sort operation. Binary trees, and sorted arrays and lists all have the data already sorted, and require no sort operation.

The complexity measures for the various operations are shown in Table 8.3. For those not familiar with this type of complexity measure, the general ordering from fastest to slowest is:

$$O(1) < O(\log n) < O(n) < O(n \log n) < O(n^2)$$

Some of the measures for the operations in Table 8.3 are rough; for example, the $O(1)$ complexity of hashing operations is slightly misleading. On average, hashing gives close to constant performance if:

a) The hash function gives a reasonable distribution, yielding few collisions; and
b) The number of elements is not significantly larger than the hash table size.

Similarly, the $O(\log n)$ performance of binary trees is an average figure. Under degenerate conditions binary trees may show the same $O(n)$ performance of sorted lists.

The *Print-Sorted* column displays the cost of printing a sorted list of entries. This cost involves the cost of printing, plus a sort operation, if required. Sorting is assumed to cost $O(n \log n)$, as this is achievable by a number of different sorting algorithms. Data structures where the data is already sorted have the best possible complexity for printing, $O(n)$.

Table 8.3. Complexity of symbol table operations

Data structure	Search	Insert	Delete	Visit	Print-sorted
Sorted array	$O(\log n)$	$O(n)$	$O(n)$	$O(n)$	$O(n)$
Unsorted array	$O(n)$	$O(1)$	$O(n)$	$O(n)$	$O(n \log n)$
Sorted list	$O(n)$	$O(n)$	$O(n)$	$O(n)$	$O(n)$
Unsorted list	$O(n)$	$O(1)$	$O(n)$	$O(n)$	$O(n \log n)$
Binary tree	$O(\log n)$	$O(\log n)$	$O(\log n)$	$O(n)$	$O(n)$
Hashing	$O(1)$	$O(1)$	$O(1)$	$O(n)$	$O(n \log n)$

The choice of data structure for implementing the symbol table ADT should be based on the cost of performing the operations most likely to occur. For example, if fast search is imperative, but sorted output is rarely needed, the hash table is ideal. However, care should be taken when choosing a complicated algorithm. These measurements are asymptotic and when the number of elements is small, the overhead of implementing a more complicated algorithm may be prohibitive. If the number of elements is very small, perhaps an unsorted array will be most efficient, as there is no memory allocation and no hash function to compute. Arrays are very good if you know in advance how many elements are to be stored in the symbol table. In this case, the generality of dynamic data structures is not an advantage. However, if it is unknown how many elements are to be stored, array implementations may be too limited.

8.8 Unsorted array version of the symbol table

Arrays are best used for data that doesn't change frequently (i.e. with few insertions and deletions). If the data is changing greatly, a dynamic structure such as a linked list or a binary tree is generally better. Arrays are most appropriate when the amount of data is known at compile-time, so that the program can reserve the right amount of memory. If the size is unknown, enough space can be reserved for the largest possible size, or a dynamic array can be allocated by `malloc`, or the `new` operator, once the required size is known.

When searching an array that is not always completely full, an integer variable is necessary to keep count of how many elements are actually stored in the array. This prevents searching the unused entries of the array. Also necessary for insertion is another integer value indicating where the next free location in the array is. Conveniently, this index can be combined with the count because the n elements in the array are stored in the locations 0..n-1, so that the next free location is n. Thus the symbol table implementation uses an array and an integer value.

An important choice concerning array implementations is whether the data should be sorted or unsorted. This section examines unsorted arrays and Section 8.9 examines sorted arrays, which offer faster search but slower insertion. Unsorted arrays offer slow search but very fast insertion.

The C++ class declaration for the unsorted array implementation is shown below. It consists of an array of records, leaving room for the addition of associated data fields, and an integer counter. The definitions for the member functions appear in subsequent sections.

```
//----------------------------------------------------------------
// Unsorted Array implementation of the Symbol Table
//----------------------------------------------------------------

#include <iostream.h>
#include <stdlib.h>

//----------------------------------------------------------------
const int MAX_ELEMENTS = 100;   // Maximum elements in symbol table

typedef int key_type;

struct key_record {
```

```
        key_type key_field;    // key field
        // .... other data fields here
};
class SymbolTable {
    private:
        key_record a[MAX_ELEMENTS];  // array
        int n;                       // number in array
    public:
        SymbolTable() { n = 0; }     // constructor
        int search(key_type key);
        void remove(key_type key);
        void insert(key_type key);
};
```

8.8.1 Searching an unsorted array

The only way to search for an item in an unsorted array is to go through every element systematically, one after the other. The simplest way is to start at the zeroth element, and go through all the rest. The C++ code for sequential search is given below. It assumes that the array is an array of `structs` with an `int` key field. The search function returns the index of the element if found, or −1 if not found. The following version uses the "looping down to zero" optimization (see Section 4.1.4), but does not use a sentinel (see Section 3.8):

```
//-------------------------------------------------------------
// Search unsorted array - sequential search
//-------------------------------------------------------------
int SymbolTable::search(key_type key)
{
    register int i;

    for (i = n - 1; i >= 0; i--) {  // For all array elements
        if (a[i].key_field == key)
            return i;               // Found, return location
    }
    return -1;            // Not found, return error
}
```

8.8.2 Insertion in an unsorted array

Insertions into unsorted arrays are very efficient. The method is to add the new key to the end of the array and then increment the integer to point to the new free location. The simple C++ code for this is:

```
//-------------------------------------------------------------
// Insert key in unsorted array
//-------------------------------------------------------------
void SymbolTable::insert(key_type key)
{
    if (n == MAX_ELEMENTS) {
        cerr << "\n Table Overflow \n\n";
        exit(1);
    }
    a[n].key_field = key;        // Store the new element
    n++;                         // Increment the counter
}
```

8.8.3 Deletion in an unsorted array

As with deletion operations for all data structures, deletions in unsorted arrays are broken into two phases — search and delete. The search for an element must use sequential search as above. If the element is found, it can be deleted.

The deletion phase can be implemented very efficiently by moving the highest record down to fill the newly created hole (i.e. copy the highest record over the one that is to be deleted). This method cannot be applied to sorted arrays, as it ruins the ordering. The C++ code for this is:

```
//------------------------------------------------------------
// Remove key from unsorted array
//------------------------------------------------------------
void SymbolTable::remove(key_type key)
{
    register int i;

    i = search(key);        // sequential search
    if (i == -1) {
        cerr << "Key not found\n";
        exit(1);
    }
    else {                  // Found it so delete it
        a[i] = a[n - 1];    // Copy the last record
        n--;                // Decrement count of keys
    }
}
```

If there is the possibility of duplicates in the array, then these duplicates must be found and deleted also. To do so, the search operation must be continued from the current location until no more are found.

8.9 Sorted array version of the symbol table

Sorted arrays have the advantage over unsorted arrays of much faster search, but have the disadvantage of slower insertions. The ordering of keys in the array permits efficient sorted output and makes possible the use of a highly efficient search algorithm called binary search. The C++ class declaration for the sorted array version is identical to that for the unsorted version in Section 8.8; only the member functions change.

8.9.1 Searching sorted arrays: binary search

When an array is known to be sorted, a much more efficient searching algorithm, called *binary search*, can be used. Binary search is so commonly used that there is a standard library function to perform binary search, called `bsearch`. However, the `bsearch` function is inefficient, not because it uses a poor algorithm but because it must call a (user-supplied) comparison function for every key comparison. This means that it must call a function just to compare two integers when searching an array of integers. For this reason it is more efficient to write your own binary search function than to use `bsearch`.

The binary search algorithm relies on the keys being sorted and cannot be applied to an unsorted array. It works by *halving* the interval to search at each iteration. Initially it considers the entire array. The algorithm repeatedly finds the key in the middle of the current search interval which is compared to the search key. If the keys are equal the search is successful. If the search key is greater than the middle key, the search key is certainly not in the first half of the interval (because the keys are sorted), and the new interval becomes the top half of the old interval. Similarly, if the search key is less than the middle key then only the bottom half need be considered. This halving process is repeated until the key is found, or there are no more keys in the interval.

A simple implementation of binary search is given below. It assumes that the array is an array of `structs` with an `int` key field. It returns the integer index of the element if found; or −1 if not found.

```
//------------------------------------------------------------
// Search sorted array - binary search
//------------------------------------------------------------

int SymbolTable::search(key_type key)
{
    register int low, high, mid, temp;

    low = 0;
    high = n - 1;

    while (low <= high) {
        mid = (low + high) / 2;
        temp = a[mid].key_field;    // Common sub-expression
        if (key > temp)
            low = mid + 1;
        else if (key < temp)
            high = mid - 1;
        else
            return mid;             // Found it!
    }
    return -1;               // Not found, return error
}
```

An important efficiency point is that equality is the least likely of the three conditions to be true during loop. Hence, the above code is more efficient than testing for equality first, as whenever the > operation succeeds, the second test is avoided.

8.9.2 Insertion in a sorted array

Insertions into sorted arrays are less efficient than for unsorted arrays. One simple but inefficient method for inserting into a sorted array is to add the new element at the end, as if the array were unsorted, then sort the array with one of the methods discussed in Section 8.16 (simple if you already have a sort function written).

A more efficient method is to find where the element should go, then shuffle the rest upwards by one. The C++ code for this method is:

```
//------------------------------------------------
// Insert key in sorted array
//------------------------------------------------

void SymbolTable::insert(key_type new_key)
{
    int pos, temp;

    if (n == MAX_ELEMENTS) {
        cerr << "\n Table Overflow \n\n";
        exit(1);
    }
```

```
    for (pos = 0; pos < n && new_key > a[pos].key_field; pos++)
        ;                       // empty loop

    for (temp = n; temp > pos; temp--)  // Shuffle others up
        a[temp] = a[temp - 1];

    a[pos].key_field = new_key;  // Store new element in place
    n++;                         // Increment counter
}
```

This implementation is less efficient than it could be. The two loops can be merged into one, by searching from the top of the array and shuffling the elements down as the search progresses. The C++ code for this is:

```
//-------------------------------------------------------
// Insert key in sorted array
//-------------------------------------------------------

void SymbolTable::insert(key_type new_key)
{
    if (n == MAX_ELEMENTS) {
        cerr <<  "\n Table Overflow \n\n";
        exit(1);
    }

    for (int pos = n; pos > 0 && new_key <= a[pos].key_field; pos--)
        a[pos] = a[pos - 1];                   // Shuffle others up

    a[pos].key_field = new_key;  // Store new element in place
    n++;                         // Increment counter
}
```

8.9.3 Deletion in a sorted array

The first part of a deletion is a search for the element. Sorted arrays can use binary search to find the element efficiently. If the element is not found, it cannot be deleted and some other action must take place (e.g. some error message).

Once found, the element is removed by shuffling all the elements above it down by one. The C++ code for this method is:

```
//-------------------------------------------------------
// Remove key from sorted array
//-------------------------------------------------------

void SymbolTable::remove(key_type key)
{
    register int i, delete_location;

    delete_location = search(key);   // binary search
    if (delete_location == -1) {
        cerr << "Key not found\n";
        exit(1);
    }

    for (i = delete_location; i < n - 1; i++)
        a[i] = a[i + 1];      // Shift down one element
    n--;                      // Decrement counter
}
```

If there is the possibility of duplicates in the array, these duplicates are just the subsequent entries in the array. They can be deleted by modifying the delete function to delete more than one item at once.

8.10 Unsorted linked list version of the symbol table

The main issue in the implementation using linked lists is the choice between a sorted or unsorted list. A sorted list allows faster search and is useful for printing out an ordered listing of the data in the symbol table. However, an unsorted list allows faster insertion because the insertion function can insert the new element at the front of the list, rather than finding the correct ordered position in the list. The class declaration for the implementation of the symbol table as an unsorted linked list is given as follows; the definitions of the member functions are given in following sections.

```
//--------------------------------------------------------------
// Unsorted Linked List Implementation of Symbol Table
//--------------------------------------------------------------

#include <iostream.h>
#include <stdlib.h>

typedef int key_type;    // Hide details of data type

class Node {             // Node on the linked list
    private:
        Node *next;      // pointer to next node in the list
        key_type key_field;
    public:
        Node(key_type k) { next = NULL; key_field = k; }
    friend class SymbolTable;    // allow easy access to nodes
};

class SymbolTable {
    private:
        Node *head;      // Pointer to head of linked list
    public:
        SymbolTable() { head = NULL; }    // constructor
        Node *search(key_type key);
        void insert(key_type key);
        void remove(key_type key);
};
```

8.10.1 Searching an unsorted list: sequential search

The only way to search for an item in an unsorted linked list is to go through every element systematically, from the start of the list to the end. The following C++ function for sequential search returns a pointer to the element if found, or NULL if not found.

```
//--------------------------------------------------------------
//  Search an unsorted linked list - sequential search
//--------------------------------------------------------------

Node* SymbolTable::search(key_type key)
{
    for (Node *ptr = head; ptr != NULL; ptr = ptr->next) {
        if (ptr->key_field == key)
            return ptr;          // Found it
    }
    return NULL;          // Not found
}
```

8.10.2 Insertion in an unsorted linked list

It is very efficient to insert into an unsorted linked list because the new node can be simply added to the front of the list. There is no need to find the correct location to place the key in the correct order. The C++ code for the member function is:

```
//---------------------------------------------------------------------
//   Insert an item into an unsorted linked list; insert at front
//---------------------------------------------------------------------
void SymbolTable::insert(key_type key)
{
    Node *new_node =  new Node(key);  // allocate new node
    new_node->next = head;
    head = new_node;                  // new head of linked list
}
```

This implementation of the insertion function assumes that duplicates either will not occur or, if they do occur, they are acceptable. If duplicates must be prevented, the entire linked list must be searched before inserting the new node, and the insertion process becomes more expensive. Hence the main advantage of unsorted lists is lost, and it becomes worthwhile to use a sorted linked list.

8.10.3 Deletion in an unsorted linked list

Deleting an element from an unsorted linked list involves a sequential search to find the element and then adjustment of pointers to remove the node from the list. The deleted node is then returned to the heap. The C++ code for this is:

```
//---------------------------------------------------------------------
// Remove element from unsorted linked list; ignore if not found
//---------------------------------------------------------------------
void SymbolTable::remove(key_type key)
{
    Node* ptr = head;
    Node* before = NULL;       // Trailing pointer to previous node

                        // Ordinary sequential search

    for (; ptr != NULL; before = ptr, ptr = ptr->next) {
        if (ptr->key_field == key)
            break;          // Found it
    }

    if (ptr != NULL) {            // FOUND IT?
        if (before == NULL) {    // Delete at FRONT
            head = head->next;   // new head of linked list
            delete ptr;          // delete old head of list
        }
        else {                   //  Delete at MIDDLE or END
            before->next = ptr->next;
            delete ptr;
        }
    }
}
```

Further deletion of duplicate elements will be inefficient as the sequential search must continue from the current node. For sorted linked lists, the duplicates would appear immediately after the node being deleted.

8.10.4 Sorting a linked list: insertion sort

It is possible to sort a list using a special routine (as discussed in this section), but it is more common and more efficient to simply keep the list sorted during every insertion. Using an insertion algorithm that maintains order can be thought of as an incremental sort algorithm!

Few of the fancy sorting algorithms devised for sorting arrays apply to linked lists, because it is difficult to calculate the address of arbitrary elements. It is possible to copy the list into an array, sort the array and then rebuild the list, but this method requires the use of extra memory and the costly creation of nodes for a new linked list.

A good method for sorting lists is *insertion sort* (see also Section 8.16.2). This method makes it possible to modify the next pointers in the existing list without requiring extra storage. Although insertion sort is not the most efficient method for sorting arrays, it is efficient on linked lists because insertion into a linked list does not require shuffling all the other elements along.

The source code for a member function that sorts an unsorted linked list is as follows; part of the algorithm uses insertion into a *sorted* linked list, and the reader should compare this code with that given in Section 8.11.2 which explains insertion in a sorted linked list.

```
//------------------------------------------------------------------
// SORT: Sort an unsorted linked list (in place - don't move nodes)
//------------------------------------------------------------------

void SymbolTable::sort()
{
    if (head == NULL)    // empty list is already sorted
        return;

    Node *sorted = head;           // sorted sub-list has one node
    Node *unsorted = head->next;   // unsorted sub-list has other nodes
    sorted->next = NULL;
    while (unsorted != NULL) {      // while more nodes to insert
        Node *temp = unsorted;
        unsorted = unsorted->next; // move to next non-inserted node

                          // modified sequential search of sorted list
        Node *prev = NULL, *ptr = sorted;
        for (; ptr != NULL && temp->key_field > ptr->key_field;
                prev = ptr, ptr = ptr->next) ;      // empty loop

        if (prev == NULL) {             // Insert at FRONT
            temp->next = sorted;
            sorted = temp;             // New head of sorted sub-list
        }
        else {                    // Insert at MIDDLE or END
            temp->next = ptr;
            prev->next = temp;
        }
    }
    head = sorted;       // new head of list
}
```

8.11 Sorted linked list version of the symbol table

The main advantage of a sorted linked list is a slightly faster search algorithm and the ease of producing ordered output, but this incurs a more expensive insertion routine. A sorted linked list is more appropriate than an unsorted linked list if sorted output is required, or if duplicates must be prevented by the insertion routine (in which case, the main advantage of unsorted lists is lost). The main body of the C++ class declaration is the same as that given for the unsorted linked list implementation in Section 8.10. Only the member functions change, and these are discussed in turn.

8.11.1 Searching a sorted list: modified sequential search

Binary search, as used on sorted arrays, cannot be used on sorted linked lists because the position of the middle element cannot be calculated easily. However, search can still be made more efficient than ordinary sequential search by searching only up until a key in a list node is *greater than* the search key (i.e. searching until a key that is too large is seen; the ordering of the list implies that all the keys following in the list will also be too large). This method increases efficiency over ordinary sequential search only when the element is not found (i.e. only on unsuccessful search).

```
//-----------------------------------------------------------------
//  Search a sorted linked list - modified sequential sort
//-----------------------------------------------------------------

Node* SymbolTable::search(key_type key)
{
    register Node *p;

    for (p = head; p != NULL && key > p->key_field; p = p->next)
        ;                    /* empty loop */

    if (p == NULL || p->key_field != key)
        return NULL;            // Not found, return NULL ptr
    else
        return p;              // Found, return pointer to it
}
```

8.11.2 Insertion in a sorted linked list

Whereas insertion into an unsorted linked list merely adds the new node onto the front of the list, insertion in a sorted linked list requires a search phase to locate the correct position for the new node. Insertion at the front of the list becomes a special case of a more general insertion routine. The following insertion routine works by searching the linked list using a similar algorithm to the one in the previous section. A trailing pointer, `before`, is maintained throughout the linked list traversal, so that the node before the final position of the new node can be accessed (to set its `next` pointer pointing at the new node). The C++ code for a simple insert function is:

```
//-----------------------------------------------------------------
//  Insert an item into a sorted linked list
//-----------------------------------------------------------------

void SymbolTable::insert(key_type key)
{
    Node* ptr = head;
    Node* before = NULL;      // Trailing pointer to previous node
```

```
                    // Search using modified sequential search
    for (; ptr != NULL && ptr->key_field < key;
           before = ptr, ptr = ptr->next) ;     // Empty loop

    if (ptr != NULL && ptr->key_field == key) { // duplicate?
        return;                                  // silently ignore it.
    }
                  //--------------------------------------------
                  //  Found its place. Now insert it in list
                  //  Insert it between "before" and "ptr"
                  //--------------------------------------------
    Node *new_node =  new Node(key);  // allocate new node

    if (before == NULL) {       // Insert at FRONT (also empty list)
        new_node->next = head; // 'head' and 'ptr' are the same node
        head = new_node;        // new head of linked list
    }
    else {     // Insert at MIDDLE or END (also single element list)
        new_node->next = ptr;
        before->next = new_node;
    }
}
```

Naturally, the efficiency of this routine can be improved if duplicates are not important, in which case the test for them can be removed. In addition, the assignment to the "before" variable inside the loop can be removed by making a slight change to the algorithm. The following insert function should be slightly more efficient, assuming that the compiler does a reasonable job of eliminating the "ptr->next" common sub-expression.

```
//-------------------------------------------------------------------
//  Insert an item into a sorted linked list - more efficient
//  Assumes no duplicates;  avoids using 'before'
//-------------------------------------------------------------------
void SymbolTable::insert(key_type key)
{
    Node *new_node =  new Node(key);             // allocate new node

    if (head == NULL || key <= head->key_field) { // insert at front
        new_node->next = head;
        head = new_node;                     // new head of linked list
        return;
    }
                      // Search using modified sequential search
    for (Node *ptr = head; ; ptr = ptr->next) {
        if (ptr->next == NULL) {       // Insertion at end
            ptr->next = new_node;
            return;                 // new_node->next is NULL already
        }
        if (ptr->next->key_field >= key) { // Found place?
            new_node->next = ptr->next;    // Insert in middle
            ptr->next = new_node;
            return;
        }
    }
}
```

8.11.3 Deletion in a sorted linked list

Deleting an element from a sorted linked list is almost identical to that for unsorted lists. The only difference is that the slightly faster modified sequential search can be used to find the key to be deleted, but even this is a minor change as the improvement is only for unsuccessful search and it seems reasonable to assume that that a key to be deleted will nearly always be found. The C++ code for the deletion routine is:

```
//-------------------------------------------------------------------
// Remove element from sorted linked list; ignore if not found
//-------------------------------------------------------------------

void SymbolTable::remove(key_type key)
{
    Node* ptr = head;
    Node* before = NULL;       // Trailing pointer to previous node

                       // Modified sequential search

    for (; ptr != NULL && ptr->key_field < key;
                before = ptr, ptr = ptr->next)
                    ; // Empty loop

    if (ptr != NULL && ptr->key_field == key) {   // FOUND IT?

        if (before == NULL) {    // Delete at FRONT
            head = head->next;  // new head of linked list
            delete ptr;
        }
        else {                       //  Delete at MIDDLE or END
            before->next = ptr->next;
            delete ptr;
        }
    }
}
```

The deletion of duplicate elements, if required, is quite simple because they appear immediately after the first node found.

8.12 Binary tree version of the symbol table

Binary trees are a well-known data structure in computer science. They aim to provide fast search without the limitation of a fixed size that inhibits the use of a sorted array and binary search. Binary search trees offer fast logarithmic search time in the average case, although they may occasionally degenerate to the linear performance of a sorted linked list. Insertions and deletions can also be performed in logarithmic time, provided the tree does not become too unbalanced. In addition, the data in the tree is sorted, and keys can be printed out in sorted order with reasonable efficiency.

As with all implementations of a symbol table, there are various ways to handle duplicates. In this implementation, duplicate entries in the binary tree will be silently prevented (i.e. they will not be inserted). Deletions must also cope with attempting to delete an item that is not in the tree, and in this implementation, no action will take place.

Since the binary tree is an inherently recursive data structure, many of the operations on trees can be coded very elegantly by using recursion. However, such recursive algorithms are inefficient and a non-recursive algorithm should be used wherever possible. In particular, all of the search, insertion and deletion routines can be implemented without recursion. Only a few operations do require recursion, such as printing out the ordered list of keys.

All of the binary tree search, insertion and deletion routines will assume the following C++ class declaration:

```
//------------------------------------------------------------
// Binary Search Tree Implementation of the Symbol Table ADT
//------------------------------------------------------------

#include <iostream.h>      // declare NULL

typedef int key_type;      // Hide details of data type

class Node {               // Node on the tree
    private:
        key_type key_field;
        Node *left, *right;      // pointers to subtrees
    public:
        Node(key_type k) { left = right = NULL; key_field = k; }
        friend class SymbolTable;    // allow easy access to nodes
};
class SymbolTable {
    private:
        Node * root;        // Pointer to root of tree
    public:
        SymbolTable() { root = NULL; }      // constructor
        Node* search(key_type key);
        void insert(key_type key);
        void remove(key_type key);
};
```

8.12.1 Searching a binary tree

Searching a binary tree is a reasonably simple algorithm. The search continues down the tree, testing the key in each node to determine if they are equal (found the key), or which of the two subtrees should be searched. The C++ implementation of an efficient iterative algorithm is as follows:

```
//------------------------------------------------------------------
//  Search the binary tree for a specified key; return pointer to it
//------------------------------------------------------------------

Node* SymbolTable::search(key_type key)
{
    Node *temp;

    for (temp = root; temp != NULL; ) {
        if (temp->key_field < key)
            temp = temp->right;              // Search right subtree
        else if (temp->key_field > key)
            temp = temp->left;               // Search left subtree
        else
            return temp;                     // Equal. Found it.
    }
    return NULL;              // NOT FOUND
}
```

It is important that the first if statement's condition uses the < operator, and not ==, as equality is the least likely condition (all but one of the nodes along the search path will *not* be the one searched for). By using the < test first, almost half of the node visits along the search path will avoid the second test. If the first test involved ==, then all node visits would cost two key comparisons.

8.12.2 Insertion in a binary tree

The following routine inserts an element into a binary tree. It functions correctly for an empty tree, changing the value of the root pointer to point to the newly created node. For a non-empty tree, it adds the new node to the "bottom" of the tree, replacing a NULL pointer. A new node is always inserted at a NULL pointer. When a duplicate is encountered, the insert function does not complete the insertion operation. This way, the insert function silently prevents duplicates. A naive C++ implementation of binary tree insertion is:

```
//-------------------------------------------------------------------
// Insert a key into a binary search tree;   prevent duplicates
//-------------------------------------------------------------------
void SymbolTable::insert(key_type key)
{
    Node* new_node = new Node(key);
    if (root == NULL) {      // if tree is empty
        root = new_node;     // new node becomes the new tree
        return;
    }

    Node *ptr = root;             // Start at root of tree
    Node *parent = NULL;          // Pointer to parent node

    while (ptr != NULL) {         // Loop until get to leaf
        if (key > ptr->key_field) {
            parent = ptr;
            ptr = ptr->right;     // Go down right subtree
        }
        else if (key < ptr->key_field) {
            parent = ptr;
            ptr = ptr->left;      // Go down left subtree
        }
        else
            return;     // Duplicate; return without inserting
    }

    if (key < parent->key_field)
        parent->left = new_node;    // Node is left of its parent
    else
        parent->right = new_node;   // Node is right of its parent
}
```

The efficiency of this version can be improved markedly. First, if it is assumed that there will be no duplicates (or that they are not important), the two comparisons of the key inside the loop can be reduced to one. Second, the use of the "parent" variable can be totally avoided, as can the final test to determine whether to set the parent's left or right pointer. The improved insertion function is:

```
//-------------------------------------------------------------------
// Insert a key into a binary search tree   (assume no duplicates)
//-------------------------------------------------------------------
void SymbolTable::insert(key_type key)
{
    Node* new_node = new Node(key);
    if (root == NULL) {      // if tree is empty
```

```
            root = new_node;    // return new node as the new tree
            return;
        }

        Node *ptr = root;        // Start at root of tree

        while (1) {              // Loop until inserted key
            if (key < ptr->key_field) {
                if (ptr->left == NULL) {    // found place to insert?
                    ptr->left = new_node;   // insert to the left
                    return;
                }
                else
                    ptr = ptr->left;        // Go down left subtree
            }
            else {      // larger or equal (but duplicates assumed absent)
                if (ptr->right == NULL) {   // found place to insert?
                    ptr->right = new_node;  // insert to the right
                    return;
                }
                else
                    ptr = ptr->right;       // Go down right subtree
            }
        }
    }
```

8.12.3 Deletion in a binary tree

The deletion algorithm operates in two parts — find and delete. The element must first be found, and then it must be deleted. The *find* part of the algorithm must deal with two cases — found and not found (successful and unsuccessful search). If the element is not found, some appropriate action must be taken (or no action, as in this implementation).

When search is successful, the element is then deleted from the tree. Deletion from a binary tree is quite complicated because of the different special cases that must be handled, as follows:

Case 1. Deleting a leaf node.
Case 2. Deleting a node with one child.
Case 3. Deleting a node with two children.

Deleting the root node is also a special case because this is the only time the value of the root pointer changes. Note that deleting the root node may involve any of the first three situations, leading to more special cases.

The first two cases are quite simple. A leaf can be deleted by setting the pointer above it to NULL. A node with one child can be deleted by setting the pointer above it to point to its only child.

The third case is more involved. A node with two children is deleted by finding the rightmost element in the left subtree, and substituting it for the node to be deleted. This rightmost node must also be deleted from the left subtree, but it is always one of the two simpler cases (leaf, or one child only). There is no reason that the leftmost node in the right subtree could not be used instead of the rightmost node in the left subtree.

Deletion has many different cases to cater for. The recursive algorithm would be slightly simpler, but is inefficient. The iterative algorithm is more complicated because it must remember whether the last iteration went left or right, but this is handled by a comparison of the key with the parent pointer at the end of the deletion function.

```cpp
//-------------------------------------------------------------------
// Remove a key from a binary tree;  no action if key not found
//-------------------------------------------------------------------
void SymbolTable::remove(key_type key)
{
    Node *ptr;          // points to the current node
    Node *parent;       // points to the parent node

    for (parent = NULL, ptr = root; ptr != NULL;) {
        if (key < ptr->key_field ) {
            parent = ptr;
            ptr = ptr->left;        // search left subtree
        }
        else if (key > ptr->key_field ) {
            parent = ptr;
            ptr = ptr->right;       // search right subtree
        }
        else                        // Found it. Now DELETE it
            break;
    }
    if (ptr == NULL)
        return;         // Not found. No deletion occurs.

    Node *subtree;      // Root of the subtree after deletion
                        // Used to later set pointer in parent

    if (ptr->left == NULL && ptr->right == NULL) {   // Case 1
        delete ptr;                 // No children - delete a LEAF
        subtree = NULL;             // Subtree becomes empty
    }
    else if (ptr->left == NULL) {   // One child only: Case 2a
        subtree = ptr->right;       // Right child is new subtree root
        delete ptr;                 // Dispose deleted node
    }
    else if (ptr->right == NULL) {  // One child only: Case 2b (reverse)
        subtree = ptr->left;        // Left child is new subtree root
        delete ptr;                 // Dispose deleted node
    }
                //---------------------------------------------
    else {      // Two children - Case 3 - the difficult case!
                // Find rightmost node of left subtree
                //---------------------------------------------

        Node *prev, *temp;
        for (prev = NULL, temp = ptr->left; temp->right != NULL;
            prev = temp, temp = temp->right)
            ;                       // empty loop

                //---------------------------------------------
                // Replace node to be deleted with this node
                //---------------------------------------------

        if (prev == NULL) {         // did not go right at all
            temp->right = ptr->right; // right subtree of deleted node
                                      // Left subtree stays the same
            delete ptr;
            subtree = temp;         // *** Case 3a ***
        }
        else {                      // went down right at least once
            prev->right = temp->left;   // delete temp from subtree
            temp->left = ptr->left;     // replace "ptr" with temp
            temp->right = ptr->right;
            delete ptr;             //  *** Case 3b ***
            subtree = temp;
        }
    }
```

```
            //-------------------------------------------------------
            // Have now reconstructed the subtrees after deletion
            // Now need to set pointers in parent node
            //-------------------------------------------------------
    if (parent == NULL)             // deleted root node?
        root = subtree;             // subtree becomes whole tree
    else
    if (key < parent->key_field)
        parent->left = subtree;      // Node was left of its parent
    else
        parent->right = subtree;     // Node to right of its parent
}
```

If there is the possibility of duplicates in the tree, then these duplicates must be found and deleted also. In a binary tree duplicates appear in the left or the right subtree of the element just found — it depends on how the `insert` function handles equality.

The efficiency of the deletion function above can be marginally improved by avoiding the need for the "`parent`" variable and also the "`prev`" variable, in a manner similar to that used for the insertion function. However, repetitions make the code too long, and the improvement is left as an exercise to the reader.

There is also a very minor inefficiency: the first three tests on the number of children could be merged into two, by making deletion at a leaf part of the first of the other two cases. However, in the interests of clarity this optimization has not been used.

8.13 Binary tree version with sentinel pointers

The efficiency improvement technique of sentinels discussed with regard to arrays in Section 3.8 can be applied to linked lists and binary trees. Instead of using NULL pointers to signify the end of the list or the edge of the tree, pointers to a sentinel node are used. The advantage is that comparisons with NULL can be avoided in the search function (and also the deletion function because it involves a search of the tree).

The C++ class declaration of a binary tree given in the previous sections can be quite simply modified to use sentinels. The sentinel node is declared as a `static` data member of the `SymbolTable` class. This involves some measure of fighting with C++ syntax and encapsulation rules, because the two classes `Node` and `SymbolTable` are mutually dependent. Both classes are declared as friends of each other to allow access to the private data members. The details are as follows:

```
//---------------------------------------------------------------
// Binary Search Tree Implementation with SENTINELS
//---------------------------------------------------------------

#define NIL   (& SymbolTable::sentinel_node)   // Sentinel pointer

typedef int key_type;

class Node;          // forward declaration of Node class

class SymbolTable {
    private:
        static Node sentinel_node;   // Static --> one node
        Node * root;
    public:
        SymbolTable() { root = NIL; }       // constructor
        Node* search(key_type key);
        void insert(key_type key);
```

```
        void remove(key_type key);
    friend class Node;      // allow Node access to sentinel_node
};

class Node {                    // Node on the tree
    private:
        key_type key_field;
        Node *left, *right;     // pointers to subtrees
    public:
        Node(key_type k) { left = right = NIL; key_field = k; }
    friend class SymbolTable;    // allow easy access to nodes
};
```

The main changes to the member functions are changing most uses of NULL to NIL, a user-defined preprocessor macro pointing to a sentinel node. The single exception is that the return value of the search function for unsuccessful search must stay as NULL, because the user of the class should not be concerned with the address of the sentinel node.

The main advantage of sentinels occurs in the search function. The algorithm used by the search function is changed to initially set the sentinel node's key equal to the search key. With this method there is no need to test the pointer with NIL (comparison with NULL would be erroneous) because the equality condition will always cause the loop to end. After the loop the pointer is tested to see if it is a "fake" success due to finding the sentinel node, or if the key has been found in the tree. The efficiency should improve because a pointer comparison on every iteration of the loop has been eliminated and replaced with one key assignment before the loop and one pointer test after the loop. The search function becomes:

```
//-----------------------------------------------------------------
//  Search the binary tree for a specified key; return pointer to it
//-----------------------------------------------------------------

#include <stdio.h>        // declare NULL

Node* SymbolTable::search(key_type key)
{
    Node *temp = root;

    sentinel_node.key_field = key;
    for (;;) {                          // Test with NULL is not needed!!
        if (temp->key_field < key)
            temp = temp->right;         // Search right subtree
        else if (temp->key_field > key)
            temp = temp->left;          // Search left subtree
        else {
            if (temp == NIL)    // Found it or sentinel.
                return NULL;    // Found sentinels; search fails
            else
                return temp;    // Found it.
        }
    }
}
```

The insertion and deletion routines can be easily implemented, and are left as an exercise for the reader. The insertion routine merely needs all NULL uses changed to NIL. This simple change to the deletion routine will allow it to work correctly, or else, its search phase can be made more efficient by modifying the loop in a manner similar to the search function above.

8.14 Hashing version of the symbol table

Hashing is an efficient method of searching for data, especially if a large number of search operations are required. The method provides fast average search and insertion times, is usually faster than arrays or linked lists (sorted or unsorted), and is often more efficient than binary trees.

The basic idea behind hashing is to use a simple function to compute an integer from the key (e.g. by adding up all the letters of a symbol). This integer then becomes an index into an array of entries. Ideally, each different symbol will map to a unique index, so that there will never be two symbols stored at the same place. If this is true, information in the table can be accessed very quickly by calculating the integer index and retrieving the array element at that location.

Unfortunately, unique mapping is not usually possible. Instead, the functions must deal with the problem of already having an entry at the location. This is called a *collision*. Collisions can be resolved by either finding a new index, or storing both keys at the same index by chaining a list at the location. The recommended method for C and C++ programs is the use of a hash table holding an array of pointers, and chaining for collision resolution.

The major disadvantage of hashing is that the data is not sorted. Any operation requiring sorted data must sort the entries explicitly (e.g. printing out). However, elements can be visited sequentially in a *non-ordered* sequence although the method is a little inefficient because all entries in the hash table must be examined to determine if there is a key stored there. Hashing is not a good data structure for processing the keys sequentially.

8.14.1 The hash table

The hash table is the data structure in which all the data is stored for hashing. It can be an array of `structs`, but this wastes space unless the hash table is likely to be very full. A hash table is often implemented in C and C++ as an array of pointers. In this way, an empty location has a `NULL` pointer and a full location has a pointer to a `struct` containing the information (or a pointer to a list of such `structs`).

It is common for the size of the hash table to be a prime number, because hash functions of the form *(key) mod TableSize* give a better distribution when *TableSize* is a prime number. The reason for this involves very advanced theory and is beyond the scope of this book.

The hash table can be initialized by setting all its entries to `NULL`. It is most efficient to declare it as a global variable or a `static` local variable, which makes the compiler automatically initialize the array to zero before the program starts. If initialization is needed again, the array must be initialized explicitly, and this can be performed by the efficient `memset` library function (although there is a portability problem with `memset` on any machines where the `NULL` pointer is not all-bytes zero).

8.14.2 The hash function

The hash function maps the key to an integer index. Any method can be used to produce an integer from the key. For example, any of the bitwise operators can be used to extract various bits from the key, and any of the arithmetic operators can be used (e.g. to add various characters of the key together).

The choice of a hash function is largely a matter of preference. A good hash function should avoid collisions on different entries as much as possible. Because the values to be stored in the hash table are usually not known in advance, a good general hash function is difficult to choose. One that is simple to calculate efficiently is probably best.

A simple hash function on strings is to add the characters up, and take the modulus with the hash table size. The modulus gives a number between $0..n-1$, where n is the size of the hash table. For a good distribution (i.e. few collisions) it is recommended that the size of the hash table be a prime number.

It is important to declare the variable as an `unsigned int`. This prevents overflow from causing problems with the modulus (%) operator. An overflow could make the variable become negative, resulting in undefined behavior from the % operator. Note that `unsigned` is necessary only for the work variable being used to compute the sum, and not in the function return type.

```
int hash(char *key)
{
    unsigned int sum;

    for (sum = 0; *key != '\0'; sum += *key++); // empty loop
    return sum % SIZE;
}
```

How well this hash function performs depends on the keys to be stored in the hash table. Any anagrams will cause collisions (e.g. "steal" and "stale"). However, this function is simple to calculate and will perform well in most situations.

8.14.3 Collision resolution — chaining

A collision occurs when two different keys map to the same hash table location. Because of this possibility, when inserting a new element into the hash table the location must first be examined to determine whether it already holds an element. If it does, this collision must be *resolved*.

There are several methods of resolving the problem of collisions. Some simple collision resolution schemes work by searching for another empty location in the hash table. One method, called *linear probing*, works by moving along the table looking for a new empty location. Another method is to try again with a second hash function (though its collisions must also be dealt with). However, the recommended method for C and C++ programs is *chaining*. The C and C++ languages have good dynamic memory allocation features and hashing may as well make use of them. In this method, a linked list of all elements that hash to the same location hangs off each hash table entry, and the hash table contains pointers to linked lists. The linked lists contain all the keys that collided at that hash table location.

Another advantage of chaining is that insertion is very efficient, particularly if there is no possibility of duplicates. To add the element, simply insert the new element at the front of the unsorted linked list (i.e. the chain).

Searching requires a traversal of the (unsorted) linked list at the hash location. The efficiency of searching depends on the length of this linked list, which in turn depends on how evenly distributed the hash values are. If the distribution is even, the lists are likely to be short. The cost of searching is certainly no worse than other methods.

Deletion is efficient when using chaining because, unlike other collision resolution schemes, deletion from the hash table causes no consistency problems. The element is simply removed from the linked list. Other collision resolution methods suffer problems when an element is to be deleted from the hash table. The problem is that a location then becomes empty, and a search for a key that collided with the deleted element will find an empty location. How is the search function to know that a collision occurred earlier and the other element is in another place in the table? To solve this problem, it must be possible to mark a location as "deleted from" and the hashing algorithms become more complicated.

Chaining does waste some space because "next" pointers are required in the linked list, but this seems a small price to pay for its convenience.

8.14.4 Implementing the symbol table: hashed chaining

An implementation of the symbol table ADT using hashing with chaining is presented as follows. The keys are character strings, and only the keys are inserted into the table — a more realistic symbol table structure would contain other data associated with each key.

The symbol table operations are quite simply implemented. Search is a matter of calculating the hash value and then searching the (unsorted) linked list for the key. Deletion involves calculating the hash value, and a find-and-delete operation on the associated linked list. Insertion involves calculating the hash value and then inserting at the front of the linked list. The insert function also performs a check for duplicates by first calling the search function. This is slightly inefficient because the hash value is calculated twice. More efficient, but slightly more complicated, would be to search the linked list within the insert function.

```
//-------------------------------------------------------------
// Hash Table Implementation of the Symbol Table ADT
//-------------------------------------------------------------

#include <iostream.h>     // declare NULL
#include <string.h>       // declare strcpy, strcmp, etc

#define TABLE_SIZE 211    // Hash Table Size: a prime number
#define STR_LEN  30       // Maximum length of string

class Node {              // Node on the chained lists
    private:
        char symbol[STR_LEN + 1]; // symbol being stored
        Node *next;               // pointer to next node in list
    public:
        Node() { next = NULL; }
        friend class SymbolTable;   // allow easy access to nodes
};
```

```
class SymbolTable {
    private:
        Node * table[TABLE_SIZE];    // Hash table - array of pointers
    public:
        SymbolTable();      // constructor
        Node* search(char * symbol);
        Node* insert(char * symbol);
        void remove(char * symbol);
};

//------------------------------------------------------------------
// Constructor - initialize the hash table to empty
//------------------------------------------------------------------

SymbolTable::SymbolTable()
{
    for (int i = 0; i < TABLE_SIZE; i++)     // all pointers are NULL
        table[i] = NULL;
}

//------------------------------------------------------------------
// HASH: Generate an integer hash value for a symbol
//------------------------------------------------------------------

int hash(char *symbol)
{
    unsigned int sum = 0;

    while (*symbol != '\0')
        sum += *symbol++;
    return sum % TABLE_SIZE;
}

//------------------------------------------------------------------
// SEARCH:  Find a symbol in the symbol table;  return pointer to it
//------------------------------------------------------------------

Node* SymbolTable::search(char *symbol)
{
    int posn = hash(symbol);         // Find hash value
    Node *temp;

               // Search linked list for the symbol

    for (temp = table[posn]; temp != NULL; temp = temp->next) {
        if (strcmp(symbol, temp->symbol) == 0)
            return temp;                   // found it
    }
    return NULL;        // not found
}

//-------------------------------------------------------------------
// INSERT: Enter a symbol in the hash table and return a pointer to it
//-------------------------------------------------------------------

Node* SymbolTable::insert(char *symbol)
{
    Node * temp = search(symbol);
    if (temp != NULL) {
        return temp;    // duplicate found; return pointer to it
    }
    else {                          // No duplicate found. Insert it
        int pos = hash(symbol);                 // get hash value
        temp = table[pos];                      // get front of list
        table[pos] = new Node;
        strcpy(table[pos]->symbol, symbol); // store symbol
        table[pos]->next = temp;                // link up the node
    }
    return temp;        // return pointer to newly created node
}
```

```
//-----------------------------------------------------------
// DELETE: delete a symbol from the symbol table
//-----------------------------------------------------------

void SymbolTable::remove(char *symbol)
{
    int pos;

    pos = hash(symbol);
    Node *temp = table[pos], *prev = NULL;
    for (; temp != NULL; prev = temp, temp = temp->next) {
        if (strcmp(symbol, temp->symbol) == 0)
            break;                  // Found it; exit for loop
    }

    if (temp == NULL) {    // Not found
        return;             // Ignore it
    }
    else {                  // Found
        if (prev == NULL)                   // Delete at front of list
            table[pos] = temp->next;
        else                                // Delete at middle/end of list
            prev->next = temp->next;
        delete temp;                        // Return deleted node to heap
    }
}
```

8.15 Searching static data — perfect hashing

In some cases the values of the keys to be stored in the symbol table are known before-hand and do not change (i.e. no insertions or deletions). Such data is usually referred to as *static* data. For example, the lexical analyzer of a C compiler must test every sequence of letters it finds in a source file to determine if it is a keyword or an ordinary identifier. This involves a search of a table containing all the C keywords. Another example is a spell checker where the most common words are known and are often stored in a table in memory (a form of handling the common cases efficiently).

Special algorithms can be used in any situation where the search data is known. Surprisingly, although there has been much research into building optimal binary search trees for static data, they are not usually the best solution. The most efficient solution is to use hashing with a specially developed hash function, designed to prevent collisions. This is called a *perfect hash function* and can only be developed for unchanging data. If a perfect hash function can be found, the symbol table can be searched with one computation of the hash function and one key comparison to determine if the key is actually there. By comparison, even the optimal binary search tree will require several comparisons on average.

The most difficult aspect of using this method is the search for a perfect hash function for a particular set of data. There are a few common methods of doing so:

• Inspired guesswork.
• Brute-force computation.

In some cases, the programmer can work out a function that has no collisions by guessing at a function. For example, if the programmer notices that all keys have a different first letter then it is easy to compute a perfect hash function as a mapping from the 26 letters to a different unique integer, the hash value. Humans are very resourceful and this method of "guessing" the function works surprisingly well.

The brute-force approach involves trying to generate the hash function using a computer which tries a number of hash functions of a particular pattern, applies the hash function to each key, and reports when a function that produces no collisions is found.

As an example of the various approaches, let us attempt to develop a perfect hash function for the set of 32 ANSI C keywords:

auto	break	case	char
const	continue	default	do
double	else	enum	extern
float	for	goto	if
int	long	register	return
short	signed	sizeof	static
struct	switch	typedef	union
unsigned	void	volatile	while

Using my own version of "inspired guesswork", involving a couple of hours of poring over ASCII tables, I managed to come up with a reasonable perfect hash function. The basic approach I took was to break up the words into groups of about five keys by using a test of the string length, and also by making single character comparisons on the larger groups of keys with the same length. Once the group was small enough I looked for letters in the keys that were unique, often the first or second letter, and then examined the ASCII binary values of these letters. This way, the hash function extracts certain bits from each letter, and generates a small integer, which is then mapped into an "interval" of values for that particular group. The function, which produces hash values in the range 0..36, is as follows:

```
int my_hash(char *s)
{
    switch (strlen(s)) {
        case 2:                         /* Only "if" and "do" */
            return (s[0] & 01) + 2;             /* 2..3 */
        case 3:
            return (s[0] & 01) + 8;             /* 8..9 */
        case 4:
            if (s[1] == 'o')        /* goto, long, void */
                return (s[0] & 03) + 26;        /* 26..29 */
            else        /* auto, case, char, else, enum */
                return ((s[1] & 14) >> 1) + 30;
        case 5:     /* break, const, float, short, union, while */
                    /* 1st letter is unique */
            return (s[0] & 07) + (s[0] == 'c') + 10;    /* 10..16 */
        case 6:
            if (s[0] == 's')    /* signed,sizeof,static,struct,switch */
                return (s[5] & 03) + ((s[5] & 8) >> 3)
                     + ((s[5] & 16) >> 2) + 18;         /* 18..22 */
            else   /* 1st letter not 's' - double, return, extern */
                return (s[0] & 03) + 23;        /* 22..24 */
        case 7:                         /* "typedef", "default" */
            return (s[0] & 16) != 0;
        case 8:         /* continue, register, unsigned,volatile */
                        /* 1st letter is unique */
            return ((s[0] & 04) >> 1) + (s[0] & 01) + 4;  /* 4..7 */
        default:            /* Can't be a C keyword */
            return 0;   /* Pick any number */
    }
}
```

The second approach is to make the computer perform a brute-force search for a perfect hash function. The following program takes a set of keys from a file and develops a hash function of the following form:

$$\left(\sum_i C_i * key[i]\right) mod\ N$$

by trying many combinations of the constants C_i and N. If any of these hash functions produces no collisions, a perfect hash function has been found. The source code below implements this concept:

```c
/*---------------------------------------------------------------*/
/* PERFECT HASH FUNCTION BRUTE-FORCE SEARCH                      */
/*---------------------------------------------------------------*/

#include <stdio.h>
#include <stdlib.h>
#include <string.h>
#include <ctype.h>

/*---------------------------------------------------------------*/

#define bool int
#define TRUE 1
#define FALSE 0

/*---------------------------------------------------------------*/

#define MAX   1000      /* Maximum number of words */
#define LEN   10        /* Maximum length of a word */

/*---------------------------------------------------------------*/

char words[MAX][LEN];       /* words being hashed */
int C[LEN];                 /* coefficients of hash function */

/*---------------------------------------------------------------*/

#define MAX_MULTIPLIER      1     /* Let Ci range 0..MAX_MULTIPLIER */
                                  /* 1 means 0..1 --> use addition */
#define MAX_MODULUS         1000

int MODULUS;
int MODULUS_START_MULTIPLIER = 5;
int MODULUS_TOP;

/*---------------------------------------------------------------*/
/* Apply the hash function to a key                             */
/*---------------------------------------------------------------*/

int compute_hash(char *s)
{
    int i;
    unsigned int hash;

    hash = 0;
    for (i = 0; i < LEN; i++) {
        hash += s[i]*C[i];
    }
    return hash  % MODULUS ;
}

/*---------------------------------------------------------------*/
/* Try all the combinations of coefficients                     */
/* This function finds the perfect hash function!               */
/*---------------------------------------------------------------*/
```

```
void find_best(int n)
{
    int num;
    bool done;
    bool flags[MAX_MODULUS];    /* has a key hashed here yet? */
    bool collision;
    int val;
    int i;


    do {
        for (i = 0; i < LEN; i++) C[i] = 0;
        do {
                /* Update C[i]'s for next attempt */
            C[0]++;
            for (i = 0; i < LEN; i++) {
                if (C[i] <= MAX_MULTIPLIER) break;
                    C[i] = 0;
                if (i + 1 < LEN) { C[i + 1]++; }
            }

            for (i = 0; i < MODULUS; i++) {
                flags[i] = FALSE;   /* clear flags for this try */
            }

            collision = FALSE;
            for (num = 0; num < n; num++) {
                val = compute_hash(words[num]);
                if (flags[val]) {
                    collision = TRUE;
                    break;
                }
                flags[val] = TRUE;
            }

            if (!collision) {               /* report success */
                printf("NO COLLISION: ");
                for (i = 0; i < LEN; i++)
                    printf("%2d ", C[i]);
                printf(", MODULUS = %d ", MODULUS);
                if (MODULUS == n) printf(" PERFECT!!!");
                printf("\n");
                break;    /* exit do loop. Do next MODULUS */
            }

            done = TRUE;    /* Finish only when all multipliers */
                            /* are up to MAX_MULTIPLIER */
            for (i = 0; i < LEN; i++) {
                if (C[i] < MAX_MULTIPLIER) {
                    done = FALSE;
                    break;
                }
            }
        } while (!done);
        if (done)
            printf("FAILED With MODULUS %d\n", MODULUS);
        MODULUS--;        /* Try the next modulus value */
    } while (MODULUS >= n);
}
/*------------------------------------------------------------------*/
/* Load the words from a text file                                  */
/*------------------------------------------------------------------*/

void load_file(char *f, int n)
{
    FILE *fp;
    int i, j;
    char s[200];
```

```
        fp = fopen(f, "r");
        if (fp == NULL) {
            perror(f);
            exit(1);
        }
        for (i = 0; i < n; i++) {
          again:
            if (fgets(s, 199, fp) == NULL) {
                fprintf(stderr, "%s: \n", f);
                perror("fgets from file");
                exit(1);
            }
            if (s[strlen(s) - 1] == '\n') /* remove fgets's newline */
                s[strlen(s) - 1] = 0;

            for (j = 0; j < LEN; j++)
                words[i][j] = 0;          /* clear to NULLs*/

            strncpy(words[i], s, LEN);
            words[i][LEN-1] = 0; /* add terminating null, just in case */

            for (j = 0; j < i; j++) {
                if (strncmp(words[i], words[j], LEN) == 0) {
                    printf("Duplicate \"%s\" found\n", s);
                    goto again;
                }
            }
            printf("Word %3d: %s\n", i, words[i]);
        }
    }

    /*-----------------------------------------------------------------*/
    /* Start of program execution                                      */
    /*-----------------------------------------------------------------*/

    int main()
    {
        int n;
        char file[100];

        printf("Enter filename: ");
        scanf("%s", file);
        printf("File: %s\n", file);
        printf("How many words? ");
        scanf("%d", &n);
        load_file(file, n);        /* Load in the keys */

        MODULUS = n * MODULUS_START_MULTIPLIER;    /* start high */
        find_best(n);     /* Find the hash function! */
        exit(0);
    }
```

As shown in the source code above, the program is set to find all hash functions where
the coefficient is either 0 or 1. These functions are a useful special case, as no multiplications are actually needed (all the characters with a 1 coefficient are simply added). When
the program is run as shown on the ANSI C keywords, the best hash function it produces
has modulus 134 and the following coefficients:

```
NO COLLISION:  1  0  1  1  1  1  0  0  0  0 , MODULUS = 134
```

This information can be coded up into a simple perfect hash function. Unfortunately, the
memset and strncpy calls are necessary to ensure that characters beyond the end of
the string are considered zero, as is assumed by the hash function generator.

```
/*------------------------------------------------------------*/
/* Computer-generated addition hash function for C keywords */
/*------------------------------------------------------------*/
int computer_hash(char *s)
{
   char s2[10];

   memset(s2, 0, 6);      /* zero the first 6 letters */
   strncpy(s2, s, 6);     /* copy up to 6 letters */
   return (s[0] + s[2] + s[3] + s[4] + s[5]) % 134;
}
```

If the records to be stored with these keys are quite large, the space wastage of 134 hash table entries may be too large. A simple method of overcoming this is to add an array of 134 small integers (i.e. using the `char` type), where each entry in this array sets each C keyword to a unique value in the range 0..31. On the other hand, this may be a de-optimization as a sparse hash table can be more efficient than a minimal perfect hash function. If the table is large, it becomes likely that an unsuccessful search will map to a location containing a NULL pointer entry, and this avoids the need for the key comparison.

As a final note about perfect hashing, all of the hash functions in this section (both human and computer-generated) are specific to the ASCII character set. They are not portable to the EBCDIC set or other character sets, although it is possible to run the generator program in these environments to find an alternative hash function.

8.16 Sorting arrays

Sorting arrays is a common procedure and there are zillions of different methods. In addition to writing your own sorting function, you can use the `qsort` standard library function, but as this always calls a function just to compare two elements, it is far more efficient to code up your own sorting algorithm.

The methods of sorting arrays presented in this chapter are: bubble sort, insertion sort, selection sort and quicksort. Quicksort is the most efficient (in general) and the others are presented for completeness, and because there are special cases for which they are well-suited.

The implementations of the sorting algorithms given here are for sorting arrays of integers. To modify the programs to sort arrays of any type, the only necessary modifications are to the lines comparing two elements.

8.16.1 Bubble sort

Bubble sort is a very simple method for sorting but has $O(n^2)$ average performance and is therefore also one of the most inefficient. It is only really useful for sorting a small number of elements, where it will perform reasonably well due to the simplicity of its algorithm.

Bubble sort works by making multiple passes over the array, looking at adjacent pairs of elements and swapping them if they are out of order. Passes over the array continue until no further swaps are made.

```
void bubble_sort(data_type a[], int n)
{
    int i, j;
    int swaps;              /* TRUE if did a swap in a pass */
    data_type temp;         /* Temporary element for use in swapping */

    for (i = 1; i < n; i++) {       /* Note: not i=0 */
        swaps = FALSE;
        for (j = n - 1; j >= i; j--) {  /* Last element downto i */
            if (a[j - 1] > a[j] ) {     /* compare two elements */
                temp = a[j - 1];        /* Do a swap */
                a[j - 1] = a[j];
                a[j] = temp;
                swaps = TRUE;           /* Set the swap flag */
            }
        }
        if (!swaps) return;         /* Exit if no swaps done */
    }
}
```

Using the swaps variable improves the efficiency of bubble sort. The algorithm would still function correctly even if all references to this variable were removed, but it would be less efficient as it would continue to make further passes even after the array was already sorted. The swaps variable allows the algorithm to terminate early when sorting a partially-sorted array, rather than terminating only when n passes over the n elements have been made.

8.16.2 Insertion sort

Insertion sort is another simple, but not particularly efficient sorting algorithm. This algorithm works by growing a sorted part of the array by repeatedly inserting a new element into this sorted subarray. At every iteration the number of sorted elements increases by one. This algorithm is inefficient if the elements are greatly out of order, because the insertion of an array element requires that all other elements be shifted upwards by one location. The following implementation maintains the locations 0..i-1 as the sorted subarray:

```
void insertion_sort(data_type a[], int n)
{
    int i, j, k;
    data_type temp;

    for (i = 1; i < n; i++) {                   /* Note: i=1 */
        for (j = 0; j < i && a[j] <= a[i]; j++) /* Where in 0..i? */
            ;           /* empty loop */
        if (j != i) {                       /* If not already in place */
            temp = a[i];                    /* Insert in place */
            for (k = i; k > j; k--)         /* by shuffling others up */
                a[k] = a[k - 1];
            a[j] = temp;
        }
    }
}
```

Despite the fact that this algorithm is $O(n^2)$ in the average case, it has very good performance if the array is almost sorted.

8.16.3 Selection sort

Selection sort also makes multiple passes over the array. Each pass increases the portion of the array that is sorted and subsequent passes ignore the sorted part. The length of each pass over the array gradually reduces as the unsorted part of the array reduces. During each pass the minimum element is found. At the end of a pass this minimum element is put in its correct place and the pass is reduced so that it no longer includes that newly sorted element. In the following function the variable i indicates the part of the array to be scanned for the minimum element (i.e. $i+1$ up to $n-1$):

```
void selection_sort(data_type a[], int n)
{
    int  i, j;
    int  min_index;          /* Index of minimum element */
    data_type min_element;   /* Value of minimum element */

    for (i = 0; i < n - 1; i++) {
        min_index = i;            /* First is minimum so far */
        min_element = a[i];

        for (j = i + 1; j < n; j++) {   /* Find minimum i+1..n-1 */
            if (a[j] < min_element ) {  /* compare two elements */
                min_index = j;          /* New minimum found */
                min_element = a[j];
            }
        }
        a[min_index] = a[i];      /* Swap ith element with the */
        a[i] = min_element;       /*  minimum of a[i] ..a[n-1] */
    }
}
```

8.16.4 Quicksort

Quicksort works by breaking down the sorting problem into smaller sorting problems. To sort an array, a single element called the *pivot element*, is chosen. This element is used to partition the array into two subarrays. In one partition, all elements are less than or equal to the pivot element; in the other partition they are all greater than the pivot element. These smaller partitioned subarrays are then sorted.

This method of partitioning reduces sorting a large array to sorting two smaller arrays. The simplest quicksort algorithm uses two recursive calls to sort the two new partitions. This works correctly but is not as inefficient as it can be.

```
/*----------------------------------------------------------------*/
/* QUICKSORT algorithm for sorting arrays                         */
/*----------------------------------------------------------------*/

void quick_sort(data_type arr[], int n, int bottom, int top)
{
    register int i, middle;
    data_type temp;                    /* used by swap macro */
    data_type pivot_value;

#define swap(x, y)        temp = arr[x], arr[x] = arr[y], arr[y] = temp

    if (top > bottom) {     /* If more than 1 element to sort */

        /* Partition into subarrays: bottom..middle-1, middle+1..top */

        pivot_value = arr[bottom];        /* arr[bottom] is pivot */
        middle = bottom;
```

```
            for (i = bottom + 1; i <= top; i++) {
                if (arr[i] < pivot_value) {
                    middle++;
                    swap(i, middle);
                }
            }
            swap(bottom, middle);    /* Move pivot to middle */

                    /* Now sort the two partitions recursively */

            quick_sort(arr, n, bottom, middle - 1); /* do bottom */
            quick_sort(arr, n, middle + 1, top);    /* do top */
        }
    }
```

The following more complex implementation of quicksort eliminates one of these recursive calls. The technique used to remove it is called *elimination of tail recursion.* Instead of having a recursive call as the last statement of a function, a branch back up to the top of the current invocation of the function is used. The branch takes the form of a while loop in the following improved function.

A further improvement in the following function is that the *smallest* subarray is sorted recursively. This reduces the *total* number of recursive calls still further. Sorting a smaller array will have fewer recursive calls at the next levels.

```
/*----------------------------------------------------------------*/
/* QUICKSORT2:  Quicksort with Tail Recursion Eliminated          */
/*----------------------------------------------------------------*/

void quick_sort(data_type arr[], int n, int bottom, int top)
{
    register int    i, middle;
    data_type       temp;         /* used by swap macro */
    data_type       pivot_value;

    while (top > bottom) {          /* Finished if zero/one element */
        pivot_value = arr[bottom];        /* arr[bottom] is pivot */
        middle = bottom;
        for (i = bottom + 1; i <= top; i++) {
            if (arr[i] < pivot_value) {
                middle++;
                swap(i, middle);
            }
        }
        swap(bottom, middle);    /* Move pivot to middle */

    /*----------------------------------------------------------*/
    /* Partitioned the array - now sort the two partitions      */
    /* Eliminate tail recursion - do only one partition recursively */
    /* Do smallest partition recursively - reduces recursion further */
    /*----------------------------------------------------------*/

        if (middle - bottom < top - middle) {
            quick_sort(arr, n, bottom, middle - 1);  /* do bottom */
            bottom = middle + 1;                      /* do top */
        }
        else {
            quick_sort(arr, n, middle + 1, top);      /* do top */
            top = middle - 1;                         /* do bottom */
        }
    }
}
```

One major aspect of quicksort not addressed properly by the preceding function is the method of choosing the pivot element for the partitioning phase. The simple choice of the leftmost element can cause worst-case behavior on already sorted arrays. A better way to choose the pivot element is by examining several different elements in the array. Commonly, the *median* of the top, middle and bottom elements is chosen as the pivot.

Another method of improving the efficiency of the quicksort algorithm is to solve small cases by using a special algorithm. When the number of elements to be sorted in a subarray drops below some level (e.g. less than 5 elements), it is better to use a simpler special-purpose sort algorithm instead of using more recursive calls. Use either special-purpose inline code for sorting this small number of elements with an optimal number of comparisons, or call one of the simpler sorting algorithms: insertion sort, selection sort. Hence, a better quicksort implementation would test how many elements are to be sorted and use the special routine if the number is small enough.

8.16.5 Choosing a sorting algorithm

Generally speaking, the quicksort algorithm is the best general-purpose sorting algorithm. However, sometimes other algorithms may be better when:

- the number of elements to be sorted is small; or
- the array is "almost" sorted (few elements out of place).

If the number of elements is small, the extra overhead in the quite complicated implementations of quicksort may be prohibitive. A simple algorithm, such as insertion sort, may be preferable.

When an array is almost sorted, the quicksort algorithm may exhibit worst-case $O(n^2)$ behavior. In this case, a simpler algorithm may be preferable.

8.17 Summary

- Abstract data types are not only good programming practice, but also aid the process of performance tuning, because it is simple to *change* the underlying data structure without affecting the code that *uses* the abstract data type.
- Stacks are most efficiently implemented as arrays, but this method is limited to a fixed size. A hybrid stack and linked list implementation is fast and general.
- Arrays are most useful for searching for a small number of elements.
- Sorted arrays have very fast search and ordered printout routines, but unsorted arrays have faster insertion and deletion.
- The main differences between sorted and unsorted linked lists is that unsorted lists have very fast insertion, but sorted lists allow easy sorted printout.
- The ordering of key tests using the <, > and == operators are important for efficiency in both the binary search algorithm on arrays, and binary tree search.
- Binary tree search, insertion and deletion can all be performed in $O(\log n)$ time on average, and can all be implemented with efficient non-recursive algorithms.

- Hashing is a good method of achieving fast search but does not allow efficient sequential processing, sorted or unsorted.
- If the keys being searched for are fixed, a perfect hash function can be tailor-made and a very fast hashing search routine implemented.

8.18 Further reading

The efficiency of data structures is a huge area of research in computer science, and this chapter has touched on only a little of that theory. The following are some of the best references in this area:

GONNET, G. H., and BAEZA-YATES, R., *Handbook of Algorithms and Data Structures (2nd edn)*, Addison-Wesley, 1991.

HOROWITZ, E., and SAHNI, S., *Fundamentals of Data Structures (3rd edn)*, Pitman Publishing, 1990.

KNUTH, Donald E., *The Art of Computer Programming (Vol. 3): Sorting and Searching*, Addison-Wesley, 1973.

STANDISH, T. A., *Data Structure Techniques*, Addison-Wesley, 1980.

8.19 Exercises

1. Improve on the insertion routine for sorted arrays by using a process similar to binary search to find where to insert the key.

2. Improve on the deletion routines for the sorted and unsorted linked list implementations of the symbol table by removing the assignment to the `"before"` variable inside the main loop.

3. Improve the deletion routine of the binary tree implementation to remove the need for the `"parent"` pointer and the `"prev"` pointer.

4. Examine the use of sentinels (see Section 8.13) for the sorted linked list implementation of the symbol table. Sentinels should allow the removal of pointer tests with NULL from the loops in the search, insertion and deletion routines.

5. Implement a quicksort routine for sorting an unsorted linked list. The sort should be performed "in place", without moving any nodes or creating new nodes, but only by changing the `"next"` pointers.

6. When the cost of key comparison is very high compared to the cost of following a `next` pointer in a linked list, the efficiency of searching a sorted linked list can be improved by using *jump search*. The idea is to jump forward a few nodes, say 10 nodes, at each iteration before performing a key comparison. If the key is before the "look-ahead" node, a sequential search of the 10 nodes is necessary; if it is after the node, jump search continues further along the list. Implement the jump search algorithm. How can its efficiency be improved if sentinels are also used?

7. How useful is a doubly-linked list for implementing the symbol table as a (sorted) linked list? What are the implications for efficiency?

8. Implement the insertion and deletion routines for the sentinel version of the binary tree in Section 8.13. Although changing all occurrences of NULL to NIL should be adequate, try to improve the search phase in the deletion routine by taking advantage of the sentinel node (i.e. eliminate a comparison with NIL inside the loop by setting the key in the sentinel node).

9. Implement a print_sorted routine for a binary tree as efficiently as possible. *Hint:* The keys should be printed by using an *inorder* traversal, and the inorder traversal can be improved with the same methods of improvement used for preorder traversal in Sections 3.9.1 to 3.9.4.

10. Complete the symbol table implementation with hashing by writing the remove function for the hash table.

11. The hash table implementation in this chapter uses an unsorted linked list to chain collisions. It is possible to use some other data structure for these collisions, such as a sorted linked lists, binary tree, or even another hash table. Examine the efficiency of these alternatives. Is an unsorted linked list the best choice?

12. Implement the symbol table using hashing with the linear probing method of collision resolution. How do you modify the search function to solve the consistency problems created by deletion?

13. Examine the addition of a count member function to return the number of keys currently stored in the symbol table. Which data structures make this easiest? How can an incremental algorithm be used to define the count function?

14. Another efficiency technique called *pairing computation* is relevant where two quantities can be calculated together faster than by computing them both separately. How can this idea be used to efficiently implement insertion in a symbol table for a compiler, which must examine the symbol table to determine if a symbol is present, and insert it if not? *Hint:* The inefficient solution is to call the search function and then call the insert function if the search is unsuccessful.

15. How can you apply the technique of *caching* commonly used values to symbol table implementation? Under what circumstances will it improve efficiency?

16. Improve the quicksort implementation by making a better choice of pivot element and by using a specialized sorting method, such as insertion sort, when the number of elements in the subarray is "small enough".

Chapter 9

Example applications

Several programs for a variety of tasks are presented in this chapter and the methods of efficiency improvement in this chapter are applied to these programs. The programs were chosen for various reasons, although they all satisfy the basic requirement of not being too small or too large. The tic-tac-toe game-playing program was chosen simply because it is an interesting little program that I had already written (although I hadn't optimized it). Checking if an integer is prime is a neat mathematical problem that is often examined when considering efficient design of algorithms.

9.1 An invincible tic-tac-toe player

When I began writing this efficiency book I looked around for a program of my own that I could try to optimize, and came across a program to make the computer play invincible tic-tac-toe. I had written the program after learning about computer game-playing in an Artificial Intelligence course. The theory of computer game-playing is quite advanced and, as you probably know, computers are already threatening the human mastery of complicated games such as chess. Let us examine how computers play games.

9.2 Game trees and the minimax algorithm

Computers are not "smart". They play two-player games using a brute-force method of examining every possible move, and then every possible opponent's reply, and then every move they could then make, etc. In complicated games such as chess, the computer can analyze only a few moves deep (usually fewer than 10), because the huge number of possible moves makes the number of variations immense. However, in the game of tic-tac-toe the computer can examine every variation, all the way to the final position, because the number of moves is always small (less than 9). In fact, the number of variations will be less than $9 * 8 * 7 * 6 * 5 * 4 * 3 * 2 * 1 = 362,880$ because at the initial position there are 9 possible moves and the number of moves for each move after that will decrease by 1. However, this is not a very accurate upper bound because not all games last 9 moves, and the number of variations is more like 250,000 (it is left as an exercise to the reader to find out exactly how many).

The variations arising from a position are usually represented as a multiway tree where each node represents a position, and each line (branch) represents a move. This is called the *game tree*, and it is the basis of all computer game-playing algorithms. An example of the game tree arising from a tic-tac-toe position close to the end of a game is shown in Figure 9.1. The game tree for a position earlier in the game would have a greater number of nodes (in fact, close to 250,000)

Figure 9.1. Game tree for a tic-tac-toe position. X to move

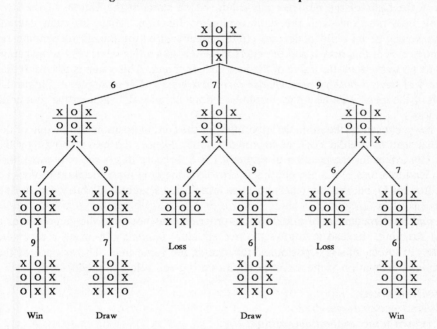

Note that, for simplicity, moves on the board are numbered as follows:

```
1 | 2 | 3
--+---+--
4 | 5 | 6
--+---+--
7 | 8 | 9
```

The computer chooses its move using a *minimax* algorithm. At positions where the game is over (either a win, loss or draw), the final position is given a value by using what is called the *static evaluation function*, as shown in Table 9.1. The end of the game need not be always at the same level in the tree; an early win or loss can occur before the 9 moves are up.

The actual values of the static evaluation function are not important, except that a loss must be weighted less than a draw which is then less than a win. If this is so, we can see that the computer would like to maximize its score and the opponent would like to minimize the score. Thus at the top level of the game tree, the computer is trying to

Table 9.1. Static evaluation function

Value	Game result
1	Win
0	Draw
−1	Loss (opponent wins)

maximize, but at the next level of the game tree it is the opponent's move, and the aim of the opponent will be to *minimize* the score.

This is the basis of the *minimax* algorithm, which starts at the bottom of the tree, evaluating final positions with the static evaluation function. Then, for each internal node, the values of its child nodes are either maximized or minimized (depending on whose move it is at this node), and the internal node is given this value. By propagation all the way up to the root, the value of the root node is found. This value is the result that the game will have *if both players choose their best moves*. For example, in Figure 9.1 the result of the game with best play would be a draw because the value of the root node is zero (draw).

The move chosen by the minimax algorithm for the current position will be one of the moves that lead to a child node of maximum value. Hence, the move chosen by the minimax algorithm for the position in Figure 9.1 is 6, because this is the only move that does not lead to a loss. To a person, this is obviously the only move because it blocks a row of three for O, but the computer must use brute-force search of all variations to find this out.

In a real implementation of minimax, the program does not build the game tree as a tree data structure. Instead it follows the tree structure *implicitly* by using a recursive algorithm. In effect, this is a postorder traversal of the game tree. The essence of the recursive implementation of the minimax algorithm is given below in pseudo-code:

```
minimax(position):
    if game won or drawn then
        return static_evaluation(position)
    else
        generate all legal moves
        generate all the new positions for these moves
        apply minimax to all the new positions (Recursive call!)
        if maximizing level then
            return maximum value and its associated move
        else
            return minimum value and its associated move
```

9.3 A simple implementation using minimax

The minimax algorithm is thus the basis of a computer game-playing program. The proper implementation of the game also needs the following routines:

- Initialize the board.
- Display the board.
- Generate all moves from a position.
- Static evaluation function.
- Make a move on the board.

The following program is the source code for the original version of the tic-tac-toe player, which was implemented without any particular concern for efficiency. The program uses the minimax algorithm but the implementation is slightly complicated by the fact that it that it doesn't just return a single move, but returns the entire "best" variation.

```
/*------------------------------------------------------------------*/
/*    Tic-Tac-Toe game playing program                              */
/*      by David Spuler,   February 1991                            */
/*------------------------------------------------------------------*/

#include <stdio.h>
#include <stdlib.h>
#include <assert.h>
#include <ctype.h>
#include <time.h>

/*------------------------------------------------------------------*/

#define DEMO    1            /* 1 if want computer v. computer */
                            /* 0 if want human v. computer */

/*------------------------------------------------------------------*/

typedef int bool;       /* A boolean-like type */
#define FALSE 0
#define TRUE 1

/*------------------------------------------------------------------*/

#define NOUGHT 0            /* Player items */
#define CROSS  1
#define EMPTY  2            /* empty square */

#define DRAWN       3        /* Game is drawn */
#define UNFINISHED  4        /* Game is not yet finished */


#define NOUGHT_CHAR   'O'    /* Characters for text screen board */
#define CROSS_CHAR    'X'
#define EMPTY_CHAR    ' '

#define VERT_CHAR     '|'    /* Characters to create board lines */
#define HORIZ_CHAR    '-'
#define CORNER_CHAR   '+'

#define INFINITY    100 /* INFINITY > max value of static_eval */
                        /* -INFINITY < min value of static_eval */

/*------------------------------------------------------------------*/

typedef struct {
    int current_move;   /* Number of the move, 1..9 */
    int player;         /* Player to move, noughts or crosses */
    int squares[3][3];  /* The 3x3 board */
```

```
}board_type;

typedef struct {
    int number;                    /* Number of moves in the list */
    int moves[9];                  /* List of possible moves */
                                   /* at most 9 moves (9 squares) */
}move_list_type;

                /* Type returned by MINIMAX analysis function */
typedef struct {
    int value;
    int path[9];                   /* List of possible moves */
                                   /* at most 9 moves (9 squares) */
} minimax_type;
/*-------------------------------------------------------------------*/
void setup_board(board_type *b)
{
    int i, j;

    b->player = CROSS;      /* Crosses to move */

    for (i = 0; i < 3; i++)/* Clear all squares */
    for (j = 0; j < 3; j++) {
        b->squares[i][j] = EMPTY;
    }

    b->current_move = 1;    /* First move */
}

/*-------------------------------------------------------------------*/
/*    Makes the move on the board  - puts the letter down         */
/*    -- Assumes that the move is legal ---                       */
/*-------------------------------------------------------------------*/
void make_move(board_type *b, int m)
{
    int x, y;
    int temp;

    temp = m-1;/* convert to 0..8 */
    x = temp % 3;/* Get X coordinate */
    y = temp / 3;/* Get Y coordinate */

    assert(b->squares[x][y] == EMPTY);
    b->squares[x][y] = b->player;          /* Put the new letter down */

    b->player = b->player == NOUGHT?CROSS:NOUGHT; /* Change player */
    b->current_move++;                        /* Count the moves made */
}


/*-------------------------------------------------------------------*/
/*    Check if the move is legal  (returns true if so)            */
/*-------------------------------------------------------------------*/
bool is_legal_move(board_type b, int m)
{
    int x, y;

    x = (m-1) % 3;
    y = (m-1) / 3;
    return b.squares[x][y] == EMPTY;  /* Legal if square is empty */
}

/*-------------------------------------------------------------------*/
move_list_type generate_moves(board_type *b)
{
    move_list_type move_list;
    int m;
```

```
          /*------------------------------------------------------*/
          /* Brute force generation:  try all squares for legality */
          /*------------------------------------------------------*/

     move_list.number = 0;   /* No moves in list yet */
     for (m = 1; m <= 9; m++) {
         if (is_legal_move(*b, m))
         {                           /* Legal move, so add to list */
             move_list.moves[move_list.number] = m;
             move_list.number++;
         }
     }
     return move_list;
}

/*----------------------------------------------------------------*/
/*  Work out who is the winner (X, O, Drawn, or Unfinished )   */
/*   Looks for rows, columns and the 2 diagonals.             */
/*   If no winners, drawn if board is full, else Unfinished   */
/*----------------------------------------------------------------*/

int winner(board_type b)
{
     int i, j;
     bool match, match1, match2;
     int temp, temp1, temp2;
     int x1, y1, x2, y2;

                                   /*-------------------*/
     for (i = 0; i < 3; i++)       /* Check all columns */
     {                             /*-------------------*/
         temp = b.squares[i][0];
         if (temp == EMPTY)        /* square empty? */
             continue;             /* Can't be a column */
         match = TRUE;
         for (j = 1; j < 3; j++) {
             if (temp != b.squares[i][j])
                 match = FALSE;
         }
         if (match)
             return temp;
     }
                                   /*----------------*/
     for (j = 0; j < 3; j++)       /* Check all rows */
     {                             /*----------------*/
         temp = b.squares[0][j];
         if (temp == EMPTY)        /* square empty? */
             continue;             /* Can't be a row */
         match = TRUE;
         for (i = 1; i < 3; i++) {
             if (temp != b.squares[i][j])
                 match = FALSE;
         }
         if (match)
             return temp;
     }

               /*----------------------*/
               /* Check both diagonals */
               /*----------------------*/
     x1 = y1 = 0;
     x2 = 0; y2 = 2;
     temp1 = b.squares[x1][y1];
     temp2 = b.squares[x2][y2];
     match1 = temp1 != EMPTY;   /* Can't match if empty */
     match2 = temp2 != EMPTY;
     for (j = 0; j < 3; j++) {
         if (temp1 != b.squares[x1][y1])
             match1 = FALSE;
```

```
                if (temp2 != b.squares[x2][y2])
                    match2 = FALSE;
                x1++; y1++;      /* Move along one diagonal */
                x2++; y2--;      /* Move along other diagonal */
        }
        if (match1)
            return temp1;
        if (match2)
            return temp2;
                        /*----------------------------------------*/
                        /* No winner yet. Drawn if board full, */
                        /*      otherwise Unfinished           */
                        /*----------------------------------------*/
        if (b.current_move > 9)
            return DRAWN;
        else
            return UNFINISHED;
}

/*----------------------------------------------------------------*/
/* STATIC_EVAL:  Static evaluation function used by Minimax */
/*    Value of position.  ( 1 : win, -1 : Loss, 0 : Draw )   */
/*----------------------------------------------------------------*/

int static_eval(board_type b, int player)
{
        int t;

        t = winner(b);
        if (t == player)
            return 1;        /* You win */
        else if (t == DRAWN)
            return 0;        /* Drawn game */
        else
            return -1;       /* Opponent wins */
}

/*----------------------------------------------------------------*/
/* MINIMAX: Do a minimax tree analysis of position          */
/*     Return value of position and move list of best path. */
/*     The first move on this path is the BEST move.        */
/*----------------------------------------------------------------*/

minimax_type minimax(board_type b, int depth, int player)
{
        int i;
        minimax_type temp;   /* Hold return value of this function */
        move_list_type move_list;
        bool max;            /* True if maximizing level */
        int best;            /* Best value found so far */

        max = ((depth & 01) == 0);     /* Maximize if level even */
        for (i = 0; i < 9; i++)
            temp.path[i] = 0;  /* Clear the path to empty initially */

        if (winner(b) != UNFINISHED) /* Stop going deeper when game over */
        {
            temp.value = static_eval(b, player);
            return temp;
        }

        if (max)                    /* Initialize for minimizing/maximizing */
            best = (-INFINITY);
        else
            best = INFINITY;

        move_list = generate_moves(&b);   /* Generate list of moves */

        for (i = 0; i < move_list.number; i++)/* For all moves */
        {
```

```
        board_type temp_board;
        minimax_type temp2;

        temp_board = b;
        make_move(&temp_board, move_list.moves[i]);
        temp2 = minimax(temp_board, depth+1, player); /* Recursion! */

        if (( max && temp2.value > best)       /* Maximizing */
            || (!max && temp2.value < best)) /* Minimizing */
        {
          int k;
          best = temp2.value;                     /* New best score */
          temp.path[depth] = move_list.moves[i]; /* add move to path */
          for (k = depth + 1; k < 9; k++)         /* get other moves */
              temp.path[k] = temp2.path[k];
        }
    }
    temp.value = best;
    return temp;
}
/*-----------------------------------------------------------*/
void computer_move(board_type *b)
{
    minimax_type temp;

    temp = minimax(*b, 0, b->player);   /* Computer uses minimax */
    make_move(b, temp.path[0]);         /* Make the chosen move */
}
/*-----------------------------------------------------------*/
void player_move(board_type *b)
{
    int move;
    bool error;

#if DEMO
    computer_move(b);
#else
    do {
        error = FALSE;
        printf("\n\nWhat is your move (1-9)? ");
        scanf("%d", &move);
        if (move < 1 || move > 9 || !check_legal_move(*b, move)) {
            printf("\nIllegal move. Try again.\n");
            error = TRUE;
        }
        else {                 /* Legal move, so make the move */
            make_move(b, move);
        }
    }while(error);            /* Until legal move */
#endif
}
/*-----------------------------------------------------------*/
void print_board(board_type b)
{
#define MARGIN 5      /* Number of spaces board is inwards */
    int i, j, k;

    if (winner(b) != UNFINISHED)
        printf("Final Position\n\n");
    else
        printf("Before move %d\n\n", b.current_move);

    for (j = 0; j < 3; j++) {
        for (k = 1; k <= MARGIN; k++)/* Space inwards */
```

```
                putchar(' ');
            for (i = 0; i < 3; i++)/* Draw the board */
            {
                if (b.squares[i][j] == EMPTY)
                    putchar(EMPTY_CHAR);
                else
                if (b.squares[i][j] == NOUGHT)
                    putchar(NOUGHT_CHAR);
                else
                    putchar(CROSS_CHAR);

                if (i + 1 < 3)
                    putchar(VERT_CHAR);
            }
            if (j + 1 < 3) {
                printf("\n");
                for (k = 1; k <= MARGIN; k++)/* Space inwards */
                    putchar(' ');
                                /* Do horizontal line */
                for (k = 0; k < 3; k++) {
                    putchar(HORIZ_CHAR);
                    if (k + 1 < 3)
                        putchar(CORNER_CHAR);
                }
            }
            printf("\n");
        }
    printf("\n");
}
/*------------------------------------------------------------*/

void announce_winner(board_type b)
{
    int temp;

    printf("\n\n");
    temp = winner(b);
    if (temp == NOUGHT)
        printf("Noughts is the winner. \n\n");
    else
    if (temp == CROSS)
        printf("Crosses is the winner.\n\n");
    else
        printf("The game goes to Jack (drawn)\n");
}

/*------------------------------------------------------------*/

main()
{
    board_type b;
    int computer_colour = CROSS;

    printf("Welcome to Tic-Tac-Toe on a 3x3 board.\n\n");
    setup_board(&b);            /* Initialize the board */
    print_board(b);

    do {
        if (b.player == computer_colour)
            computer_move(&b);
        else
            player_move(&b);
        print_board(b);
    }while(winner(b) == UNFINISHED );/* Until game over */
    announce_winner(b);
    exit(0);
}
```

9.4 Improving the efficiency of the program

To improve the efficiency of this program it is necessary to have some measure of the time it takes. For this program, it was a simple matter of using demo mode and measuring the execution time with the `clock` library function. Note that in the following discussion, the timings were taken from a powerful mainframe computer.

First, I set out to improve the program without using any special algorithm improvement (i.e. without using alpha-beta pruning; see Section 9.5), and without profiling. The first version took 56 seconds to run. I removed the pass-by-value of the large board structures by using pointers; this reduced execution time by about 9% to 51 seconds.

I unrolled completely all of the fixed-length loops in the `print_board`, `generate_moves` and `winner` functions (this involved rewriting the `winner` function). This reduced execution time by 33% to 34 seconds.

I converted the program to use a one-dimensional array of 9 squares, instead of a two-dimensional array of 3x3 squares, reducing execution time by 35% to 22 seconds. This removed not only array calculations but also the need for the `%` and `/` operators in the `make_move` function.

Converting all the smaller functions to macros reduced execution time by 13% to 19 seconds.

Rewriting the call to `static_eval` as inline code, allowing the removal of the duplicated calls to the `winner` function, reduced execution time by 10% to 17 seconds.

Removing from the program all the unnecessary references to the `path` variable reduced execution time by 35% to 11 seconds.

I added a "common case" test to the `winner` function whereby if the move number was less than 6, it would immediately return a result saying that the game was unfinished. However, this decreased efficiency slightly, indicating that the early moves are not really a common case (because the number of positions examined increases exponentially with the number of moves) and the extra test costs time rather than gaining it.

As a final improvement, I moved the base case in the `minimax` function up one level by testing if the game was finished before recursively calling `minimax` for the next level. This improved efficiency by approximately half a second, an improvement of about 5%, making the program require about 11 seconds. A summary of these optimizations is given in Table 9.2

Table 9.2. Improvements to the tic-tac-toe program

Technique	Improvement	Execution time
Pass pointers to structures	9%	51 seconds
Unrolled fixed length loops	33%	34 seconds
Conversion to one-dimensional array	35%	22 seconds
Replace functions with macros	13%	19 seconds
Removed duplicate call to `winner`	10%	17 seconds
Removed unnecessary code	35%	11 seconds

I had run out of ideas for minor optimizations. The run-time had been improved from 56 seconds to just 11 seconds, a massive improvement. However, readability had suffered and the original program was now beyond recognition; in particular, the `minimax` function was much more complicated. In making all these improvements I had also introduced a number of bugs at various stages, and these had taken some time to remove (thankfully, it was easy to detect them by noting when the move sequence of the demo game changed). The next step was to try a different algorithm: alpha-beta pruning.

9.5 Alpha-beta pruning

Alpha-beta pruning is a method of avoiding the evaluation of entire subtrees of the game tree. It takes advantage of the fact that the minimax algorithm doesn't generate the entire tree before evaluating internal nodes (in fact, minimax performs a postorder traversal of the game tree). By maintaining two extra cut-off values, traditionally called *alpha* and *beta*, the improved algorithm can avoid evaluating many subtrees. The term "pruning" comes from the fact that branches are pruned from the game tree.

The improved alpha-beta algorithm improves on minimax in that it does not always make a recursive call to evaluate all moves from a given position. Once a cut-off occurs, no more moves from the position are evaluated. The procedure is similar at minimizing and maximizing levels. At a minimizing level, the beta value is continually updated so as to be the current maximum value of a move found at this position. At the same time, a test for an alpha cut-off is performed. The beta value is propagated down to the next level of the tree, which will be a maximizing level, and the value is used for a beta cut-off. The alpha value is continually updated at a minimizing level, and tracks the minimum value found so far at the current position.

The occurrence of a cut-off, either alpha or beta, indicates that the current position will never arise with best play because there is a better variation available at a higher level node in the tree. An alpha cut-off indicates that at the current position the opponent has a good move, but you can avoid this variation by choosing a better move earlier in the move sequence. Similarly, a beta cut-off indicates that you have a good move, but the opponent can avoid the variation in favor of a better one.

I took the original 56-second program and changed the `minimax` function to use alpha-beta pruning. It took about 2 seconds to run. The use of a different algorithm should have been the first attempt at efficiency improvement, not the last. However, the smaller improvements were not wasted, because modifying the 11-second program to use alpha-beta pruning reduced execution time further to 0.46 seconds. The alpha-beta pruning function is shown below:

```
/*--------------------------------------------------------------------*/
/* MINIMAX:  Do an alpha-beta pruning minimax analysis of game tree */
/*           Returns value of position and the BEST move           */
/*--------------------------------------------------------------------*/
minimax_type minimax(board_type b,int d,int player,int alpha,int beta)
{
    int i;
    minimax_type temp;  /* Use to hold return value of this function */
    move_list_type move_list;
    bool max;                /* True if maximizing level */
    int best;                /* Best value found so far */
```

```
    max = ((d & 01) == 0);     /* Maximize if level even */

    if (winner(b) != UNFINISHED) /* Stop going deeper when game over */
    {
        temp.value = static_eval(b, player);
        return temp;
    }

    if (max)                   /* Initialize for minimizing/maximizing */
        best = (-INFINITY);
    else
        best = INFINITY;

    move_list = generate_moves(&b);    /* Generate list of moves */

    for (i = 0; i < move_list.number; i++)/* For all moves */
    {
        board_type temp_board;
        minimax_type temp2;

        temp_board = b;
        make_move(&temp_board, move_list.moves[i]);
        temp2 = minimax(temp_board, d + 1, player, alpha, beta);

        if (max) {                      /* Maximizing */
            if (temp2.value > best) {
                temp.best_move = move_list.moves[i];   /* store move */
                best = temp2.value;              /* New best score */
                alpha = temp2.value;             /* New alpha bound */

                if (best >= beta) {      /* Check for beta cut-off */
                    temp.value = best;
                    return temp;
                }
            }
        }
        else {                          /* Minimizing */
            if (temp2.value < best) {
                temp.best_move = move_list.moves[i];   /* store move */
                best = temp2.value;              /* New best score */
                beta = temp2.value;              /* New beta bound */

                if (best <= alpha) {     /* Check for alpha cut-off */
                    temp.value = best;
                    return temp;
                }
            }
        }
    }
    temp.value = best;
    return temp;
}
```

The initial values of `alpha` and `beta` are important, being negative and positive infinity. The first call to the `minimax` function is:

```
temp = minimax(*b, 0, b->player, -INFINITY, INFINITY);
```

There is one very important detail in the implementation of alpha-beta cut-offs: the operators >= and <= in the check for cut-offs are crucial for efficiency. The program will still perform correctly with the > and < operators, but many cut-off opportunities will be lost, particularly in the tic-tac-toe game because, with only three possible values from the static evaluation function, equality is fairly common.

9.6 Total precalculation

Although there seems to be no obvious method of improving the efficiency still further, it is possible to precalculate the best moves for every possible position, store these moves in an array, and thereby replace the call to the `minimax` function with a super-efficient table lookup. To do so we would need two programs — one to generate the array of moves, and one to play the game using this array. To generate the moves, we apply the program already written to all possible board positions. Since we have $3^9 = 19683$ board positions and our program requires at most 0.46 seconds, the data generating program should run in less than 9000 seconds (about 3 hours). In fact, it runs much faster than this because 0.46 seconds is required only when starting with the empty board.

For simplicity, we work by encoding each position as a number in the range $0..3^9$, by regarding the position as a base-3 number with digits X, O and the empty square. The functions to *decode* an integer to a position and *encode* a position as an integer are shown in the following source code. The basic algorithm to generate the precalculated array of best moves is also shown (with the code to perform the position analysis omitted for the sake of brevity).

```c
/*------------------------------------------------------------*/
/*  Create precalculated array of best moves                  */
/*------------------------------------------------------------*/

#define TABLE_SIZE  19683        /* 3^9 different positions */

/*------------------------------------------------*/
/* ENCODE: Convert board position to an integer */
/*------------------------------------------------*/

int encode(const board_type *b)
{
    int i, code = 0;

    for (i = 0; i < 8; i++)
        code = code * 3 + b->squares[i];
    return code;
}

/*---------------------------------------------*/
/* DECODE: Convert integer to a board position */
/*---------------------------------------------*/

void decode(board_type *b, int code)
{
    int i;

    b->current_move = 1;
    b->player = COMPUTER_PIECE;
    for (i = 8; i >= 0; i--) {
        b->squares[i] = code % 3;   /* extra ternary digit */
        code /= 3;
        if (b->squares[i] != EMPTY) /* count how many moves made */
            b->current_move++;
    }
}

/*------------------------------------------------------------*/

main()
{
    board_type b;
    int code;
    char filename[100];
```

```
    char c;
    minimax_type ret;
    FILE *fp;

    printf("Enter name of resulting file: ");
    scanf("%s", filename);
    fp = fopen(filename, "r");   /* Check doesn't already exist */
    if (fp != NULL) {
        printf("That file already exists!!\n");
        printf("Do you want to overwrite it? (y/n): ");
        scanf(" %c", &c);
        if (tolower(c) != 'y') {
            fclose(fp);
            exit(1);
        }
        fclose(fp);
    }
    fp = fopen(filename, "w");       /* Create/truncate file */
    if (fp == NULL) {
        perror(filename);
        exit(1);
    }
    /*------------------------------------------------------------*/
    /* Now produce the C declaration for initialized array */
    /*------------------------------------------------------------*/
    fprintf(fp, "char board_table [%d] = {\n", TABLE_SIZE);
    fflush(fp);
    for (code = 0; code < TABLE_SIZE; code++) { /* for 3^9 positions */
        decode(&b, code);
        if (b.current_move <= 9) {
            ret = minimax(&b, 0, COMPUTER_PIECE);
        }
        else
            ret.best_move = 0;  /* dummy move; board is filled up! */
        fprintf(fp, "%d", ret.best_move);

        if (code + 1 < TABLE_SIZE) { /* comma after all but last */
            fprintf(fp, ", ");
            if (code % 20 == 19)      /* new line every 20 digits */
                fprintf(fp, "\n");
        }
    }
    fprintf(fp, "\n};\n");   /* finish the array declaration */
    fclose(fp);
    exit(0);
}
```

The tic-tac-toe program can be made much smaller by removing any functions related to the minimax algorithm, and rewriting the `computer_move` function as follows. Naturally, the final game-playing version still uses many other functions, such as `setup_board` and `print_board`, but these are omitted for the sake of clarity.

```
/*------------------------------------------------------------------*/
/* Tic-tac-toe player using total precomputation               */
/*------------------------------------------------------------------*/

#include "table.c"     /* Include computer-generated file */

void computer_move(board_type *b)
{
    int code;

    code = encode(b);
    assert(1 <= board_table[code] && board_table[code] <= 9);
    make_move(b, board_table[code]);
}
```

This version of the tic-tac-toe player takes only 0.03 seconds to play an entire game against itself.

9.7 Testing for prime numbers

Testing if an integer is a prime number is a well-known problem in number theory. An integer is prime if it is divisible only by 1 and itself. For example, 5 is prime because it is divisible only by 1 and 5, but 9 is not prime because it is divisible by 3.

Our first attempt at testing if an integer is prime is to test whether it can be divided by the numbers $2..n-1$, where the test for divisibility is to compare the result of the remainder operator, %, with zero. n is divisible by i if and only if n%i is zero. The function is:

```
bool prime1(long n)
{
    long i;

    for (i = 2; i < n; i++) {      /* Try 2..n-1 */
        if (n % i == 0)            /* Does i divide n evenly? */
            return FALSE;          /* Yes, so not prime */
    }
    return TRUE;                   /* None divide, so must be prime */
}
```

To examine its run-time efficiency, calling the function for the numbers from 1 to 10,000 was timed. This algorithm took 12.59 seconds.

The best optimization to apply to this technique is to choose a better algorithm. A little thought will show that there is no need to test for divisors up to $n-1$. Only divisors up to $\sqrt{n}$ need be tested. If a number has a divisor greater than $\sqrt{n}$, then it also has a divisor less than $\sqrt{n}$, and the smaller divisor will be found by our algorithm. The improved algorithm can be coded up as:

```
bool prime2(long n)
{
    long i;
    long max;

    max = (long) sqrt( (double) n);
    for (i = 2; i <= max; i++) {   /* Try 2..sqrt(n) */
        if (n % i == 0)            /* i divides n evenly? */
            return FALSE;          /* Yes, so not prime */
    }
    return TRUE;
}
```

Care has been taken not to compute sqrt in the condition of the for loop, since this would call sqrt for every iteration.

The improved algorithm takes only 0.34 seconds to test the primes from 1 to 10,000, compared to 12.59 seconds for the first version. This incredible speedup occurs because the first algorithm performs approximately n^2 remainder tests, whereas the second algorithm performs only approximately $n\sqrt{n}$ tests (note that remainder tests on composite numbers are much fewer for both algorithms because a divisor can be found quickly). Even so, the speedup seems incredible until the way the timings are performed is taken into consideration — the numbers from 1 to 10,000 are tested. By using some simple mathematics to estimate how much speedup should be expected, the cost of testing 1..10,000 for the two algorithms can be approximated by the formulae:

$$\sum_{i=1}^{10,000} i^2 \equiv 333,383,335,000$$

$$\sum_{i=1}^{10,000} i\sqrt{i} \equiv 4,000,500,012$$

where the values have been calculated by a small computer program. Hence, our estimate of the speedup factor is around $333/4 \equiv 83$, and we estimate that the second algorithm should take around $12.59/83 \equiv 0.15$ seconds, which is far better than the actual result. The fact that the algorithm does not do as well as the estimate can be traced to the fact that the summation formulae do not take into account that the algorithms do not take as long to detect a non-prime integer as they do for a prime.

The algorithm can be improved still further by noting that the program should never test for divisibility with an even number larger than 2 since numbers which are divisible by large even numbers will have already been identified as non-prime by the fact that they are divisible by 2. Hence, the algorithm can be modified to skip over even numbers:

```
bool prime3(long n)
{
    long i;
    long max;

    if (n <= 2)
        return TRUE;
    if (n % 2 == 0)      /* divide by 2 as special case */
        return FALSE;

    max = (long) sqrt( (double) n);
    for (i = 3; i <= max; i += 2) {   /* 3..sqrt(n) odds only */
        if (n % i == 0)
            return FALSE;
    }
    return TRUE;
}
```

This improvement reduced the execution time from 0.34 to 0.20 seconds. The remainder operation n%2 was then replaced by a bitwise-and operation, reducing the time further by 10% to 0.18 seconds. The fact that this small change improved the speed by such a large percentage shows that the divisibility test succeeds frequently (in fact, half the time).

The idea of avoiding dividing by even numbers can be generalized to avoiding dividing by any multiples of numbers already tested. This is difficult to do for all numbers, but it was possible to remove the remainder tests for all multiples of 3 by using the improved function:

```
bool prime4(long n)
{
    long i;
    long max;
    int count3;

    if (n <= 3)
        return TRUE;
    if ((n & 1) == 0)        /* Divide by 2 as special case */
        return FALSE;

    if (n % 3 == 0)          /* Divide by 3 as special case too */
        return FALSE;

    max = (long) sqrt( (double) n);
    count3 = 3;                       /* 3rd decrement sets to zero */
                                      /* as i's first value is 5 */
    for (i = 5; i <= max; i += 2) {   /* 3..sqrt(n), odds only */
        count3--;
        if (count3 == 0) {
            count3 = 3;               /* multiple of 3 */
            continue;                 /* skip it */
        }
        if (n % i == 0)
            return FALSE;
    }
    return TRUE;
}
```

This small improvement to the algorithm improved the efficiency from 0.18 seconds to 0.16 seconds.

9.8 Precomputing arrays of primes

Interestingly, a first attempt at precalculation failed to improve efficiency, and actually increased run-time. The following function took 0.17 seconds, and in fact, when the number of primes in the precalculated array was increased, efficiency went down. Conversion of the array references to use a pointer traversal of the array (see Section 4.1.9) improved the situation slightly, but it was still less efficient than earlier algorithms. Presumably, the problem is the extra processing performed each loop iteration.

```
bool prime5(long n)
{
    long i, max;
    int j;
    static long primes[] = { 2, 3, 5, 7, 11, 13, 17, 19, 23, 29 };

#define NUM_PRECALC  ( sizeof(primes) / sizeof(long))

    for (j = 0; j < NUM_PRECALC; j++) {
        if (n <= primes[j])        /* Must be prime; <= catches 1 */
            return TRUE;           /* == would require 1 in array */
        if (n % primes[j] == 0)
            return FALSE;          /* Divides, so not prime */
    }
    max = (long) sqrt( (double) n);
    i = primes[NUM_PRECALC - 1] + 2;    /* Start at next odd */
    for (; i <= max; i += 2) {   /* up to sqrt(n), odds only */
        if (n % i == 0)
            return FALSE;
    }
    return TRUE;
}
```

Finally, a boolean array indicating whether an integer in the range 0..1000 was prime or not was used (this was calculated by another program). Surprisingly, this had no noticeable improvement over the best algorithms, taking 0.16 seconds. However, when all the numbers up to 10,000 were precalculated, the execution time was reduced to 0.03 seconds.

```c
bool prime6(long n)
{
    long i;
    long max;
    int j;

    static bool is_prime[] = {
#include "primes.h"          /* Include precalculated array */
    };

#define NUM_PRECALC  ( sizeof(is_prime) / sizeof(bool))

    if (n < NUM_PRECALC)
        return is_prime[n];  /* Look up result in table */
    else
        return prime5(n);    /* Call a general prime routine */
}
```

9.9 How the prime functions were timed

The scaffolding used to time the various functions is quite interesting in itself. Clever use of an array of pointers to functions meant that adding another function to evaluate was just a matter of adding its name to the initialization of the array of pointers to functions.

```c
main()
{
    long n;
    long i;
    int alg;
    clock_t start;

    static bool (*fns[])(long) = {    /* pointers to functions */
        prime1, prime2, prime3, prime4, prime5, prime6
    };

#define MAX  10000        /* How many primes to test */

#define NUM_ALG   \
    (sizeof(fns) / sizeof(fns[0]))  /* number of algorithms */

    static double times[NUM_ALG];        /* array of run-times */
    static bool arr[NUM_ALG][MAX + 1];   /* flags indicating primes */

                /*---------------------------*/
                /* Time all the algorithms */
                /*---------------------------*/

    for (alg = 0; alg < NUM_ALG; alg++) {  /* for all algorithms */
        start = clock();

        for (i = 2; i <= MAX; i++)
            arr[alg][i] = fns[alg](i);        /* test if i is prime */

        times[alg] = (clock() - start) / (double) CLOCKS_PER_SEC;
    }
```

```
/*----------------------------------------------------------*/
/* Perform debugging check to ensure all return same values */
/*----------------------------------------------------------*/

for (i = 2; i <= MAX; i++) {
    bool value = arr[0][i];
    for (alg = 0; alg < NUM_ALG; alg++) { /* for all algorithms */
        if (arr[alg][i] != value) {
            printf("Fails i = %ld,  prime%d = %d, prime1 = %d\n",
            i, alg + 1, arr[alg][i], value);
            exit(1);
        }
    }
}

/*--------------------------------*/
/* REPORT the times of execution */
/*--------------------------------*/

for (alg = 0; alg < NUM_ALG; alg++) {     /* for all algorithms */
    printf("Version %d took %5.4f seconds\n", alg + 1, times[alg]);
}
exit(0);
}
```

9.10 Further reading

My artificial intelligence textbook was by Elaine Rich, and the minimax and alpha-beta
algorithms are adapted from there (although she uses a slightly more efficient method
where testing if the level is minimizing or maximizing is avoided by negating the value at
each level). An excellent book on writing games such as tic-tac-toe, chess, checkers, go,
poker, and many others, is *Computer Gamesmanship* by David Levy.

LEVY, David, *Computer Gamesmanship*, Century Publishing, 1983.

RICH, Elaine, *Artificial Intelligence*, McGraw-Hill, 1983.

9.11 Exercises

1.   Make the tic-tac-toe player a more user-friendly game by adding features such as
     interactive choice of demo mode, take back move, hint, etc.

2.   Modify the minimax and alpha-beta versions of the tic-tac-toe player to determine
     how many nodes are evaluated by the static evaluation function. By what percent-
     age does alpha-beta pruning reduce the number?

3.   Modify the tic-tac-toe program to play tic-tac-toe on an NxN board.

4.   Modify the precalculated tic-tac-toe player so that it can play either player. At
     present, it does not correctly precalculate moves for alternating players, but always
     assumes X is to play from the current position.

5.   Modify the prime5 function in 9.8 to remove the loop overhead by completely
     unrolling the first loop.

Chapter 10

Ideas for compiler optimization

Whereas previous chapters have examined the issue of efficiency from the point of view of the programmer, this chapter looks at efficiency from the point of view of the compiler implementor. The design of optimizing compilers is still an area of current research, and there are many techniques that could be covered. However, rather than discuss the many issues of code optimization, this chapter focuses upon optimizations that are relevant to the C and C++ languages. In particular, the effect of the ANSI C standard on compiler optimization is given special emphasis.

The fundamental principle of optimization is to replace a computation with a more efficient method that computes the same result. The ANSI C standard specifies the *results* of computations as if on an "abstract machine", but the *methods* used by the compiler are not specified. The compiler's optimizer is free to choose any method that produces the correct result. This is commonly called the "as if" rule, since the program must run as if it were executing on the abstract machine.

One important consideration for optimizers is whether they are allowed to remove code that may produce some form of exception, such as a NULL pointer dereference or arithmetic overflow (which might cause program termination, or some other side effect). Fortunately, such effects are classed as "undefined behavior" in the ANSI C standard and the compiler is free to treat them in any way. Ignoring such exceptions is one possible behavior, and hence the compiler's optimizer may remove such statements (provided the statements cause no other useful side effects, of course).

10.1 Well-known optimization techniques

The fundamental design of an optimizer for a C or C++ compiler is largely the same as an optimizer for any other procedural programming language. For an introductory discussion of compiler optimization, the reader is referred to any good compiler textbook, such as Aho, Sethi and Ullman (1986). This section examines well-known optimizations when applied to C and C++.

Naturally, all operations and statements should be implemented with the most efficient instructions. Some of the more difficult areas are the `switch` statement (see Section 4.2.3 for a brief discussion), and the conditional operator. The conditional operator should produce code identical to the `if` statement wherever its result is not used; hence it is worthwhile to determine if the result is used when deciding on the code sequence to use.

10.1.1 Code motion and common sub-expression elimination

Large-scale code transformations such as code motion and common sub-expression elimination suffer from problems because of C's system level ancestry, and are often avoided by compiler implementors (and rightly so!). These transformations can cause problems when a location has special properties, such as a memory-mapped I/O port, and a useful reference may be "optimized out" because it appears redundant to the compiler. This fact, along with bugs in optimizers, helps explain the well-known phenomenon of a program that works without optimization, but fails if the optimizer is used. The `volatile` keyword is a partial solution to the problem, but it is limited in that it must be added to existing code. For further discussion, refer to Section 10.8.

An interesting possibility for improving these optimizations is to use knowledge about the standard library functions. In particular, the knowledge that some library functions never produce a side effect can be used to generalize the sub-expressions to which code motion and common sub-expression can be eliminated. The library functions which don't produce side effects include, for example, `strlen`, `strcmp` and all of the `<ctype.h>` functions. Consider the following code fragment:

```
for(i=0; i < strlen(s); i++)
        hash += s[i];

if(strcmp(s1,s2) == 0)
    printf("equal");
else if(strcmp(s1,s2) < 0)
    printf("less than");
else
    printf("greater than");
```

In theory, a compiler could optimize the following code using knowledge of `strlen` and `strcmp`. The `strlen` call can be moved *before* the loop and the second `strcmp` call, which is a common sub-expression, can be removed by storing and reusing the result from the first call. I'll be very impressed when I see a compiler that can do this!

10.1.2 Constant folding

The well-known technique of "constant folding" can be applied in C and C++ to both integral and floating point constants, and also to objects declared as `const` (see Section 10.9). Although the ANSI C standard specifies that a compiler must honor the presence of brackets, even for commutative-associative operators, this was mainly introduced to solve problems programmers had when they were trying to reduce the size of relative error in floating point computations. Hence, although brackets should be honored for floating point expressions, a compiler can often rearrange integral expressions. In fact, if done properly, the "worst" that rearranging an integral expression can do is to cause an overflow condition. This is no problem on the many 2's complement implementations where integer overflow has no effect and cannot be detected; nor is it a problem for other compilers since overflow is "undefined behavior" and the comments made in the introduction to this chapter apply.

Constant folding can be extended to include the "propagation" of a constant assigned to a variable, provided that the variable is not `volatile`. For example, the constant assigned to i in the code fragment:

```
i = 0;
j = i;
```

can be propagated to its next use, so that j is also assigned the constant 0. Note that this optimization will cause problems in traditional C if a variable has special properties (i.e. if it would be `volatile` in ANSI C), but it is unlikely that an `int` variable is intended to be special. A pointer variable is more likely to point to a special location, and it is perhaps too dangerous for the compiler to propagate constants assigned via a pointer dereference.

10.1.3 Algebraic identities

There are many small optimizations that can be applied at the expression level. An integer multiplication involving a constant power of two can be changed into a bit shift. The same can be done for integer division if the bitwise right shift operator sign extends (as opposed to filling with zeros), or if the operand being shifted has an `unsigned` type (why?). Similarly, a remainder involving a power of two can be changed to use bitwise-and on implementations where the result of `%` on negative values is identical to that of bitwise-and (and for `unsigned` operations).

The compiler could also check for common cases such as assigning zero to a variable if a fast set-to-zero assembly instruction is available. If this optimization is used, the compiler should also watch for zero assigned through a non-trivial assignment, such as:

```
x = y = 0;
```

It is also worth finding expressions that add 1 to a value using ordinary + for a number of reasons:

- ++ is not valid in situations where the operand is not an l-value;
- novice programmers may forget to use ++;
- #define constants may have the value 1.

On some machines, adding small constants (e.g. 2) may be more efficiently implemented as a sequence of increment operations, and these special cases should be optimized.

There are many simple algebraic identities that can be used to improve efficiency. It is usually safer to apply these optimizations only to integer expressions, but floating point expressions may also be considered if it is clear that the result will not be changed. Some identities are as follows:

```
x + 0   == x
x * 1   == x
x * -1  == -x
x / 1   == x
x * 0   == 0
```

Although it is unlikely that the programmer will knowingly place such expressions in the code, they can arise if symbolic constants have values such as 1 or 0, or if complicated constant expressions evaluate to these values.

Another very common form of identity involves the ! operator. Expressions of the form:

```
! (x == y)
```

are quite common, as they can arise when the ! operator is applied to a macro expansion. Obviously, the more efficient expression is x!=y. This form of expression is easy for the compiler to detect, and the compiler can also generate more of this form of improvement by using the identities:

```
! (x && y) == !x || !y
! (x || y) == !x && !y
```

However, these identities are only really useful if the x and y sub-expressions contain relational operators, thus allowing the ! operations to be removed. If neither x nor y contain relational operators, it is more efficient to use the identities in reverse (from right to left) to remove one of the ! operations. Fortunately, these algebraic identites preserve all the same semantics, even those involving short circuiting and side effects.

A very sophisticated optimizer might notice some less obvious algebraic identities. For example, in the expression:

```
x * (y != 0)
```

the multiplication operator is always applied to either 0 or 1, so the optimizer could generate code for this statement as if it had the equivalent form which totally avoids multiplication:

```
y != 0 ? x : 0
```

Another very advanced optimization, although perhaps it will only rarely be used, is illustrated by the code sequence:

```
#define ABS(x)  ( (x) >= 0 ? (x) : -(x))

y = ABS(y)
```

which expands out to become:

```
y = ( (y) >= 0 ? (y) : -(y))
```

Although it isn't obvious immediately, this has a redundant assignment in the second part, effectively assigning: y=y. The compiler should optimize any redundant assignments of this form and do so *after* the code is generated for the conditional operator.

A similar form of optimization, where the compiler must recognize the same sub-expression on both left and right sides of the = operator, is that statements such as the following can usually be implemented as a single machine instruction:

```
x = -x;
x = ~x;
```

10.1.4 Evaluating boolean expressions

It is interesting to note that the common code optimization technique of "short circuiting" a logical expression is absolutely necessary in C and C++, as it is part of the definition of the && and || operators. However, there are still some improvements possible in the evaluation of boolean expressions, depending on what context a logical or relational operator is used in. The restriction that operators such as < and && must return either 0 or 1 limits efficiency, but in some cases this isn't important, such as when the results of these operators are the *operand* to either && or || (which permit any non-zero value for true), or the conditional expression for an if statement or loop condition. For example, the expression:

```
x != y && ...
```

might well be optimized to use subtraction:

```
x - y && ...
```

although when the result of the != operator must be stored, then the code must return either 0 or 1, as in:

```
z = (x != y);    /* difficult to optimize */
```

A boolean expression, either as an operand to && or ||, or as a conditional expression for an if statement or loop, can have quite efficient generated code. As an example, the statement:

```
if (x < y)
```

can be implemented using instructions like:

```
cmp     x, y           ; compare x and y
bls     somewhere      ; branch if less than
```

However, if this test were used in the assignment statement:

```
z = x < y;
```

the assembly instructions are less flexible because of the need to actually evaluate < as either 0 or 1:

```
        cmp     x, y           ; compare x and y
        bls     true           ; branch if less than
        store   z, 0           ; z = 0
        jmp     after          ; skip the next statement
true:   store   z, 1           ; z = 1
after:  ....
```

10.2 Prototypes and argument widening

The addition of prototypes to C by the ANSI standard gives the implementor more freedom in efficient implementation of function calls. The main areas of improvement are the avoidance of widening `char`, `short` and `float` types, and the flexibility to pass parameters in registers. These optimizations apply also to C++, where fortunately they cause no problems since non-prototyped function calls are not allowed.

In traditional C, no functions are prototyped, and implicit argument promotion of smaller types occurs in function calls. `char` and `short` types are promoted to `int`, and `float` is promoted to `double`. These conversions cost both time and space, and can often be avoided in ANSI C. When an ANSI compiler sees a call to a function that is governed by a prototype, the compiler is free to dispense with these promotions, and can instead pass the arguments as their actual types. Of course, this rule for prototypes must be consistently followed for both function calls and function definitions (i.e. if arguments to a prototyped call are not widened, the function definitions should know to expect the arguments as having non-widened size).

Unfortunately, this new policy does make function calls slightly more brittle, because if the programmer accidentally calls this function in a file where no prototype is declared, the default argument promotions will occur. A larger argument than expected by the function definition will be passed on the stack, and a run-time failure is the most likely result. Although ANSI does give the compiler this freedom by requiring that such a function is always called with a prototype in scope, this is little consolation to the programmer whose program is failing. This is a trade-off between speed and robustness.

10.3 Prototypes and the function call mechanism

The traditional method of passing arguments to a function in C has been to push them all onto the program stack. This was simple to implement and provided support for variable-argument functions (e.g. `printf`, `scanf`). In fact, since without prototyping there is no way to tell if a function call is to a variable-argument function or a fixed-argument function, the function call mechanism had to support both, and pushing arguments onto the stack was the simplest method of achieving this.

The introduction of prototyping allows the use of different function call mechanisms, such as passing arguments in registers, in certain situations. The ANSI standard introduces one very important constraint on programs:

All calls to variable-argument functions must be governed by a prototype.

In other words, calls to variable-argument functions can no longer be non-prototyped.

One of the main effects this has on programs is that any programs using library functions in the `printf` or `scanf` families must include `<stdio.h>` (which should declare prototypes for these variable-argument functions). In addition, the declaration of user-defined non-prototyped variable-argument functions (e.g. those using the old `<varargs.h>` header file) is not allowed in ANSI C, nor is a call to a variable-argument function allowed to be non-prototyped, even if defined by using the ANSI header `<stdarg.h>` (i.e. the call must be governed by a prototype containing the ellipsis).

This new rule has important consequences for the compiler implementor. Non-prototyped function calls can be assumed to be calls to fixed-argument functions, and hence non-prototyped calls can use a function call mechanism other than pushing arguments onto the stack, such as passing arguments in registers (after the argument value promotions of `char` and `short` to `int`, and `float` to `double`). Calls to functions declared by fixed argument prototypes can also be passed by using this same mechanism. In fact, the mechanisms for fixed-argument prototyped and non-prototyped calls must be identical; otherwise, there will be a run-time failure if a call is made to a prototyped function definition, where that function call is not actually governed by a prototype (this situation must be supported by an ANSI compiler).

Any method of passing arguments could be used, provided that function calls as well as function definitions rely on it. For example, a reasonable rule, based on the assumption that structures and `float`/`double` arguments can't be placed in registers, would be to pass the first n scalar arguments in registers, for some fixed n that depends on the number of available hardware registers in the machine. Thus, a function definition would expect its first n scalar arguments in registers, and any non-scalar arguments or extra scalar arguments on the stack.

Variable-argument functions must be implemented slightly differently because they have to support a variable number of arguments. When a function is called with a prototype in scope that contains the ellipsis, such as:

```
void printf(char *format, ...);
```

any mechanism can be used, provided it supports both the use of the declared arguments (i.e. `format`) within the function definition, and the extraction of any remaining arguments via the `va_start`, `va_arg` and `va_end` macros in `<stdarg.h>`. For example, the same mechanism as for fixed-argument prototyped calls could be used for the declared arguments, and the remaining arguments (after the default non-prototyping promotions of `char`, `short` and `float`) could be pushed onto the stack as in traditional C. The stack is just one possible implementation (albeit the most common) and the implementor can choose any method provided the macros in `<stdarg.h>` are modified to correctly receive the arguments.

Unfortunately, relying on the assumption that all variable-argument functions will be called via a prototype can cause old code to fail, and provides no safety net for the programmer who accidentally omits a prototype. The compiler could partially solve this problem by producing warnings about all non-prototyped calls, especially those involving calls to variable-argument standard library functions such as `printf` and `scanf`. Another alternative is to limit the situations in which the faster argument passing mechanism is used, and this is now discussed.

A slightly safer but less powerful optimization is to relax the assumption that non-prototyped calls are always to fixed-argument functions and to use the traditional stack method for *all* non-prototyped calls. Hence, a function call or definition can be optimized only if it can be guaranteed that all calls to a function will be governed by a prototype; according to p247 of Harbison and Steele's book, *C: A Reference Manual*, these situations are when a function is called with a prototype in scope (or defined as a prototyped function) and:

• at least one argument is of `char`, `short`, or `float` type; *or*
• the prototype uses the ellipsis token \"f(CW..." *(variable-argument function).*

Hence, a call to a prototyped function with a `char`, `short`, or `float` argument can be handled in a different manner than required for non-prototyped function calls (which would be handled in the traditional stack-based method). Unfortunately, any such rule will still lead to run-time errors if the programmer accidentally forgets to declare a prototype for this type of function; the situation is the same as for argument widening as discussed in the previous section.

This safer rule also loses the opportunity for optimizing non-prototyped calls and even prototyped calls which do not use `char`, `short` or `float` arguments (i.e. using only `int`, `long`, `double`, pointers and structures). The reason for this restriction is that an ANSI compiler must still support calls to a prototyped function that doesn't use `char`, `short` or `float` parameters, even if no prototype is in scope at the time of the call. Hence, any difference in the handling of this function when it is prototyped or non-prototyped will cause run-time failure and thus violates ANSI. This support for programs that mix prototyping and non-prototyping for the same function limits the optimization of prototyped calls if we do not choose to also optimize non-prototyped calls.

One practical alternative for the implementor is to provide a user option to force all prototyped function calls to use a faster calling mechanism. This imposes on the programmer the burden of always using prototypes correctly (compilation warnings about non-prototyped calls become almost a necessity in such an environment). To reduce the risk of failures due to accidental non-prototyping, this option could also ensure that the same calling mechanism is used for non-prototyped functions so that programs will not fail unless a variable-argument function is called without a prototype, or unless a prototyped function with a `char`, `short` or `float` argument is called without a prototype.

In summary, the ANSI standard gives the implementor new freedom of choice over the function call mechanism. The implementor can choose between the traditional (safe) method of pushing arguments onto the stack, or use a more efficient method which may fail if the programmer does not correctly follow ANSI guidelines — in particular, a variable-argument function must be called via a prototype, and prototyped and non-prototyped calls can be mixed only when no argument type is `char`, `short` or `float`. Unfortunately, any method that relies on variable-argument function calls always being prototyped may break existing code. Perhaps the best practical choice is to provide a user option to set the level of optimization, based on different choices of argument widening (as discussed in the previous section) and argument passing through hardware registers. Some of the possible levels, roughly ordered from "fast and unsafe" to "slow and safest" are as follows:

1. Use registers for non-prototyped and fixed-argument prototyped arguments; widen only non-prototyped arguments.
2. Use registers for non-prototyped and fixed-argument prototyped arguments; widen all arguments.
3. Use registers for fixed-argument prototyped functions involving `char`, `short` or `float` parameters; widen only non-prototyped arguments.
4. Treat all prototyped calls as traditional non-prototyped calls; widen all arguments.

The difference between levels 1 and 2 is that, although both will fail if a variable-argument function is called or defined without a prototype, an accidentally non-prototyped call to a prototyped function with a `char`, `short` or `float` parameter will not cause a run-time failure in level 2.

Level 3 optimization will not cause a program to fail due to a non-prototyped call to a variable-argument function, but a program will fail due to a non-prototyped call to a prototyped function with a `char`, `short` or `float` parameter. Note that since there are no failures due to prototyped calls, there is no advantage in widening small arguments in prototyped calls.

The lowest level of optimization is to treat prototyped function calls and definitions as if they are non-prototyped; all `char`, `short` or `float` parameters in prototypes are still widened in both the function definition and function call (even in the presence of the prototype). This will prevent any failures, except those that would have occurred in non-ANSI C anyway, but the prototypes provide no efficiency advantage.

The function call mechanism in C++ is far easier to change. Since all function calls are prototyped and variable-argument functions must use the elipsis, no run-time problems can arise in passing arguments in registers. Hence, C++ makes it far easier for the compiler to generate optimized code.

10.4 Single precision float arithmetic

The ANSI C standard permits arithmetic operations involving `float` to be performed by using single-precision arithmetic, whereas in traditional C all `float` values were converted to `double` before applying double precision arithmetic. This new rule allows the compiler implementor to choose the most efficient method of computing results involving `float`. If single-precision arithmetic is faster, the compiler may use it. However, the compiler may also choose to use `double` or even `long double` arithmetic if it is actually faster (e.g. if double-precision arithmetic has hardware support).

There are a few situations in C where double precision arithmetic is actually required by ANSI, but does not necessarily produce different results to single-precision arithmetic. Consider the following statements:

```
float f1,f2,f3;
  ....
f1 = f2 * 10.0;
f1 = f2 * sqrt(f3);
```

Because the constant `10.0` is a `double` constant, and `sqrt` is a `double` function, both of these statements will cause `f2` to be promoted from `float` to `double` and double-precision arithmetic is used. However, since the result is immediately being truncated to `float`, the use of double-precision arithmetic is of dubious merit. One optimization which a compiler implementor might consider is to use single-precision arithmetic in these special situations (where the result of a double-precision computation is immediately converted to `float`). The constant `10.0` could be treated as a `float` constant, and the call to `sqrt` could even be replaced by a call to a single-precision (hidden) library function, say `sqrtf`, which returns a `float` value and (possibly) accepts a `float` argument.

Unfortunately, this optimization is not strictly ANSI-conforming unless the results are identical to those that would occur if double-precision arithmetic were used. For many implementations the results will differ markedly if the `float` values are close to the maximum or minimum representable values, and for any `float` values the results may differ in the last decimal place of the result (a very small difference). On such machines the optimization may make the program produce slightly different behavior, and should probably be a configurable option allowing the user to choose between slow and accurate versus fast and inaccurate.

10.5 Widening of char and short in expressions

Traditional C required that whenever a `char` or `short` value appeared in an arithmetic expression, it would undergo promotion to `int`. The ANSI C standard relaxes this requirement and permits operations involving only `char` or `short` values to avoid the conversion when the narrower representation range of the result has no effect. For example, if `c1` and `c2` are both of type `char`, the expression:

```
c1 + c2
```

would normally promote both `c1` and `c2` to `int`. However, if this expression is immediately converted back to `char`, such as by type casting, assignment or prototyped argument passing, the promotions are unnecessary. Even if the addition did produce a value not representable by `char` (e.g. greater than 255 if `char` is `unsigned` by default), the conversion of the result back to `char` is actually an instance of overflow and the loss of the higher order bits does not violate any ANSI constraint. The optimization is possible because the result will be identical regardless of whether the operands to + are promoted or left unchanged.

10.6 Macros for standard library functions

A common method for improving the efficiency of the library functions is declaring them as macros in the standard library header files. In fact, a number of functions have traditionally been macros, including most functions in `<ctype.h>` and a few others, such as `putchar` and `getchar`. ANSI permits all library functions to be macros, provided that the macros are "safe", and that there is a "real" function that can be accessed by applying `#undef` to the macro name.

A safe macro must not cause any precedence errors (requiring brackets around the entire replacement text and around every occurrence of a macro parameter in the replacement text) and must also evaluate any side effects in its arguments *exactly once* (which usually means that each macro parameter must appear exactly once in the replacement text). This second requirement severely limits the functions that can be implemented as macros. For example, the obvious macro definition for `abs`:

```
#define  abs(x)   ((x) >= 0 ? (x) : -(x))
```

is not safe, as a side effect to x will be evaluated twice. A clever attempt to overcome this problem using a "hidden" global variable such as:

```
#define  abs(x)  ( _temp = (x), _temp >= 0 ? _temp : - _temp )
```

solves the problem of side effects, but introduces some obscure errors. For example, it can fail for the expression:

```
abs(i) + abs(j)
```

because of the (obscure) order of evaluation ambiguities. In addition, a signal occurring after the assignment to _temp where the signal handler calls the abs function will cause errors when the handler returns because the value of _temp has been changed. Hence, there seems to be no way to declare a safe macro for abs.

Some of the "small" library functions that are good candidates for macro expansion are floor, ceil, putchar, getchar and most of the functions in <ctype.h>. Functions for which it appears difficult (impossible?) to declare a safe macro include abs and fabs.

10.7 Intrinsic standard library functions

The ANSI C standard clearly defines the names of functions that are part of the library, and their names are reserved in the sense that the programmer should not define new functions using these names (doing so results in "undefined behavior"). This means that an optimizer has a great deal of power in its handling of ANSI C library functions. Because the names of the library functions are reserved, the optimizer can examine every call to a library function and optimize it by using built-in knowledge about the behavior of the library function. Note that these techniques can also be applied to functions in a non-standard C library or a C++ library provided that the implementation reserves their names in the same way.

While the declaration of library functions as macros is effective and simple to implement, a better method is to inline the functions in a manner that is totally transparent to the programmer. To achieve this, the library functions to which this technique is applied are defined as *intrinsic functions*. The front-end of the compiler treats these functions as any other function call, but the back-end of the compiler recognizes them as intrinsic and knows the correct inline code to generate. This method has a number of advantages over macros:

- Ensures type-safety: macros lose all type checking information.
- Avoids scrambled error messages: semantic analysis of the program uses the original text, instead of a macro expanded version.
- *All* library functions can be inlined.
- More powerful "smart" optimizations can be used.

However, this method is more time-consuming to implement than the simple addition of a macro to a system header file. The optimizer must detect all calls to intrinsic functions and then produce an optimized version of that function call. Built-in knowledge is required about each library function being optimized.

The obvious optimization that can be applied to calls to any library functions considered "small" enough is to inline the function call. This requires some representation (possibly assembly language) of the inline code to be generated for each library function being inlined. Some of the many good candidates are: `abs`, `fabs`, all of the `<ctype.h>` functions, `floor`, `ceil`, `feof`, `ferror`, `clearerr`, `putchar`, `getchar`, etc.

Many of these functions could also be macros, but the use of intrinsic functions has the advantages discussed above, if the implementor has enough time to add these optimizations to the compiler. Furthermore, some of these functions are difficult to implement as safe macros; and macros are restricted to use features of the C language, whereas intrinsic functions can work directly at assembly level.

10.7.1 Constant folding and intrinsic functions

Inlining function calls is not the limit to the optimizations available using this method. The well-known optimization of *constant folding* can be generalized in the sense that if the optimizer notices that arguments to a function call are constants, then it may be possible to replace the function call with a constant. For example, the function call `log(1.0)` could be replaced by `0.0` at compile-time.

Functions to which this optimization can be applied are those where the return value is determined only by the arguments and which produce no other side effects. This class of functions includes: `abs`, `labs`, `div`, `ldiv`, all functions in `<ctype.h>`, and all functions in `<math.h>` that do not have pointer arguments.

Perhaps the simplest method of implementing this optimization is to *call* the library function within the optimizer and replace the function call with the result returned (although this may fail for cross-compilers).

Care is required to handle the `<math.h>` functions correctly so that their error-handling characteristics are preserved (i.e. setting `errno`). One method of handling this problem is to check the ranges of the (constant) arguments in the function call and inline the call only if the arguments are within satisfactory bounds. Another alternative is to detect whether the function call would set `errno` and if so, generate an extra machine instruction that sets `errno`.

Library functions that take string arguments, such as `atof`, `atoi`, `atol`, and many functions in `<string.h>`, can also be evaluated at compile-time if their argument is a string constant. ANSI specifies that string constants should not be modified, and that any program that does so has "undefined behavior". Hence, the optimizer can assume that the characters in a string constant are fixed, and replace function calls with their result. For example, `strlen("abc")` can be replaced by 3.

10.7.2 Built-in knowledge about intrinsic functions

Even this replacement of constant result library function calls with a constant value does not show the full power of optimization based on the compile-time analysis of arguments of calls to library functions. Heuristic knowledge about the behavior of library functions can be built into the optimizer to allow it to handle special cases very efficiently. This can be done more generally than requiring all arguments to be constant.

For example, one area of optimization is the analysis of calls to the `printf` and `scanf` families of functions when the format string is a string constant (even if other arguments are not constant). The analysis of the format string required within these library functions could be performed at compile-time. For example, in the function call:

```
printf("%d", i);
```

the format string would be analyzed and it would be discovered that only a call to an internal routine is necessary to print out an integer. Thus the assembly code output would be of the same form as generated by:

```
_print_int(i);
```

Note that if the argument, `i`, were actually an integer constant, the result could be even more efficiently coded as direct calls to `putchar`; one for each output digit.

Another good area for applying optimizations is in unrolling the loops inside the `<string.h>` functions such as `strcpy`. For example, the `strcpy` call:

```
strcpy(s, "abc");
```

could be more efficiently coded as:

```
s[0] = 'a';
s[1] = 'b';
s[2] = 'c';
s[3] = 0;
```

Another opportunity for optimizing calls to generalized functions occurs in examining `malloc` calls where the argument is a constant (e.g. from the `sizeof` operator). Rather than calling the general `malloc` function, it is possible to use a call to a function that is specially designed to handle allocation requests of that size.

Yet another example occurs the second argument to the `pow` function is a constant that is an integer, as in:

```
y = pow(x, 2.0);
```

A more efficient specialized function for handling integer powers could be called, or, in fact, the above call to `pow` could be replaced by `x*x`.

In summary, the well-defined meaning of the library functions allows the optimizer to produce far more efficient code sequences for special cases by using built-in knowledge about the behavior of these functions. All of the library functions supported by a particular environment are candidates for the optimizations, whether they are ANSI standard library functions or not. The scope of the optimizations is limited only by the need to mimic exactly a call to these functions.

10.8 The volatile qualifier

C is traditionally a low-level systems programming language, and systems programmers often use special locations in their programs (e.g. memory mapped I/O, shared memory variables, etc). The introduction of the `volatile` qualifier by the ANSI C standard provides the programmer with a method of specifying that a location is special and accesses of it should not be "optimized away". For example, the location of a memory-mapped I/O port can be declared using a pointer to `volatile`:

```
volatile unsigned char *port = 0x0100;    /* I/O port at 0100 */

*port = 1;    /* send byte 1 */
*port = 2;    /* send byte 2 */
```

Without the `volatile` qualifier the compiler does not know that the location pointed to by `port` is special, and could, in theory, remove the first assignment statement as its value is apparently overwritten by the second assignment. If the optimizer does this, it will introduce a strange bug into the program. For this reason alone, optimizers for traditional C were restricted in the transformations that could be safely applied. For example, transformations such as dead code elimination and code motion out of loops could introduce bugs.

In ANSI C, the programmer can use the `volatile` qualifier to inform the compiler that a variable or location is special. The optimizer is allowed to treat any non-volatile qualified location as if it has no special properties. Thus the optimizer in an ANSI C compiler has far more latitude in the choice of optimizations that can be performed. Unfortunately, this new freedom can lead to problems because the onus of the use of `volatile` is on the programmer. There is a high risk of breaking existing pre-ANSI code, and also of forgetting to use `volatile` in new code. There are a few choices for the implementor, ordered from the most risky to the most conservative:

- Assume that all programs will use `volatile` correctly.
- Produce a warning whenever a dangerous transformation is used.
- Apply dangerous transformations only in restricted situations.
- Don't apply any of the dangerous transformations (i.e. as done in traditional C).

To leave the optimizer as it was for traditional C is obviously the safest approach, but it loses many opportunities for optimization. A better approach would be to apply transformations whenever a location is unlikely to be special. For example, it is unlikely that an automatic local variable is special, but more likely that a pointer dereference could be accessing a special location such as a memory port. Global variables might be safe, or they might be shared memory with other processes. Which locations are safe depends on the environment (e.g. a single-user computer needn't worry about shared memory).

Another option is to warn at compile-time about transformations that might be dangerous. For example, the elimination of a "dead" assignment statement could be warned about, as it indicates either a minor bug in the program or the need to qualify a variable with `volatile`. The warnings might be produced for all dangerous transformations, or else produced only for those transformations involving locations that may not be safe (as discussed in the previous paragraph).

10.9 The const qualifier

The const qualifier provides some room for optimization in both C and C++, although less than one would hope. It can be assumed that a const variable will never change throughout the program's execution, and this provides the opportunity for extra *constant folding*. For example, given the const declaration and assignment statement:

```
const int x = 1;

y = x;
```

the compiler can replace the x in the assignment statement with the constant 1. By using hacked code a const object can be modified at run-time by a program, but such a modification is moving into the territory of "undefined behavior"; hence the compiler can replace any const objects with constants and still conform to the ANSI standard.

Similarly, there is nothing stopping the compiler from optimizing accesses to const aggregate objects, such as arrays or structures. For example, an access to an array element or struct field could be replaced by a constant as follows:

```
const int arr[2] = { 0 , 1 };
const struct { int f1, f2; } s = { 0 , 1 };

x = arr[0];        /* arr[0] can be replaced by 0 */
x = s.f1;          /* s.f1 can be replaced by 0 */
```

However, accesses through pointers to a const type (or equivalently, const array parameters) are a different story. For example, consider the declaration of p to point to a "const int":

```
int i;
const int *p = &i;
```

ANSI does not guarantee that an access via a pointer to const ensures that the object pointed to will not change. For example, although p is declared as a pointer to const, pointing at i, the value of i can be legally changed by direct assignment to i. In this situation, the const qualifier merely means that the value pointed to cannot be changed *via this pointer*. Also note that this declaration of p does not mean that p will have constant value; the declaration to ensure this is:

```
int * const p = &i;
```

This declaration would allow all uses of p to be changed to &i at compile-time, as with any other const variable.

Unfortunately, this form of optimization is not as useful in C as it is in C++ simply because const is not used as frequently. The ANSI standard for C disallows (somewhat arbitrarily) the use of const variables in constant expressions (e.g. sizes in array declarations and case constants). Hence, C programmers tend to use #define more than const because it is more flexible. However, the optimization will increase speed if const is used to declare scalar constants, or aggregate variables, and the frequency of such instances will increase as more C programmers become aware of the advantages of using const (and as more compilers actually start to implement this optimization!).

10.10 The register qualifier

The `register` qualifier is used by programmers to indicate to the compiler that a variable is likely to be heavily used, and that the programmer wishes that variable to be placed in a hardware register for efficiency. However, the `register` qualifier is merely a "hint" to the compiler and does not force it to use a register for that variable. For example, if the programmer declares too many variables as `register`, the compiler obviously cannot place all of them in registers.

Programmers are often poor at guessing which variables are heavily used, whereas the compiler can analyze the number of uses of a variable inside a function. Thus the compiler is better placed to choose which variables to store in registers, and it is reasonable for an advanced optimizing compiler to simply ignore all `register` requests made by the programmer. Sophisticated algorithms can be used to choose which variables to place in registers and, in fact, a well-known problem in code generation is the allocation of registers for values of variables and sub-expressions. There are rare situations where the compiler will make the wrong choice, such as when the programmer has better information about the probability of certain branches being executed at run-time. The compiler implementor might consider providing an option to force the honoring of `register` requests, but if the register scheduling algorithm is well designed, such situations are so rare that they could be ignored.

10.11 Register allocation and small objects

An interesting feature of C++ optimization is that they should be able to handle small objects, where the object contains only one or two scalar data members. In particular, it should be possible to include these objects in the register allocation algorithm.

This optimization is particularly necessary in C++ because it is quite common to define an object that contains either a pointer to an object (e.g. in reference counting, or for "smart" pointers), or only a single integer (e.g. declaring your own `Integer` class). Whereas in C these objects would probably be implemented as basic types (i.e. using `typedef` names), the C++ class facility effectively makes them `structs`, and it is unlikely that the C++ optimizer will be able to treat them as simpler objects. This is particularly true if the C++ translator produces C output code, since a class will be implemented as a `struct`, and the C compiler is unlikely to place a `struct` in a register.

If C++ programmers are to use small objects without a degradation in performance, the compiler must be clever enough to recognize when an object is small enough to be treated as a scalar type. Without this optimization, the C style of declaring such objects as type aliases, rather than C++ classes, will be more efficient.

This section seems to contradict the claim made in Chapter 5 that a C++ program won't run more slowly than the equivalent C program. This is still true in the sense that a C program can be converted to C++ with no performance degradation. However, this section can be seen as a limitation of using the object-oriented programming paradigm with C++, because converting small scalar types into objects may reduce performance (at least until the current generation of C++ compilers catches up).

10.12 The C++ inline qualifier

By adding the inline qualifier to a function definition, C++ programmers can indicate to the compiler that they wish a particular function to be replaced by inline code wherever it is called. Hence, C++ compilers should support the inlining of reasonably complicated functions, in order to give the programmer the required efficient improvement.

However, the `inline` qualifier is only a "hint" to the compiler, and the compiler is free to ignore it completely and decide for itself which function calls to inline. It would be valid for a C++ compiler to inline no function calls at all, but this would be a very poor quality compiler. It is more realistic for a compiler to inline simple functions, but refuse to inline overly complicated functions (possibly emitting a warning to inform the programmer). For example, the compiler may refuse to inline functions that are too large or where the control flow is too complicated.

One interesting point to note is that a C++ compiler could legitimately choose to generate inline code for non-`inline` function calls (providing that the function body has already been defined earlier in the file). The facility for inlining functions is already present and it would be simple to apply inlining to whatever functions the compiler considers simple enough.

For any `inline` function (or non-`inline` function that the compiler decides to inline), there are occasions where there must be a "real" function available at link-time, such as:

- the compiler decides not to inline calls to this function;
- the function is called when its function body has not been previously defined; or
- the address of the function is used as a pointer-to-function constant.

Note that the last two reasons merely require the function body to be linked, and the compiler can still inline any ordinary calls to these functions.

10.13 virtual function calls in C++

As discussed in Chapter 5, the only time that a call to a virtual function need generate different code from an ordinary function call is when the function is called through a *pointer or reference*. Any calls involving an object can be statically bound to the correct function, as illustrated below:

```
ObjectPtr->virtual_print();      // must be virtual call
Object.virtual_print();          // can be statically bound
```

Unfortunately, all calls via pointers and references must generate the slower dynamic binding call sequence. It would seem that calls via a pointer or reference to a *derived* class (with no other classes derived from it) could also be statically bound. However, C++'s ability to handle multiple file programs may prevent this optimization, because it is impossible to tell when examining a single file whether a class will have a new class derived from it *in a separate file*. The optimization is therefore possible in any compiler environments where the compiler has access to *all* of the source files at once, such as an integrated development environment.

10.14 Implementing enum's as a small type

Although traditional C treated `enum` types as if they were `int`, the range of values which an `enum` type can hold is restricted to the values of its declared enumerated constants. For example, in the declaration:

```
typedef enum { FALSE = 0, TRUE = 1} bool;
```

the `bool` type can legitimately hold only 0 or 1. The compiler can use this restriction to implement `bool` as a small data type such as `char`. This saves space and often increases speed because smaller data types are more efficiently manipulated.

The ANSI C standard allows compilers to implement enumerated types as an integral type different from `int`, and although it does not state so explicitly, nothing in the standard prohibits the declaration of different enumerated types as different sizes. Thus, the `bool` type above could be implemented as a `char`, and a separate enumerated type with larger values could be implemented as a `short` or `int`.

The problem with this optimization is that existing code may rely on an `enum` type having the same size as an `int`. For example, any use of the address of an enumerated type, such as in a call to `scanf`, will cause problems if the enumerated type is not stored as an `int`. Thus, this optimization is not ideal in environments which must support traditional C code.

10.15 Space reduction by merging string literals

A common space optimization performed by C compilers is to store identical string literals at the same address. This is valid as ANSI prohibits the modification of a string literal. However, traditional C did not have this restriction and the few programs that modify string literals may fail if the compiler does merge string literals.

A generalization of merging identical string literals is to merge string literals where one string is the *suffix* of another. For example, consider the two literals below:

```
"the cat"
"cat"
```

The second literal can be replaced by a pointer to the *c* in the middle of the first literal. Another very common example is that the empty string literal `""` is the suffix of any other string literal.

10.15.1 Miscellaneous optimizations

There are several other methods by which the efficiency of a program can be increased marginally. The start-up time used to process command-line arguments can be avoided if `main` is declared without arguments and if no other method is used to access them. For example, some environments define a global variable `__argv`, and the start-up sequence can be avoided only if this variable is not used (detectable at link time). Similarly, any startup processing of environment variables can be omitted if `getenv` is not used, and if no global variable is used (e.g. many UNIX-based environments define the `environ` variable).

One neat way of improving run-time efficiency at the cost of space is to ignore all `struct` bit-field requests and use `int` instead. This avoids the cost of packing and unpacking bit-fields whenever they are accessed.

10.16 Summary

- C compilers have traditionally avoided large-scale transformations such as code motion and common sub-expression elimination as they could "optimize away" useful references.
- ANSI C prototypes permit the compiler to use a faster function call mechanism, at some risk to existing code. C++ compilers can always use faster mechanisms.
- ANSI C permits `float` arithmetic to be performed in single-precision arithmetic, whereas traditional C required double-precision arithmetic.
- Macros are a simple method of removing the function call overhead of some library functions, but some functions are difficult to implement as "safe" macros.
- Intrinsic functions are a more powerful method of optimizing calls to library functions. Knowledge about the library functions can be used because the function names are reserved.
- The `volatile` qualifier only partially solves the problem of "optimizing away" useful code.
- References to `const` variables can be optimized, as by constant folding, but access via a `const` pointer cannot.
- The compiler may choose to ignore `register` and `inline` keywords if the implementor believes the compiler can make better choices.
- Merging identical string literals is a common and efficient space optimization. Merging *suffixes* of string literals is a possible extension.

10.17 Further reading

Code optimization is a huge area of compiler design, and anyone not familiar with it should consult a good compiler textbook, such as the one by Aho, Sethi and Ullman listed here. Thomas Plum's book contains a good chapter on the implications of the ANSI C standard for implementors of optimizing C compilers. A good discussion of mixing prototyping and non-prototyping in C is given by Harbison and Steele, and their book book also contains useful material on many of the complicated issues in both traditional and ANSI C.

AHO, Alfred V., SETHI, Ravi, and ULLMAN, Jeffrey D., *Compilers — Principles, Techniques and Tools*, Addison-Wesley, 1986.

HARBISON, Samuel P., and STEELE, Guy L. Jr., *C: A Reference Manual (3rd edn)*, Prentice Hall, 1991.

PLUM, Thomas, *Notes on the C Draft Standard*, Plum Hall Inc., 1987.

10.18 Exercises

1. Design an efficient safe macro for the `tolower` and `toupper` library functions. Note that they must return the character unchanged if it is not a letter.

2. [advanced] Given the following definition and call of the `abs` macro, find an order of evaluation allowed by the ANSI C standard where incorrect results will occur:

    ```
    #define abs(x) (_temp = (x),_temp >= 0 ? _temp : -_temp)
     ...
    abs(i) + abs(j)
    ```

3. [advanced] Consider the following attempt to overcome the deficiencies of the `abs` macro in the previous exercise. Does it have problems due to order of evaluation?

    ```
    /* Pseudo code: push(x), top() >= 0 ? pop() : -pop()   */
    /* _s is a global variable; the stack pointer   */
    #define abs(x) (((*++_s)=(x)) >= 0 ? *(_s--): -(*(_s--)))
    ```

4. There are a large number of standard library functions that return values which are commonly ignored, including: `printf`, `scanf`, `strcat`, `strcpy`. What possibility does the idea of intrinsic functions provide for optimization in this situation?

5. The `strcmp` function is quite general in that it allows tests for equality and ordering on strings. How can (most) calls to `strcmp` be optimized by detecting whether the program is using `strcmp` for an equality or ordering test?

6. [advanced] The inherent efficiency limitation of `qsort` and `bsearch` is that they must call the user-supplied function for each comparison. Can the optimizer improve calls to `qsort` and `bsearch` so that the overhead of calls to the comparison function is avoided?

7. What are the dangers of assuming references via a `const` pointer always access the same value? When can this optimization safely be used?

8. When would the assumption that an automatic local variable won't have special properties (i.e. `volatile`-like semantics) be invalid? In other words, when would common sub-expression elimination involving automatic local variables lose an important reference?

9. [advanced] What opportunities for optimization are provided by C++ `const` member functions? This language feature was added so that `const` objects could have methods applied to them without violating their "const-ness". *Hint:* `const` member functions are not allowed to modify the object to which they are applied.

10. Can the compiler optimize the space used by `enum` variables by storing `enum` fields of structures as bit-fields? For example, this would mean that a variable of type `bool` (see Section 10.14) would be stored as 1 bit inside a structure.

11. Build a list of impediments to efficiency that are imposed by the ANSI C standard. What reasons justify the limitations on efficiency?

Appendix

Answers to selected exercises

Chapter 2. Measurement and estimation

1. It fails because the measured loop overhead will be lower than the value for the main loop, since the main loop's assignment operation will be slower. The assignment statement could be changed to x=x, which will be a proper assignment (it isn't a redundant statement since x is `volatile`).

2. The placement of the call to `clock` at the end of `start_clock` and the beginning of `stop_clock` aims to reduce the overhead time included in the clock measurements. The macros aim to reduce this further by leaving out the function call overhead in the times. A global variable of type `clock_t` is needed to store the value of the `clock` function call.

    ```
    clock_t ticks;        /* global variable for stop_clock */
    #define stop_clock(s)  ((ticks = clock()), stop_clock(s))
    ```

    and the `stop_clock` function must use this global variable instead of calling `clock`. A global pointer variable is needed for `start_clock`, and it must be set to the address of where to store the clock ticks (i.e. &p->last_time).

    ```
    clock_t *glob_ptr;    /* global pointer for start_clock */
    #define start_clock(s) (start_clock(s),(*glob_ptr=clock()))
    ```

5. Certainly, estimation is far less important once the program has been completed. However, estimation is still needed because it may be difficult to measure some of the quantities. In addition, the dynamic quantities will depend on the program inputs and it may not be possible to provide worst-case inputs to a program.
    Executable size can be estimated by many methods, ranging from a simple line-count of the program to a token-by-token analysis using estimates of how large each instruction will be. Plum and Brodie's book *Efficient C* contains a good discussion of this issue.

Static data size includes the memory from global variables, static local variables, string constants and possibly floating point constants. By using knowledge about the sizes of various types, it is a simple matter of counting the number of such variables and adding their sizes. The memory used by string constants and floating point constants can be estimated by finding all of them, but the possibility that identical constants may be merged should also be taken into consideration.

Stack and heap usage are very difficult to estimate because they depend on the run-time execution path. In the absence of recursion, a reasonable estimate of the worst case stack usage can be found by finding the worst function call sequence. This is by no means trivial and a software tool to do so is sorely needed.

Estimating run-time efficiency from source code is well-nigh impossible. Perhaps the cost of each function can be roughly estimated by using a simple metric based on the number of loops and the nesting depth of these loops.

Chapter 3. Algorithm improvements

2.   Re-display only those squares on the chess board that have changed in the move. The number of squares is usually 2, and at most 4 (castling), so the method compares well with re-displaying 64 squares.

Chapter 4. Code transformations

2.   The test of `maximizing` is constant throughout the loop, and hence the test should be moved so that is comes before the loop. The simplest method of doing so is to repeat the loop code, as follows:

```
                    /* Compute either maximum or minimum */
result = a[0];
if(maximizing) {
    for(i = 1; i < n; i++)
        result = a[i] > result ? a[i] : result;
}
else {
    for(i = 1; i < n; i++)
        result = a[i] < result ? a[i] : result;
}
```

3.   By examining the effect of this statement, you will see that it has the same behavior as:

```
if (a[i] > result)
        result = a[i];
else
        result = result;   /* REDUNDANT */
```

Hence the more efficient code is simply:

```
if (a[i] > result) result = a[i];
```

4.   Since the computations of the two roots are very similar, the idea of common sub-expression elimination can be employed. The sub-expression $b^2 - 4ac$ should be calculated only once, and `sqrt` should be called only once. It is doubtful whether eliminating the sub-expressions $-b$ or $2a$ will make any difference. The multiplication $2a$ can be avoided using $a + a$ (it might also be worthwhile to do this for $4ac$, by precomputation ac and adding the result 4 times). Because the computation involves `double` arithmetic the constants in the expression should be expressed as 4.0, and not 4, to avoid possible conversion costs (although most compilers will do this automatically). The resulting efficient code is:

```
temp1 = sqrt ( b * b - 4.0 * a * c);
r1 = (-b + temp1) / (a + a);
r2 = (-b - temp1) / (a + a);
```

5.   Reorder the `enum` declaration to place NO_ERROR first, giving it the value of zero, because comparison with zero is often slightly more efficient.

6.   The crucial point to note is that the multiplication is always either by 1 or −1, so a boolean flag can be used to decide which value to multiply by, as follows:

```
#define   TRUE   1
#define   FALSE  0

int my_atoi(char *s)
{
    int value, sign;

    if (*s == '-') {
        sign = TRUE;
        s++;            /* skip over the '-' */
    }
    else
        sign = FALSE;

    for (value = 0; isdigit(*s); s++)
        value = 10 * value + *s - '0';

    if (sign)
        return -value;
    else
        return value;
}
```

7.   This method will seldom be faster than a plain assignment. If the flag is not set, there has been the extra comparison as overhead. If the flag is set, the assignment is avoided, but the difference in cost between a comparison and an integer assignment will most likely be slight. The optimization is valid only if:

    1. comparison is faster than assignment; and
    2. the assignment is avoided often enough to justify the extra comparison.

8.   Yes, to a limited extent. In C any automatic local variables *with explicit initializations* will involve run-time instructions. Hence, the initialization should take place where the variable is first used, in case this initialized value is never actually used

(causing inefficiency). Variable declarations can be moved to inner blocks in some cases; the alternative is to remove the initialization from the declaration, and use an explicit assignment statement to set the variable immediately before its first use. For example, in the code:

```
int fn()
{
  int i;        /* Not initialized */
  int n;

  scanf("%d", &n);
  if (n >= 0) {
       i = 1;        /* Initialize immediately before use */
       /* .. use i here */
  }
}
```

9. Any multiplication can be written as a mixture of shift and addition operations. The expression `x*17` can be rewritten as:

```
(x << 4) + x
```

but on many implementations the cost of a shift and an addition will be greater than the cost of multiplication.

10. The pointer expression idioms `*ptr++` and `*--ptr` will be very efficient because the compiler can translate these directly to the special addressing modes.

11. We will assume that the field has type `FIELD_TYPE` and the `struct` has type "`struct node`". An obvious method is to use a pointer to a structure as follows:

```
struct node * ptr;
for (ptr = &arr[0]; ptr < &arr[n]; ptr++)
    process(ptr->field);
```

Another solution that will probably be more efficient is to use a pointer to the field and increment it by the size of a structure each iteration. This avoids the addition of the offset of `field` implicit in the `->` operation. Pointer type casts are needed to get the correct increment (`ptr++` would fail).

```
FIELD_TYPE *ptr;
for (ptr = &arr[0].field; ptr < &arr[n].field;
       ptr=(FIELD_TYPE*)((char*)ptr+sizeof(struct node)))
     process(*ptr);
```

Note that using "`ptr=(FIELD_TYPE*)((struct node*)ptr+1)`" as the increment condition could be dangerous on machines with alignment restrictions. Perhaps the most efficient version is to avoid the pointer comparison each loop by decrementing n (assuming its value is not needed afterwards):

```
for (ptr = &arr[0].field; --n >= 0;
       ptr=(FIELD_TYPE*)((char*)ptr+sizeof(struct node)))
     process(*ptr);
```

12. The simplest method is to use a neat mathematical identity involving bitwise arithmetic: for $x > 0$, $x \& (x-1)$ evaluates the rightmost set bit in x. Thus if this equals x (and x is not zero) then x must contain only a single binary bit and be a power of 2. The macro is:

    ```
    #define is_power2(x)   ( x != 0 && x == (x & (x-1)))
    ```

13. If you went in for minor changes to the bitwise arithmetic then you should go back and read Chapter 3. Since there are only 16 distinct nibbles, the most efficient method is to use a small lookup table:

    ```
    int nibble_table[16] = { 0, 3, 12, 15, 48, 51, 60, 63,
                    192, 195, 204, 207, 240, 243, 252, 255 };

    #define nibble_extend(x)     nibble_table[x]
    ```

Chapter 5. C++ Techniques

1. Not inlining functions with loops is a compiler limitation because theoretically there is no difficulty in doing so, although inlining functions with loops is by no means an easy task in practice! The main theoretical limitation of `inline` functions is that recursive functions cannot be inlined fully because this would cause an infinite loop in the compiler. More generally, functions that form a link in a mutually recursive function call sequence cannot be inlined fully (e.g. two functions that both call each other).

4. Yes, the idiom is usually necessary, because omitting the copy constructor or assignment operator can lead to an `aliasing` problem. (It makes no difference whether the default operations are bitwise copying, as in early versions, or memberwise copying as in C++ 2.0 and above, because member-wise copying will still perform bitwise copying of pointer members.) Two objects will have pointers to the same allocated memory. Any change to one object's allocated data will change both objects. Hence, the idiom can be avoided only if:

   1. the contents of allocated memory are not modified except in the ordinary constructors; or
   2. neither copying nor assignment of the objects ever occurs (i.e. the copy constructor and assignment operator are never called).

   To answer the second part, the copy constructor and assignment operator must still allocate new memory for an object even if the destructor does not de-allocate the memory. True, the problem of de-allocating memory twice is gone, but there is still the aliasing problem as discussed above.

5. The idea is to use a dynamically allocated object, as its lifetime is not governed by braces. The improved code becomes:

```
double d;
Object *ptr;

while (....) {
        cin >> d;
        ptr = new Object(d);   // construction at first use
}
cout << *ptr;           // Use the object
delete ptr;             // de-allocate the object
```

The optimization is beneficial only when the cost of the assignment operator for an incredibly complicated object is higher than the combined cost of allocation by new, de-allocation by delete, and a few pointer operations.

6.   Instead of declaring the data member(s) as static, use two global objects of the class type. The zero-argument (default) constructor must be either absent or performs no actions. Implicit initialization of global objects to all-bytes zero will efficiently set the data values to zero. Unfortunately, this is not valid if the data members must contain values other than zero or NULL.

7.   Yes, returning a reference would avoid the need for a temporary in the expression. However, there is no way to return a reference from the operator. Returning a reference to an automatic local variable will cause a run-time failure because the stack space storing the local variable may be overwritten after the function returns. Returning a reference to a global or local static variable will lead to errors when the + operator is used twice in the same expression, because both calls to the operator function will be attempting to store their result in the same place. Returning a reference to a dynamically allocated object on the heap will work, but creates garbage (unused and unaccessible dynamic memory) and will probably be slower than using a temporary object anyway. Returning a reference to one of the Complex parameters of the operator will not work because either (a) they are not passed by reference in which case they are equivalent to automatic local variables; or (b) they are passed by reference in which case storing the result there will overwrite one of the operands. The common "return *this;" idiom for returning references from an overloaded = or += operator works only because the first operand is being changed by the function, and is identical to the result of the function.

Chapter 6. The ANSI C standard library

3.   The simplest method is to use a switch statement such as:

```
switch (n) {
    case 0:  return 1.0;
    case 1:  return x;
    case 2:  return x * x;
    case 3:  return x * x * x;
    case 4:  x2 = x * x;   return x2 * x2;
    case 5:  x2 = x * x;   return x2 * x2 * x;
    ... etc
    default:  ...    /* General algorithm here */
}
```

5.
```
char *temp = s;

for (; *temp != '\0'; temp++);  /* empty loop */
*s++ = 'a';
*s++ = '\0';
```

6. There should be brackets around these two character constants. To do so requires changing a + to a − operator:

```
#define TOLOWER(c)   (isupper(c) ? ((c) - ('A' - 'a')) : c)
#define TOUPPER(c)   (islower(c) ? ((c) - ('a' - 'A')) : c)
```

8. The trick is to declare `strcpy` as having most of its code inside a new block, and declaring local variables at the start of this block. The macro is:

```
#define  strcpy(s1,s2)        \
    { char * temp1 = (s1), *temp2 = (s2);          \
      while ((*temp1 ++ = *temp2++) != '\0')      \
          ;          /* empty loop */    \
    }
```

Another fine point is that this macro will cause a syntax error due to the semicolon following a right brace when the macro is used as a single statement body before an `else` keyword, as in:

```
if (...)
    strcpy(a, b);   /* syntax error: if(..) {...} ; else */
else
    ...
```

The solution is to use a pair of `do..while(0)` wrappers around the block. The improved macro is:

```
#define  strcpy(s1,s2)      \
    do {  char * temp1 = s1, *temp2 = s2;           \
      while ((*temp1 ++ = *temp2++) != '\0')      \
          ;     /* empty loop */   \
    } while (0)     /* no semicolon here */
```

9. The `memset` library function provides very fast byte copying. Hence the efficient method is:

```
memset(arr, 0, SIZE * sizeof(int));
```

Unfortunately, this method is non-portable to environments where integral zero does not have all bytes zero.

Chapter 7. Space-efficiency

3. The use of the word "store" in the question was deliberately misleading. The most space-efficient way to "store" these numbers is to use a function to represent them (i.e. use a function to calculate a Fibonacci number each time it is required). The only storage cost is the cost of the machine language instructions. Naturally, run-time efficiency is sadly lacking if you use this method.

4.   Before the deletion phase, simply seed the random number generator again with the same seed value and use `rand` to regenerate the same sequence of numbers.

5.   Since these functions are so similar, it is reasonable to assume that they will all use mostly the same executable code (possibly all calling an internal function). Hence, avoiding `scanf` but still using `sscanf` or `fscanf` will probably not reduce executable size greatly.

6.   Possibly. A good compiler will notice the shorter lifetimes of these local variables and reuse the space on the stack after the enclosing block has finished execution. However, an even better compiler would automatically examine the usages of a variable to determine its lifetime and perform any optimization regardless of whether the variable is moved to its inner block.

7.   Since there are only 201 distinct values they can be stored in the small data type `unsigned char` which can represent values from 0..255. To convert this value to the floating point value of the grade is a simple matter of multiplication by 0.5. This is time-inefficient, but storage space will be saved, especially if there are many grades to be stored.

Chapter 8. Abstract data types in C++

6.   Jump search is a tricky algorithm to implement. The C++ code for one implementation, where the search jumps ahead five nodes is as follows:

```
//-------------------------------------------------------------
//  Search a sorted linked list - JUMP SEARCH
//-------------------------------------------------------------
Node* SymbolTable::search(key_type key)
{
    register Node *p = head, *save;

    if (p == NULL)          // empty list?
        return NULL;
    do {
        save = p;                       // Save current position
                                        // Jump ahead 5 nodes
        if(p != NULL) p = p->next;
        if(p != NULL) p = p->next;
        if(p != NULL) p = p->next;
        if(p != NULL) p = p->next;
        if(p != NULL) p = p->next;
    } while (p != NULL && key > p->key_field);

    if (p != NULL && key == p->key_field)  // key at lookahead?
        return p;
                            // sequential search of 0..5 nodes
    for (; save != p; save = save->next) {
        if (key == save->key_field)
                return save;
    }
    return NULL;     // not found
}
```

If sentinel pointers are being used, there is a simple trick to avoid the need for the five tests "p!=NULL". By setting the sentinel node's `next` pointer to point at itself, these test can be omitted without causing an access violation. At the end of the linked list the assignments p=p->next will be redundant, as they set p to be the same value, but this is a small price to pay for removing five tests from the main loop.

7. The obvious disadvantage is the space wastage due to an extra pointer in each node. The improvements to be gained are that the insertion and deletion routines elegantly avoid the need for a "prev" pointer, reducing the cost of loops. Both insertion and deletion are also slightly less efficient due to setting the "prev" pointer, but this is only one assignment statement. The search routine is unaffected by the change.

8. The insertion routine is simply a matter of changing NULL to NIL. The deletion routine can be improved to make use of the sentinels during the search phase of deletion, as follows:

```
//-----------------------------------------------------------------
// Remove a key from a binary tree with SENTINELS;
//-----------------------------------------------------------------
void SymbolTable::remove(key_type key)
{
    Node *ptr;          // points to the current node
    Node *parent;       // points to the parent node

    sentinel_node.key_field = key;      // Set the sentinel node
    for (parent = NIL, ptr = root;;) {  // test with NIL omitted
        if (key < ptr->key_field ) {
            parent = ptr;
            ptr = ptr->left;            // search left subtree
        }
        else if (key > ptr->key_field ) {
            parent = ptr;
            ptr = ptr->right;           // search right subtree
        }
        else                            // Found it or sentinel
            break;
    }

    if (ptr == NIL)     // Was it the sentinel?
        return;         // Not found. No deletion occurs.

    Node *subtree;      // Root of the subtree after deletion
                        // Used to later set pointer in parent

    if (ptr->left == NIL && ptr->right == NIL) {   // Case 1
        delete ptr;                     // No children - delete a LEAF
        subtree = NIL;                  // Subtree becomes empty
    }
    else if (ptr->left == NIL) {   // 1 child: Case 2a
        subtree = ptr->right;      // Right child is new subtree
        delete ptr;                // Dispose deleted node
    }
    else if (ptr->right == NIL) {  // 1 child: Case 2b (reverse)
        subtree = ptr->left;       // Left child is new subtree
        delete ptr;                // Dispose deleted node
    }
                   //---------------------------------------------
    else {         // Two children - Case 3 - the difficult case!
                   // Find rightmost node of left subtree
                   //---------------------------------------------
```

```
                    Node *prev, *temp;
                    for (prev = NIL, temp = ptr->left; temp->right != NIL;
                       prev = temp, temp = temp->right)
                    ;                                   // empty loop

                       //-----------------------------------------------
                       // Replace node to be deleted with this node
                       //-----------------------------------------------

                    if (prev == NIL) {               // did not go right at all
                       temp->right = ptr->right; // right subtree of dead node
                                                 // Left subtree stays same
                       delete ptr;
                       subtree = temp;           // *** Case 3a ***
                    }
                    else {                       // went down right at least once
                       prev->right = temp->left;  // delete temp from subtree
                       temp->left = ptr->left;    // replace "ptr" with temp
                       temp->right = ptr->right;
                       delete ptr;                //  *** Case 3b ***
                       subtree = temp;
                    }
                 }
                    //-----------------------------------------------------
                    // Have now reconstructed the subtrees after deletion
                    // Now need to set pointers in parent node
                    //-----------------------------------------------------

             if (parent == NIL)          // deleted root node?
                root = subtree;          // subtree becomes whole tree
             else
             if (key < parent->key_field)
                parent->left = subtree;     // Node was left of its parent
             else
                parent->right = subtree;    // Node to right of its parent
          }
```

12. When using linear probing, hash table locations must have a special value indicating "deleted from". The deletion routine marks a location as such. The search routine must treat these special locations as if there was a key present. The search cannot terminate there because a deleted key may have had more keys placed after it by linear probing collision resolution, and this would cause the search function to fail to find some keys in the table.

13. The array representations make the count function most efficient, as they already maintain a count of the number of elements. The linked list versions must implement a traversal of the list nodes such as:

```
int SymbolTable::count()
{
    int sum = 0;
    for (Node *p = head; p!=NULL; p = p->next)
        sum++;
    return sum;
}
```

Binary trees must implement a tree traversal counting the number of nodes. The hash table with chaining must examine each hash table location and count the nodes on each non-empty chained list.

A simple incremental algorithm can be easily added to all these versions. An extra integer field, n, is stored as a data member of class SymbolTable. This is set to zero in the constructor, incremented in the insert function and decremented in the remove function. This is a small amount of overhead each time, but it speeds up the `count` function incredibly, and the cost of the increments/decrements will likely be much less than the extra difficulty of traversing a list, tree or hash table.

14. The idea of combining two operations can be applied by designing a specialized `search_insert` routine that performs a search of the data structure, at the same time keeping track of enough information to insert the symbol if it is not found. For example, a `search_insert` routine for a sorted linked list would need to keep a "prev" pointer as it searches along the linked list. This idea of pairing computation gains efficiency since in most data structures the insertion routine performs similar processing to the search routine.

15. Caching can be applied by keeping track of a small number of the recently accessed symbol records, possibly in an extra array data member. Before searching the main data structure, the small array is searched for the symbol. If the symbol has been cached, the search of the complex data structure has been avoided. This idea works well if there is *locality* in the references to symbols in the table, so that it is reasonably likely that the record will be cached. For example, in a compiler's symbol table the same symbol is usually accessed many times (i.e. wherever a variable name appears in the code).

Chapter 10. Ideas for compiler optimization

1. Use a precalculated table of 256 bytes for each function.

2. ANSI C has sequence points at the end of the first operand to the comma operator, and the order of evaluation of operands to + is not defined. Hence a legitimate order is:

```
_temp = i;
_temp = j;
TMP1 = ( _temp >= 0 ? _temp : - _temp );
TMP2 = ( _temp >= 0 ? _temp : - _temp );
result = TMP1 + TMP2;
_temp
```

3. No, it suffers from the problem that expressions such as `abs(i)-abs(j)` are affected by order of evaluation. In particular, the operands of the conditional operator can be interleaved and one valid order would be to "push" both `i` and `j` and then have the first macro "pop" `j` (the wrong value). Note that this macro seems to solve the problem of signal handlers calling `abs`.

4. Situations where return values are ignored can be detected easily, and the compiler implementor has several options. The simplest optimization would be to call a different version of the function, declared as a `void` function, which will be marginally more efficient. Another option would be better inlining of the function by using a different sequence of assembly instructions.

5. The most common use of `strcmp` is to immediately test its return value with zero, either explicitly via a comparison with the constant 0, or implicitly as the value of a conditional expression or as an operand to a logical operator (`&&`, `||`, `!`). A simple

analysis of the expression can determine what form of test it is using `strcmp` for, and this information can be used to choose a faster version of `strcmp`. For example, the expression `strcmp()==0` could be replaced by a call to a (hidden) string equality function which will be marginally faster because it need not worry about returning a positive or negative value if the strings are not equal. Of course, this optimization cannot be applied where the return value of `strcmp` is used more fully, such as being assigned to a variable.

6.   Yes, in some cases. Wherever the function passed to `qsort` or `bsearch` is a pointer-to-function constant (i.e. a function name) the compiler may be able to examine the body of the comparison function (if it is available) and produce an in-line version. A special version of the `qsort` or `bsearch` function could then be generated and called instead of the general function.

7.   The danger is that the object pointed to may be modified between two accesses by either an assignment via another (aliased) pointer, direct modification to the object pointed to (e.g. if the pointer points to a local variable of the function, or a global variable), or modification inside a function call (using any method). Note that there is no cause to worry if the pointer points at a volatile object because, if it does, it should be qualified by `volatile`. Detecting situations via source code analysis where this optimization can be used safely is probably a research problem. One sufficient, but not necessary, condition for the safety of the optimization is that there should be no assignments, increments or function calls between the two pointer accesses.

8.   The local variable could be changed via a symbolic debugger. In addition, a function which contains a `setjmp` call may have the values of the local variables in an indeterminate condition when a `longjmp` call is executed. However, this is not a problem as ANSI requires that any local variables whose values are desirable after a `longjmp` call must be declared as `volatile`.

9.   `const` member functions offer very few opportunities for optimization. The knowledge that a function call will not change the object can be used in rare cases, such as to eliminate the common sub-expression in the code below:

```
x = object.data;
object.const_fn();      // call the const member function
y = object.data;        // y = x would be equivalent
```

Unfortunately, the fact that a member function is `const` is not, in itself, enough to guarantee that the function will not cause a side effect, and this limits the optimizations that can be applied. For example, the common sub-expression elimination of two consecutive calls to the same `const` member function cannot be applied without a detailed analysis of the function body (e.g. it may contain an important output statement).

In addition, it may even be possible for a `const` member function to *change* its object through coding hacks, or via an aliased pointer. This is surely an abuse of C++, but there is as yet no ANSI C++ standard to state that such uses are "undefined". Hence, the optimization of the common sub-expression given above may be dangerous for a few poorly written programs.

10. This will fail for any program that takes the address of the `enum` field of the structure by using the address-of operator (`&`) or the ANSI standard macro `offsetof` in `<stddef.h>`.

11. Some of the many efficiency problems in ANSI C are:

- The `strcat` and `strcpy` library functions return values that are rarely used. They should be `void` functions as this would allow them to be declared as macros, and would reduce the complexity of their definition as functions.

- There are no equivalents of the `<math.h>` library functions for `float` arguments.

- Arguments to variable-argument functions are promoted to `int` or `double`. It would be more efficient to modify the calling mechanism and the macros in `<stdarg.h>` to handle `char`, `short` and `float` arguments.

- Objects accessed via `const`-qualified pointers cannot be assumed to be unchanging, and this reduces the compiler optimizations that can be applied.

- Macros for standard library functions must be "safe" (no side effect problems), which makes it difficult to define macros for many library functions.

- `const` variables cannot be used everywhere `#define` constants can be (although many implementations allow this as an extension).

The main reasons for these limitations are historical. The ANSI standard set out to break as little existing code as possible, and hence, many minor inefficiencies remain in the language definition.

Bibliography

A large number of books on C, C++ and data structures were consulted while I wrote this book. Few of them cover efficiency in any great detail, but many of them contain sections that helped me to discover the many techniques of improving efficiency of C and C++ programs. For further discussion of the contents of some of these books, refer to the "Further reading" sections in most of the chapters. In particular, Chapter 1 examines books that contained a large amount of material on efficiency.

AHO, Alfred V., SETHI, Ravi, and ULLMAN, Jeffrey D., *Compilers — Principles, Techniques and Tools*, Addison-Wesley, 1986.

AMMERAAL, Leendert, *Programs and Data Structures in C*, John Wiley and Sons, 1987.

AMSBURY, Wayne, *Data Structures from Arrays to Priority Queues*, Wadsworth Publishing Company, 1985.

ANDERSON, Paul, and ANDERSON, Gail, *Advanced C: Tips and Techniques*, Hayden Books, 1988.

BENTLEY, Jon Louis, *Writing Efficient Programs*, Prentice Hall, 1982.

COPLIEN, James O., *Advanced C++ Programming Styles and Idioms*, Addison-Wesley, 1992.

GONNET, G. H., and BAEZA-YATES, R., *Handbook of Algorithms and Data Structures (2nd edn)*, Addison-Wesley, 1991.

HARBISON, Samuel P., and STEELE, Guy L. Jr., *C: A Reference Manual (3rd edn)*, Prentice Hall, 1991.

HOROWITZ, E., and SAHNI, S., *Fundamentals of Data Structures (3rd edn)*, Pitman Publishing, 1990.

KELLEY, Al, and POHL, Ira, *A Book on C (2nd edn)*, Benjamin/Cummings Publishing Company, 1990.

KERNIGHAN Brian W., and PLAUGER, P. J., *The Elements of Programming Style*, McGraw-Hill, 1974.

KERNIGHAN, Brian W., and RITCHIE, Dennis M., *The C Programming Language (2nd edn)*, Prentice Hall, 1989.

KNUTH, Donald E., *The Art of Computer Programming (Vol. 3): Sorting and Searching*, Addison-Wesley, 1973.

KORSH, James F., and GARRETT, Leonard J., *Data Structures, Algorithms and Program Style Using C*, PWS-Kent Publishing, 1988.

LAPIN, J. E., *Portable C and UNIX System Programming*, Prentice Hall, 1987.

LEVY, David, *Computer Gamesmanship*, Century Publishing, 1983.

MASTERS, David, *Introduction to C with Advanced Applications*, Prentice Hall, 1991.

PLAUGER, P. J., *The Standard C Library*, Prentice Hall, 1991.

PLUM, Thomas, *Notes on the C Draft Standard*, Plum Hall Inc., 1987.

PLUM, Thomas, and BRODIE, Jim, *Efficient C*, Plum Hall Inc., 1985.

PRESS, W. H., FLANNERY, B. P., TEUKOLSKY, S. A., and VETTERLING, W. T., *Numerical Recipes in C: The Art of Scientific Computing*, Cambridge University Press, 1988.

PUGH, Ken, *All on C*, Scott, Foresman/Little, Brown Higher Education, 1990.

REINGOLD, Edward M., and HANSEN, Wilfred J., *Data Structures in Pascal*, Little, Brown and Company, 1986.

RICH, Elaine, *Artificial Intelligence*, McGraw-Hill, 1983.

SCHILDT, Herbert, *C: The Complete Reference*, Osborne-McGraw-Hill, 1987.

SHAPIRO, Jonathan S., *A C++ Toolkit*, Prentice Hall, 1991.

SPULER, David A., *Comprehensive C*, Prentice Hall, 1992.

STANDISH, T. A., *Data Structure Techniques*, Addison-Wesley, 1980.

STROUSTRUP, Bjarne, *The C++ Programming Language (2nd edn)*, Addison-Wesley, 1991.

STUBBS, Daniel F., and WEBRE, Neil W., *Data Structures with Abstract Data Types and Pascal*, Brooks/Cole Publishing Company, 1985.

Perhaps the most important reference for C is the ANSI C standard, although the majority of people won't need to read it. The standard is more properly called American National Standard ANS-X3.159-1989 "Programming Languages—C", and has also been adopted as the international standard ISO/IEC 9899:1990 (which differs only in section and page numbering). The standard is not a public domain document and can be purchased from:

American National Standards Institute
1430 Broadway
New York, NY 10018
USA
(+1) 212 642 4900

and also from:

> Global Engineering Documents
> 2805 McGaw Avenue
> Irvine, CA 92714
> USA
> (+1) 714 261 1455
> (800) 854 7179 (within USA and Canada only)

Within Australia, a version of the standard (equivalent to ISO/IEC 9899:1990) can be purchased from Standards Australia, and is called Australian Standard AS 3955-1991 "Programming Languages—C". The mailing address of the National Sales Center is:

> PO Box 1055
> Strathfield 2135
> AUSTRALIA
> (02) 746 4600 (within Australia only)

Index

Z